The American History Series

SERIES EDITORS

John Hope Franklin, *Duke University*

A. S. Eisenstadt, *Brooklyn College*

D0324502

Carl Abbott
PORTLAND STATE UNIVERSITY

Urban America in the Modern Age
1920 to the Present

SECOND EDITION

HARLAN DAVIDSON, INC.
WHEELING, ILLINOIS 60090-6000

Copyright © 1987, 2007
Harlán Davidson, Inc.
All Rights Reserved

Visit us on the World Wide Web at www.harlandavidson.com.

Library of Congress Cataloging-in-Publication Data

Abbott, Carl.
 Urban America in the modern age : 1920 to the present / Carl
Abbott.— 2nd ed.
  p. cm. — (The American history series)
 Includes bibliographical references and index.
 ISBN-13: 978-0-88295-247-5 (alk. paper)
 ISBN-10: 0-88295-247-1 (alk. paper)
 1. Metropolitan areas—United States—History—20th century.
2. Cities and towns—United States—History—20th century.
3. Urban policy—United States. I. Title. II. Series: American history
series (Arlington Heights, Ill.)
 HT334.U5A56 2007
 306.760973—dc22

                              2006007409

Cover photograph: View of the Chicago River.
Courtesy of the Chicago Chamber of Commerce

Manufactured in the United States of America
10 09 08 07 06 1 2 3 4 5 VP

FOREWORD

Every generation writes its own history for the reason that it sees the past in the foreshortened perspective of its own experience. This has surely been true of the writing of American history. The practical aim of our historiography is to give us a more informed sense of where we are going by helping us understand the road we took in getting where we are. As the nature and dimensions of American life are changing, so too are the themes of our historical writing. Today's scholars are hard at work reconsidering every major aspect of the nation's past: its politics, diplomacy, economy, society, recreation, mores and values, as well as status, ethnic, race, sexual, and family relations. The lists of series titles that appear at the back of this book will show at once that our historians are ever broadening the range of their studies.

The aim of this series is to offer our readers a survey of what today's historians are saying about the central themes and aspects of the American past. To do this, we have invited to write for the series only scholars who have made notable contributions to the respective fields in which they are working. Drawing on primary and secondary materials, each volume presents a factual and narrative account of its particular subject, one that affords readers a basis for perceiving its larger dimensions and importance. Conscious that readers respond to the closeness and immediacy of a subject, each of our authors seeks to restore the past as an actual present, to revive it as a living reality. The individuals and groups who figure in the pages of our books appear as real people who once were looking for survival and fulfillment. Aware that historical subjects are often matters of controversy, our authors present their own findings and conclusions. Each volume closes with an extensive critical essay on the writings of the major authorities on its particular theme.

The books in this series are designed for use in both basic and advanced courses in American history, on the undergraduate and graduate levels. Such a series has a particular value these days, when the format of American history courses is being altered to accommodate a greater diversity of reading materials. The series offers a number of distinct advantages. It extends the dimensions of regular course work. Going well beyond the confines of the textbook, it makes clear that the study of our past is, more than the student might otherwise understand, at once complex, profound, and absorbing. It presents that past as a subject of continuing interest and fresh investigation. The work of experts in their respective fields, the series, moreover, puts at the disposal of the reader the rich findings of historical inquiry. It invites the reader to join, in major fields of research, those who are pondering anew the central themes and aspects of our past. And it reminds the reader that in each successive generation of the ever-changing American adventure, men and women and children were attempting, as we are now, to live their lives and to make their way.

John Hope Franklin
A. S. Eisenstadt

CONTENTS

Maps, Tables, Diagrams

PREFACE
TO THE SECOND EDITION

The study of American cities has flourished in the years since the first edition of this book appeared in 1987. In undertaking a second edition, I have drawn on the recent work of historians who have explored issues of urban growth, municipal politics, immigration and ethnicity, "suburbanization," and environmental change. I have also benefitted from the scholarship in fields closely related to history such as geography, political science, sociology, and planning. An academic position in which I work with students in interdisciplinary programs in Community Development, Urban Studies, and Urban and Regional Planning constantly reminds me that fascination and concern with growth and change in the nation's metropolitan regions spans a wide range of scholarly disciplines and fields of public policy.

The most obvious change for this edition is the addition of a fourth chapter covering the years since 1980. I have tried to explore the continued development of the themes and topical areas delineated in the earlier chapters—the physical form of metropolitan areas, their sources of growth, their mix of ethnic and racial groups, public policy responses, and community planning ideas about the best way to shape efficient and just cities. In this new chapter, as in the earlier edition, I have tried to maintain regional balance in examples. New York, Boston, and Chicago are indispensable anchors for the urban history of the United States, but so are Los Angeles, Atlanta, and San Francisco—

not to mention Seattle, Denver, San Antonio, Miami, Charlotte, Washington, Detroit, and Cleveland.

In addition to the new chapter, I have revisited the introduction and the earlier chapters to update statistical information and incorporate the findings of important and influential new books. Alert readers who are familiar with recent urban history will spot new sentences and paragraphs for which I am indebted to the scholarship of Lizabeth Cohen, Becky Nicolaides, Earl Lewis, Alison Isenberg, Robert Fogelson, Andrew Wiese, Julia Blackwelder (to name a few examples from Chapter One) and many others. As might be expected, most of these changes lead to a more nuanced history with more attention to alternatives and exceptions of the central narrative.

The proliferation of scholarship is also apparent in the bibliographical essay, which includes a wide selection of new books in addition to the earlier references. The essay concentrates on books by historians but also includes a number of titles by other social scientists, city planners, and policy specialists. My task was aided by the excellent bibliographies of new books and articles that are a regular feature of the Urban History Association newsletter.

INTRODUCTION

The Metropolitan Era

The modern metropolis is a huge and intricate machine, a three-dimensional network of houses, skyscrapers, highways, parks, and power grids. Those of us who live in cities or visit them see only parts and pieces. We use a few neighborhoods, a freeway, downtown offices, a coliseum, or a convention center. The closest anyone can come to a view of the entire metropolis is a satellite photograph that spans fifty or a hundred miles, from one suburban fringe to another.

Every city dweller spends his or her daily life as a member of specific groups and a resident of an individual neighborhood. At the same time, each citizen shares connections and concerns with all other members of the metropolitan community. If we are to meet our present responsibilities, we need to understand how we have built the parts and assembled them into the immense artifacts that we call modern American cities.

At our starting point in 1920, the most successful machine in the United States was Henry Ford's Model T automobile, available to most citizens for under $600. The Volstead Act went into effect in January of that year, ending a campaign for a national prohibition on the sale of alcoholic beverages that had pitted small towns and middle-class suburbs against the working class neighborhoods of large cities. The Nineteenth Amendment to the U.S. Constitution was ratified in August 1920, in time to allow women as well as men to vote Republican Warren G. Harding into office as president.

In 1920 the Census Bureau reported that the United States had become an urban nation; 51.2 percent of all Americans lived in towns and great cities rather than in country villages and on farms. Urban America in that year included 54,158,000 people who lived in 2,700 communities with populations of 2,500 or more—the official cutoff between rural and urban (Table I.1). The "cities" ranged from mining centers hidden in the high Rockies to fashionable resorts, from upper-crust suburbs to grimy mill towns. There were places of global importance like New York and Chicago, and farm-market centers like Thomaston (population 2,502) in the heart of Georgia, and Colfax (population 2,504) along Iowa's Skunk River.

Historians now look upon the 1920s as a new departure for urban America. For the three generations from 1920 to the twenty-first century, American society has been preoccupied with the problems and possibilities of its large cities. The cities themselves experienced a new scale and type of growth, changing from relatively compact communities with densely packed populations to huge sprawling metropolitan areas covering tens of millions of acres.

The degree of urbanization in any country is measured by the increase in the proportion or percentage of the population that lives in urban areas. Urbanization involves both increases in the size of existing cities and the appearance of new cities (see Table I.1). Between 1920 and 1950, jobs, housing, and services had to be provided for more than 42 million new residents of American cities—and this figure does not include the starting population in 1920. Between 1950 and 1980 we had to build streets, schools, fire stations, and water systems for an additional 70 million city dwellers—the equivalent of one hundred Tulsas or two hundred Spokanes—and for an additional 55 million urbanites in the century's last two decades.

Another way to measure urban population is to count the residents concentrated in major metropolitan areas. In 1920, the Census Bureau defined metropolitan districts as cities of 200,000 or more, plus the inhabitants of adjacent suburban areas. It made a similar cal-

TABLE I.1 **Urbanization of the United States in the Twentieth Century**

Year	Number of Urban Places	Total Urban Population (millions)	Percentage of U.S. Population in Urban Locations
1900	1,743	30.2	39.7
1910	2,269	42.0	45.7
1920	2,728	54.2	51.2
1930	3,183	69.0	56.2
1940	4,385	74.4	56.5
1950	4,077	96.5	64.0
1960	5,445	125.3	69.9
1970	6,433	149.3	73.6
1980	7,749	167.1	73.7
1990	8,510	187.1	75.2
2000	See note*	222.4	79.0

*In 2000, the Census Bureau radically changed the definition of urban areas so that no compatible figure is available.

culation for cities of 100,000 to 200,000 people, adding the population within ten miles of their boundaries. As Table I.2 shows, these fifty-eight metropolitan districts housed just over one-third of the American population. New York, Chicago, Philadelphia, Boston, Detroit, and Pittsburgh—the six largest—housed one-sixth of all Americans. As metropolitan areas have grown in importance, the definition for them has changed repeatedly. Since 1950, "Metropolitan Statistical Areas" have consisted of central cities with populations of at least 50,000 and the surrounding counties that are tied closely to those cities. Using the new definition, the first census after World War II found that more than half of all Americans lived in 168 metropolitan areas. Almost 30 percent lived in the fourteen metropolitan areas with a million or more people. Between 1950 and 1980, the number of individual metropolitan areas continued to grow as the populations of smaller cities passed the 50,000 threshold. For 1990 and 2000, the Census grouped a number of adjacent metropolitan ar-

TABLE I.2 **Metropolitan Population, 1920–2000**

Year	All Metropolitan Areas or Districts			Metropolitan Areas or Districts of 1,000,000+		
	Number	Population (millions)	Population as percent of U.S.	Number	Population (millions)	Population as percent of U.S.
1920[1]	58	35.9	33.9	6	17.6	16.6
1930[2]	96	54.8	44.4	10	30.6	24.8
1940[2]	140	63.0	47.6	11	33.7	25.5
1950[3]	168	84.5	55.8	14	44.4	29.4
1960[4]	212	119.6	66.7	24	62.6	34.9
1970[4]	243	139.4	68.6	34	83.3	41.0
1980[4]	318	169.4	74.8	38	92.9	41.1
1990[5]	268	197.5	79.4	40	135.9	54.3
2000[5]	276	226.2	80.3	49	161.2	57.1

[1]1920: Twenty-nine Metropolitan Districts plus 29 cities of 100–200,000 with adjacent territory.

[2]1930,1940: Metropolitan Districts

[3]1950: Standard Metropolitan Areas

[4]1960, 1970, 1980: Standard Metropolitan Statistical Area

[5]1990, 2000: Metropolitan Statistical Areas or Consolidated Metropolitan Statistical Areas

eas as Consolidated Metropolitan Statistical Areas such as Washington-Baltimore, reducing the total count. The metropolitan share of national population continued to grow, however, passing 79 percent by 1990. Sometime in the 1980s, metropolitan areas of 1 million or more accounted for more than half of all Americans and reached the 57 percent level in 2000.

The decades covered by this book represent a distinct period in the history of the United States and its cities. For the nation as a whole, this is the period in which city and then suburban votes came to shape national policy, in which the problems of race and poverty within cities became national concerns, and in which the growth or decline of urban centers determined the prosperity or decline of entire regions. Cities have led the transition from the industrial economy of the 1910s and 1920s to the service-based economy of the 1960s and 1970s and the information-based economy that ushered in the twenty-first century

This examination of urban America in the metropolitan era centers on four topics: (1) the evolution of the national system of cities from 2,700 urban areas and 58 metropolitan areas in 1920 to 8,500 urban areas and 276 metropolitan areas in 1990; (2) the changing arrangement of neighborhoods, communities, factories, and shopping districts within urban areas; (3) the changing balance of ethnic and racial groups within cities and suburbs and the efforts made by urban populations to deal with ethnic diversity; and (4) competing ideas about the most sustainable and equitable ways in which to build cities. All of these factors have significantly shaped national politics and have, in turn, been shaped by federal government initiatives.

Each chapter covers two decades in the history of modern America. One dividing point is the beginning of World War II, which fundamentally altered the economic balance within the United States. The second is the discovery of an urban crisis in the early 1960s, which changed the ways in which we have thought about cities and their problems. The third turning point is the accelerating transformation of the global economy that began in the later 1970s and increasingly shaped urban society and politics in the 1980s and 1990s. Because of the book's chronological organization, it may be helpful to summarize the key points within each topic.

The evolution of the national urban system has meant a shift in our urban balance from the Frostbelt to the Sunbelt as many of the major cities in the Northeast and Middle West have experienced a slow erosion of their economic base. The major reasons for this shift include the devastating impact of the Great Depression on industrial cities, the effect of wartime and Cold War defense spending, and the relative advantage of younger cities in competing for the growth industries that depend on new technologies.

These decades have also been the era of the exploding metropolis. Mass production of automobiles, paving and construction of hundreds of thousands of miles of streets and highways, and mass merchandising of new single-family dwellings allowed middle-class Americans to move up socially by moving out to new suburban communities. By the 1950s and 1960s, one result was the splitting of nearly every urban area into a relatively poor central city and a relatively wealthy ring of suburbs. By 1970, there were more suburbanites than central-city residents (see Table I.3). At the same time it was clear that many suburban areas had succeeded in socially isolating themselves and becoming politically and economically independent of their core cities.

TABLE I.3 Suburban Population, 1920–2000

Year	Suburban Population (millions)	Suburban Population as Percentage of U.S.	Suburban Proportion of all Metropolitan Population
1920	9.7	9.1	26.9
1930	16.9	13.7	30.9
1940	20.3	15.2	32.0
1950	35.1	23.2	41.5
1960	54.9	30.5	45.9
1970	75.6	37.2	54.2
1980	101.3	44.8	59.9
1990	120.0	48.0	60.5
2000	145.9	51.8	64.5

An important factor in the accelerated metropolitan explosion was the great northward movement of the twentieth century. In the 1910s and 1920s, the migration of black Americans from the rural South to northern cities was a largely new phenomenon. In the 1940s and 1950s, migration to northern and western cities swelled as more African Americans, Puerto Ricans, and whites from the depressed counties of Appalachia sought economic opportunities. With reforms in immigration law in 1965, the northward movement took on an international character involving millions of new urbanites from the Caribbean nations, Central America, Mexico, and East Asia. The increasingly multiracial character of U.S. cities has changed their politics, created new points of conflict, and reinforced the tendency toward suburban isolationism.

When critics, planners, and reformers have contemplated the growing metropolis, they have defined the basic choice as going up or going out. Some writers have argued that the solution to urban problems is to spread cities outward and devise sustainable regional systems that balance city and countryside. Others have claimed that the great advantage of cities is their density and concentration, with the creative energy that can be sparked in intense settings. From 1920 to 1960, the first school of thought spoke more loudly and convincingly. In the more recent decades, advocates of focused cities and urbanism have been gaining ground.

Suburbs and Sunbelt, ghettos, barrios, and everyday neighborhoods have all been part of the metropolitan challenge. The building of humane cities has been the great task and the great adventure of modern America. Our cities have mirrored both the weaknesses and strengths of our society. They have been the centers of persistent problems of economic inequality and of deep gulfs among racial and ethnic groups. They have also been the places with the greatest concentration of human energy for creating new industries, ideas, and solutions to longstanding problems.

Seventy years ago, a number of the nation's leading specialists on urban growth summed up the promise of the American city in a report to President Franklin Roosevelt on *Our Cities: Their Role in the National Economy*. Their words are still appropriate for the new century:

The city has seemed at times the despair of America, but at others to be the Nation's hope, the battleground of democracy. Surely in the long run, the Nation's destiny will be profoundly affected by the cities which have two-thirds of its population and its wealth. . . . There is fertility and creation in the rich soil of the broad countryside, but there is also fertility and creativeness in the forms of industry, art, personality, emerging even from the city streets and reaching toward the sky. The faults of our cities are not those of decadence and impending decline, but of exuberant vitality crowding its way forward under tremendous pressure—the flood rather than the drought.

CHAPTER ONE

The First Modern Cities

George F. Babbitt, the hero of Sinclair Lewis's best-selling 1922 novel, *Babbitt*, was thoroughly up to date. He awakened each morning to "the best of nationally advertised and quantitatively produced alarm-clocks, with all modern attachments, including cathedral chime, intermittent alarm, and a phosphorescent dial." His God was Modern Appliances. His bathroom was sleek with glazed tile and silver metal, with "tooth-brush holder, shaving-brush holder, soap-dish, sponge-dish, and medicine-cabinet, so glittering and so ingenious that they resembled an electrical instrument-board." Best of all was his motor car, a symbol of poetry and heroism that sometimes started on cold mornings and sometimes did not.

Babbitt lived in the thoroughly modern (and mythical) city of Zenith in an unidentified state in the Middle West. His green-and-white Dutch Colonial house stood in the bright new subdivision of Floral Heights. Three miles away at the center of town, the tower of the Second National Bank building pushed thirty-five stories of Indiana limestone into the sky. In between, nearly 400,000 Zenithers lived in an assortment of rich, poor, and middling neighborhoods. Babbitt

admired each part of the city in turn on his daily drive to his downtown real estate office:

> The one-story shops on Smith Street, a glare of plate-glass and new
> yellow brick; groceries and laundries and drug-stores to supply the more
> immediate needs of East Side housewives. The market gardens in Dutch
> Hollow, their shanties patched with corrugated iron and stolen doors.
> Billboards with crimson goddesses nine feet tall advertising cinema
> films, pipe tobacco, and talcum powder. The old "mansions" along Ninth
> Street, S.E., like aged dandies in filthy linen; wooden castles turned
> into boarding-houses, with muddy walks and rusty hedges, jostled by
> fast-intruding garages, cheap apartment-houses, and fruit-stands. . . .
> Across the belt of railroad-tracks, factories with high-perched water-
> tanks and tall stacks. . . . Then the business center, the thickening dart-
> ing traffic, the crammed trolleys unloading, and the high doorways of
> marble and polished granite.

To sophisticated critics, "babbittry" was to become a synonym
for smug self-satisfaction, but Babbitt's city was instantly recognizable to readers in the 1920s. Lewis had spent weeks in towns like
Indianapolis and Kansas City soaking up the flavor of city life. Minneapolis celebrated a "Babbitt week" after the book's publication. Newspapers in Cincinnati, Milwaukee, Kansas City, and Duluth
each proclaimed proudly that their own community was the model
for Zenith. As far as George Babbitt's contemporaries were concerned,
Zenith was the typical industrial city at the peak of heavy industrialization in the United States.

Core and Periphery

The American urban system in the 1920s was the geographical cli-
max of the age of steam and steel that had begun in the second half of
the nineteenth century. Economists define primary industries as the
producers of raw materials and secondary industries as those that make
raw materials into manufactured goods. For the United States as a
whole, national employment in primary and secondary industries
reached its 56 percent peak around 1920, before the balance in the
labor force began to shift toward commerce and services.

To paint the regional picture with the broadest strokes, the United States economy at the start of the 1920s was divided into two parts. In one, the West and South furnished wheat, cotton, lumber, copper, and hundreds of other raw materials; in the other, northern cities emptied the ships and boxcars and turned the raw resources into finished products. This division of labor was possible because of the American railroad network, which had grown from 60,000 miles of track in 1870 to 254,000 miles at its apex in 1916. Manufacturers had found that they were able to serve the entire national market from single huge factories. The heart of a city like Zenith was its factory zone, "a high-colored, banging, exciting region: new factories of hollow tile with gigantic wire-glass windows, old red-brick factories stained with tar . . . and, on a score of hectic side-tracks, far-wandering freight-cars from the New York Central and apple orchards, the Great Northern and wheat-plateaus, the Southern Pacific and orange groves."

Like the cities on which it was modeled, Zenith also specialized. Its factories made paper boxes, condensed milk, and lighting fixtures. A real city like Dayton made cash registers for the country's booming retail business. Akron manufactured tires. Bethlehem, Gary, Youngstown, and Pittsburgh turned out steel. Grand Rapids was known for furniture pieced together from the forests of the Great Lakes. Farm machinery rolled off the line in Moline and tractors did the same in Peoria. Detroit was the grandest of all of these manufacturing capitals. It furnished roughly two-thirds of the world's motor cars in the early 1920s, with half its labor force employed by auto plants and their suppliers. Good wages attracted 600,000 new Detroiters in the 1910s and 900,000 in the 1920s. Its symbol was Ford Motor Company's giant new plant on 2,000 acres along the Rouge River. The plant was an autonomous industrial complex in which a network of low-slung buildings allowed Henry Ford to realize his ideal of a continuous flow of work that could be performed on one level. For industrialists and artists alike, it was one of the marvels of the age.

From the Merrimack River of New England to the Mississippi, these specialized cities made up the American industrial belt. Draw a line on a map from Waterville, Maine, to Minneapolis, turn south to St. Louis, and return to the Atlantic coast by way of Louisville, Cincinnati, and Baltimore, and you will find that the entire area includes less than 10 percent of the land area of the United States. In the 1920s, it also included more than 70 percent of the nation's manufacturing jobs and industrial output. Perhaps a simpler way to think of the area is as the home territory of major-league baseball in the era of Ty Cobb and Babe Ruth—from the Boston Braves to the Washington Senators to the St. Louis Cardinals.

Among all the cities of the industrial heartland, New York was the uncontested capital in the 1920s, an energetic and flamboyant city that was second only to London as a world metropolis. To novelist Thomas Wolfe, New York in the 1920s was the essence of opportunity. "New York lays hands upon a man's bowels," he wrote in *The Web and the Rock*. "He grows drunk with ecstasy; he grows young and full of glory." The city was the hinge between the United States and the rest of the world. Huge maritime terminals in Brooklyn and New Jersey handled goods from every continent, while executives and office workers in lower and midtown Manhattan controlled the shipments. Greater New York was the location of heavy industries like oil refining in New Jersey (where pipelines and rail lines from Pennsylvania and the Middle West reached the seaboard). The center of the frantic garment district was 34th Street and Seventh Avenue. Above all else, however, New York was the center of the nation's nervous system. There were located the major stock exchanges, the biggest banks, the most expensive law firms, the publishing industry, and the most important of all the new advertising firms that were influencing the decade's consumerism. "After you leave New York," said entertainer George M. Cohan, "every town is Bridgeport."

The Manhattan skyline reflected the city's role as a business center. Wall Street was rebuilt in the 1910s and 1920s with an array of magnificent corporate towers. Wealthy New Yorkers moved into the new elevator apartment buildings that turned Park Avenue into a fashionable two-and-a-half mile corridor of brick and limestone extending from Grand Central Station at 46th Street north to 96th Street. Three great monuments climaxed New York's skyscraper boom. The Chrysler Building, which opened in 1930, was the pet project of auto tycoon Walter Chrysler; six stories of stainless steel capped the 77-floor spire. Done in the full art-deco style of the twenties, a frieze of abstract automobiles ran in a band around the tower, and the gargoyles

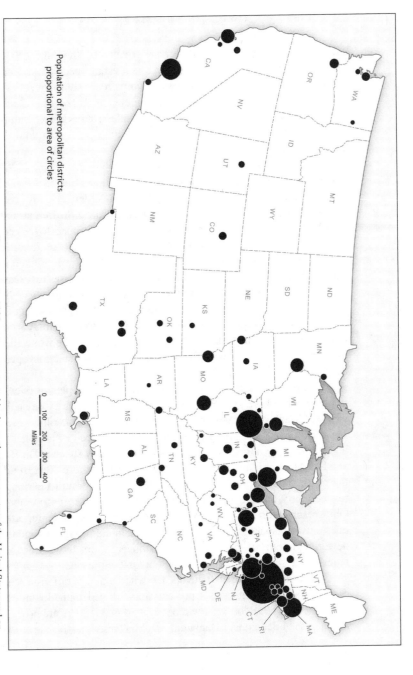

Metropolitan Districts in 1930. Major metropolitan centers in 1930 were concentrated in the northeastern quarter of the United States and on the Pacific Coast. Adapted from U.S. National Resources Committee. *Our Cities. Their Role in the National Economy* (1937).

Population of metropolitan districts proportional to area of circles at the top were copied from radiator cap ornaments. The Empire State Building, completed a year later, was a real-estate speculation. Construction was so efficient that its steel frame rose one story per day until all 102 floors were finished. The builders of Rockefeller Center worked throughout the 1930s to cover seventeen acres in the heart of the city with an integrated complex of buildings massed around the soaring wafer of the RCA Building.

Chicago also ranked among the world's top ten cities by the 1920s. Its skyline not only reflected its role as hog butcher and tool maker, but also as banker, insurance agent, freight forwarder, and salesman. Old and new skyscrapers packed the central business district, around which the elevated rail loop brought workers and shoppers to the center of the city. "Although it is relatively but a small part of the city," wrote a local publication about the Loop in 1923, "it is a giant in power. Here are gathered the main offices of big businesses that serve the world . . . a business section in which are 300,000 workers, to say nothing of 20,000 streetcars passing in and out of this area every 24 hours." A new bridge across the Chicago River took Michigan Avenue north and opened a new architectural frontier for the white-tiled Wrigley Building, the neo-Gothic Tribune Tower, and a lakefront apartment zone for the rich.

One historian has counted 377 American skyscrapers of twenty or more stories built by 1930. The overwhelming majority rose on the island of Manhattan or within two miles of State and Randolph streets in Chicago. However, dozens of smaller cities were just as eager to boast of their own towers as symbols of community success. Buffalo and Los Angeles built high-rise city halls. The Baltimore Trust Building reached thirty-four stories, Pittsburgh's "Cathedral of Learning" reached forty, and the American Insurance Union tower in Columbus, Ohio, reached forty-six. "Des Moines is ever going forward!" reported one of its newspapers. "With our new thirteen-story building and the new gilded dome of the Capitol, Des Moines towers above the other cities of the state like a lone cottonwood on the prairie."

The twenties were also the decade when a number of cities carried out grand public works projects that framed their downtown areas. Even if they don't know it, American moviegoers are now familiar with Philadelphia's Benjamin Franklin Parkway—it's the broad, tree-lined avenue that Rocky Balboa views exultantly from the steps of the Philadelphia Art Museum after his early morning run in the original *Rocky*. First opened in 1919 and completed over the next several years, it realized a twenty-year-old dream of having a magnificent entrance to the city. Chicagoans built on an even greater scale, spending a billion dollars on their lakefront between the world wars. Landfill and landscaping turned nearly twenty miles of ill-kept shoreline into parks and beaches. For the past half century, the view from Lake Shore Drive across Grant Park and northwestward into the heart of Chicago has provided the most visually impressive cityscape in the nation.

Downtowns were increasingly shaped by and for women. Nineteenth-century business districts had been rough-and-tumble areas that mixed offices, warehouses, docks, and shops. The evolution of the massive department store with its multiple block-wide floors of clothing and household goods, however, provided a safe environment for middle-class shoppers from the new neighborhoods. Experts calculated that women controlled 85 percent of consumer spending and store owners strove to attract "Mrs. Consumer" to their particular locations. Working women added to the numbers of women on downtown streets. Since the introduction of the typewriter and telephone in the late nineteenth century, female stenographers, secretaries, bookkeepers, telephone operators, and receptionists had replaced male clerks in most office settings. They took the streetcar to work, ate in downtown lunch rooms, and shopped in downtown stores after work. Meanwhile, the bars, hotels, flophouses, and brothels that served single male workers were increasingly concentrated in Skid Row districts on the edge of downtown.

Urban development in the South during the 1920s involved a small-scale industrial takeoff in which northern companies began to relocate or to open branch plants in small southern cities where land and labor were relatively cheap. The new manufacturing cities formed a wedge into the South along both sides of the Appalachians. The small towns of the central Carolinas grew at the expense of the textile-mill cities of New England. The iron and steel city of Birmingham, Alabama, with a statue of the god Vulcan as its civic symbol, prospered as the "Pittsburgh of the South." Kingsport, Tennessee, designed by noted planner John Nolen in 1916, burgeoned from a few hundred to 12,000 residents in 1930.

Finance, marketing, and distribution of goods from the North were handled by southern centers that were themselves tributaries to St. Louis and New York. Atlanta was the South's major railroad hub and New Orleans its major port. Nashville's ambitious leaders promoted finance and manufacturing simultaneously. Nashville's businessmen worked through their chamber of commerce and commercial club to lure northern textile and shoe manufacturers to the city, while Du Pont converted a wartime gunpowder plant to one that produced rayon in 1923. Nashville's bankers also reached through the middle South so that the expansion of local insurance companies made it possible to tout Union Street as "the Wall Street of the South."

In the western half of the nation, the biggest story was the growth of Los Angeles. Boosters used an "All-Weather Club" to attract tourists and retirees, but the city's real strengths were agriculture, oil production, and new industries like aircraft manufacturing and movies. Los Angeles replaced San Francisco–Oakland as the West Coast's largest manufacturing center and port during the 1920s boom. Given that the city's population grew from 1.2 million to 2.3 million in a single decade, it is not surprising that the price of real estate rose in a speculative spiral. Potential buyers could take free bus tours in which the homes of Hollywood celebrities like Mack Sennett and Mary Pickford were pointed out. These tours would end at the new subdivision with the expected come-on.

> And now here we are . . . buy one, or ten, of these lots, regardless of the sacrifice it might mean. Ten thousand banks may close, stocks may smash, bonds may shrink to little or nothing, but this tract and Los Angeles real estate stand like the Rock of Gibraltar for safety, certainty, and profit.

The Climax of Immigration

The great transatlantic migrations that brought millions of new Americans from northern, eastern, and Mediterranean Europe combined with economic patterns to establish the individual character of American cities. The United States welcomed 17 million immigrants between

1890 and 1914 and another 2.9 million between 1919 and 1924, the vast majority of whom settled in urban areas. As of 1920, the largest immigrant sources were (in decreasing order) Russia (including ethnic Russians, Ukrainians, and Jews), Italy, Germany, Poland, Ireland, and the Scandinavian countries. Russians, Italians, and Irish tended to concentrate in the cities of the Northeast and in major ports such as New Orleans and San Francisco. A band of heavily German cities ran across the Middle West, anchored by the beer-producing centers of Cincinnati, St. Louis, and Milwaukee. Poles and other central Europeans also gravitated toward the industrial cities of the Middle West. Scandinavians settled in the country's northwestern quadrant (see Table 1.1).

Urban immigrants and their children lived in highly structured cities as the neighborhoods in a typical metropolis fit together like slices of a pie, with a set of wedges radiating outward from the thriving downtown to the surrounding suburbs. The local elite usually appropriated the most attractive land for their own homes—typically hills, ridge lines, and shoreline areas backed by high bluffs—with middle-class residents locating as close to these areas as possible. Heavy industrial sectors tended to develop on lower land where freight transportation was cheapest, particularly along riverfronts and railroad corridors. Laborers, factory workers, and skilled tradesmen filled in the remaining sectors with a hodgepodge of neighborhoods that ranged from the least expensive and most crowded housing in the inner-city slums and boarding-house districts to stable, family-oriented areas with newer houses and apartments.

These wedges of working-class housing were further subdivided into a checkerboard of ethnic districts. Old-stock Americans, observing the industrial city from the comfortable distance of their affluent neighborhoods, tended to assume that immigrant districts meant simple divisions in which all Italians (and almost no one else) lived in "Little Italy," all Germans lived in "Yorkville" or "Over-the-Rhine," and all Jews lived on the Lower East Side. In fact, in most cities several neighborhoods housed each major immigrant group. For example, Polish immigrants to Philadelphia settled in at least twelve distinct neighborhoods. Although the heart of Polonia in Chicago was the northwest side, which counted about 180,000 ethnic Poles in 1930, more than 10,000 Poles lived in each of five other areas. Even in a smaller city like Portland, Oregon, Italian immigrants and their children were living in two distinct neighborhoods by the 1920s and 1930s.

Nor did any one group monopolize most neighborhoods. There were single blocks where everyone was Polish or Jewish or Croatian, but the larger neighborhood, the one that everyone in the city could identify by name, was shared by residents of different backgrounds. The Japanese, who began to spread through Boyle Heights in Los Angeles in the 1920s, shared the district with Mexicans, Jews, and Anglo Americans; even the heart of Little Tokyo was only 37 percent Japanese. Elderly Italians in Portland remember South Portland as an Italian community while older Jews remember it as a Jewish neighborhood; each group dominated a few blocks, but neither formed a majority in the neighborhood as a whole. The situation was similar in Philadelphia. Slovaks lived in at least five neighborhoods and Ukrainians in at least six. "Although the vast majority of Philadelphia's Italians lived in that part of South Philadelphia directly adjacent to Center City," historian Caroline Golab points out, "it is unfair to speak of South Philadelphia as if it held only Italians or only one Italian colony. Rather, South Philadelphia housed innumerable Italian colonies, each separated by seas and bands of Irish, Germans, Jews, blacks, British, and Anglo-Americans."

Even when several groups shared the physical space in a particular neighborhood, that neighborhood was still able to be their focus because of the distinct churches, businesses, fraternal associations, and social networks through which each immigrant group maintained its own community. What made a neighborhood "Jewish" or "Greek" was not that Jews or Greeks were the sole residents, but that its streets, stores, newspapers, and social clubs served as centers of activity, communication, and practical assistance for residents who thought of themselves as Jews or Greeks. At the same time, the ethnic community provided the base of loyal customers from which a small entrepreneur could build a substantial business. Economically successful immigrants or their children might move upward and outward, but the ethnic neighborhood, its institutions, and its main street with Polish or Italian signs helped to maintain

TABLE 1.1 **Origins of European-Born Population of Twenty-five Large Cities, 1920**

City	Leading Country of Birth	Second Leading Country of Birth
New York	Russia	Italy
Philadelphia	Russia	Ireland
Washington	Russia	Ireland
Baltimore	Russia	Germany
Jersey City	Italy	Ireland
Newark	Italy	Russia
Rochester	Italy	Germany
New Orleans	Italy	Germany
San Francisco	Italy	Germany
Boston	Ireland	Italy
Cleveland	Poland	Hungary
Buffalo	Poland	Germany
Detroit	Poland	Germany
Chicago	Poland	Germany
Pittsburgh	Germany	Poland
Milwaukee	Germany	Poland
Cincinnati	Germany	Russia
St. Louis	Germany	Russia
Kansas City	Germany	Russia
Indianapolis	Germany	Ireland
Los Angeles	England	Germany
Minneapolis	Scandinavian nations	Germany
Portland	Scandinavian nations	Germany
Seattle	Scandinavian nations	England
Denver	Scandinavian nations	Russia

and broadcast its ethnic identity. In the Lawndale neighborhood of Chicago, for example, the main thoroughfare of Douglas Boulevard was lined with half a dozen synagogues, a home for the Jewish blind, the Hebrew Theological College, the Jewish People's Institute, and Herzl Junior College. Close by were dozens of other synagogues, Jewish social service agencies, and the Jewish *Daily Forward* offices. On the High Holy Days, automobile traffic on Douglas and its side streets virtually ceased.

In most of the larger and middle-sized cities, the ethnic neighborhood and the community-forming institutions were created in the decades around 1900, a time when the volume of immigration was greatest and the problems of adjusting to the new world the most overwhelming. By the 1920s and 1930s, ethnic neighborhoods had increasingly become remnants or survivals. Thanks to the research of Stephen Thernstrom, we know more about economic mobility in Boston than any other city. And if Bostonians are representative of other large cities, immigrants began to show significant gains relative to native-born Americans early in the last century. Although old-stock Yankees still dominated the professions between the two world wars, second-generation ethnics probably matched them in other white-collar jobs. There were important differences in the rates of economic success from one ethnic or religious group to another: Jews outpaced Italians in Boston and New York, for example, and Romanians reached middle-class status more rapidly than did Slovaks in Cleveland. But the most important conclusion overall is that white immigrants and their children were able gradually to close the gap that separated them from the native born.

Economic mobility allowed immigrant families to choose newer and/or better housing than the crowded apartments of the congested urban center. Residential segregation for immigrant groups declined steadily. Sociologist Stanley Lieberson's study of ten northern cities found declines in segregation between 1910 and 1920 and again between 1930 and 1950 (gaps in the available data prevent a 1920–30 comparison). In addition, the children of European immigrants were less segregated from whites of American-born parents than were their immigrant mothers and fathers. These facts and figures reflect the outward expansion of ethnic neighborhoods. Half of Chicago's Italians lived within two miles of the city's center in 1920; by 1930 the halfway line was 3.3 miles. New York's Jewish families followed what Samuel Lubell has called the "tenement trail" from Manhattan to the Bronx, especially to the west side of the Grand Concourse "beyond which rolled true middle-class country" where "janitors were called superintendents."

The newer neighborhoods offered important opportunities for capital accumulation and upward mobility through home ownership. Slovaks in Cleveland and Italians in Pittsburgh used the homes they owned to both gain control of the family's living conditions and build up a savings account. In Chicago, an estimated 33,000 Polish families had purchased homes in northwest and southwest neighborhoods by 1928. Milwaukee's fourteenth ward, also heavily Polish, had a higher percentage of home ownership than the city average by 1940. A federal report commented that most families started with a four-room frame house.

> When this has been paid for, it is raised on posts to allow a semi-basement to be constructed underneath. . . . This basement or the upstairs flat is then let by the owner, who, as soon as his funds permit, substitutes brick walls for the timber of the basement, but the ambition of a Polish house-owner is not crowned until he is able to have cement walks and iron railings in front of his house.

In the same decades, the narrow horizons of ethnic identity and neighborhood also broadened under the influence of mass culture. Historian Lizabeth Cohen has described the transition in Chicago from an ethnically divided city in 1920 to one with a unified working-class by the 1930s. Much of the change came from the erosion of the city's ethnic grocery stores, banks, and churches, as well as its foreign-language newspapers and radio. Instead, working-class Chicagoans increasingly shopped at chain stores, listened (in English) to the new national radio networks, and viewed Hollywood movies. The Roman Catholic diocese worked to replace ethnic parishes with neighborhood churches that served everyone regardless of national background. Out of this engagement with mainstream culture came a white working class whose members retained their sense of ethnic identity but also recognized common needs that would support a strong labor union movement during the Great Depression.

The Transition of Reform

The business boosterism of George Babbitt and the maturing of urban ethnic groups combined to establish the context for city politics in the 1920s and early 1930s. During the first two decades of the century, urban politics had tended to reflect the social geography of the metropolis. The immigrant poor in central-city neighborhoods provided the votes that kept professional politicians and their machines in control of city governments. Members of the native-born middle class, who had moved in increasing numbers to new neighborhoods at the outer end of trolley lines, were the heart of reform movements that attempted to replace the machines with businesslike and progressive administrations. At the very least, members of the articulate middle class worried about city governments that were inefficient and unresponsive to urban needs. Many reform campaigns for clean government were also struggles between suburban and inner-city lifestyles. In these sometimes bitter cultural contests, it was difficult to discern whether the key conflict was native born versus immigrant, Protestant versus Catholic, or middle class versus working class.

Reformers had good reason to be concerned about the corruption and demagoguery of many machine politicians. Chicago's William Hale Thompson, mayor from 1915 to 1923 and again from 1928 to 1931, typified the problem with political bosses and machine politics. "Big Bill" has been described by Paul M. Green as "an easygoing hustler, a sometimes adolescent showman, and probably the greatest political campaigner in Chicago history." Thompson won his first election by appealing to the most blatant ethnic prejudices. He attacked Catholics in middle-class Protestant neighborhoods; at the same time, he courted the German and Irish vote with anti-British speeches. A few years later, he played to Irish audiences by threatening to punch King George in the nose if the British monarch decided to make a Chicago side trip while on a tour of Canada. Thompson presided over deep corruption. In the early 1920s, bootlegger John Torrio bought protection from Thompson and the city authorities with regular payoffs. When Al Capone became the king of organized crime in Chicago, Thompson was little more than a front man for his mob.

Middle-class urbanites in the 1920s also feared the immigrant neighborhoods' propensity for being recruiting grounds for militant labor unions that threatened their economic position. The first two decades of the century had brought a long series of violent labor-management confrontations in industrial cities like Lawrence, Massachusetts, and Paterson, New Jersey. Events in 1919 fed the urbanites' fears, as unions tried for wage increases to match salaries during wartime inflation. A walkout by Seattle shipyard workers led the Seattle Central Labor Council to take the radical step of calling a general strike. Mayor Ole Hanson quickly proclaimed that the city was menaced by Reds and used troops to break the strike within five days. In September of 1919, the Boston police struck, leaving the city open to looting and vandalism. The governor of Massachusetts, Calvin Coolidge, made a national reputation by sending in the National Guard to restore order.

Along with major strikes in the coal and steel industries, the events in Seattle and Boston created a situation that enabled U.S. attorney general A. Mitchell Palmer to manufacture a national "Red scare." Palmer was an opportunistic politician who found it convenient to announce that foreign-born radicals were leading a concerted movement to destroy the foundations of the nation. In August 1919, he appointed young J. Edgar Hoover to head a new general intelligence bureau within the Justice Department and gave Hoover instructions to root out Reds. With his eye on the Democratic presidential nomination, Palmer directed mass arrests in New York and deported 249 radicals in November and December. He greeted 1920 with coordinated raids in thirty-three cities, detaining 4,000 suspected communists. Although an increasingly skeptical public tired of the Red scare within the year, Palmer's actions would not have been possible had the urban middle class not been deeply concerned that the immigrant residents of central-city districts were a threat to their economic position and way of life. The level of concern was expressed in miniature Red scares and militant union-busting in a number of cities.

The success of the Ku Klux Klan in many southern, western, and midwestern cities in the early 1920s derived from the same concern about protecting an established way of life that seemed threatened by rapid modernization. Founded by Georgian William J. Simmons in 1915, the Klan, for its first five years, was an unsuccessful fraternal organization. In 1920, however, Simmons hired professional organizers for a membership drive that soon had scores of "Kleagles" recruiting throughout the cities and towns of the South. The Klan played on fears of social change. In the age of motor cars, movies, and mass merchandizing, Klansmen shared a commitment to a nostalgic Americanism. Membership in the Invisible Empire meant an assault on "outsiders" who were pushing their way into positions of influence—Jews, African Americans who dared to violate race-caste lines, and especially Roman Catholics.

Klan membership grew from 2,000 in 1920 to a peak of more than 2 million in 1924. It was especially strong not only in the South, but also in such states as Indiana, Oklahoma, Colorado, and Oregon. Given its anti-Catholicism, it is no surprise that the Klan made few gains in the heavily immigrant Northeast and Great Lakes cities. However, half of its membership came from cities of more than 50,000—Knoxville, Dallas, Memphis, Indianapolis, Portland. Many urban politicians decided that Klan support could make them sure winners. In Denver, Mayor Benjamin Stapleton appointed a Klansman as director of Public Safety. When threatened with a recall election, Stapleton vowed·that "I will work with the Klan and for the Klan . . . heart and soul. And if I am reelected, I will give the Klan the kind of administration it wants."

The KKK faded out nearly as rapidly as it had grown. In part, the prosperity of the mid-1920s stilled the insecurities that had made the Klan's scapegoating seem plausible and reassuring. Moreover, it was difficult to turn fear into legislation. Klansmen or Klan sympathizers who were elected to public office found that it was easier to criticize than to offer constructive solutions that went beyond legislative attacks on communion wine or parochial schools. By 1928, membership was down to 100,000 and dropping fast, and civic leaders were trying to forget the whole embarrassing episode.

The negative effects of the Red scare and the KKK were balanced by more rational responses to urban change. Members of the native-born middle class turned to the tools of municipal government to insulate themselves from the turmoil of their cities. The city council–city manager system was intended to take the politics out of local government and to provide inexpensive, effective services by giving all administrative responsibilities to a single appointed executive. First adopted in 1908 in Staunton, Virginia, the system spread widely in the 1920s, with several hundred cities adopting it. It was especially popular in small- and middle-sized cities such as San Diego, Cincinnati, Dallas, and Charlotte where voters agreed on the basic goals of their local government. In such communities, the city manager system provided "businesslike" government that met the needs and interests of comfortable managerial and professional families.

Middle- and upper-class neighborhoods were also committed supporters of land-use zoning, the system of public regulation whereby a local government divides its territory into districts, with limitations placed on the types and densities of development allowed. Between the adoption of the first comprehensive zoning ordinance by New York in 1916 and the end of the 1920s, nearly a thousand cities and towns had implemented zoning.

Many of the early zoning ordinances made a simple division among single-family, apartment, commercial, and industrial zones. The strongest support came from the middle- and upper-middle-class neighborhoods that were protected through designation as exclusive zones for single-family housing. Apartment development was usually confined to lower-middle- and working-class neighborhoods, and commercial strips were relegated to the fringes of residential areas. The goal and the result were stable residential neighborhoods for city families with clout and status, while the pressures for land-use changes were channeled toward cheaper land in poorer neighborhoods. Independent suburbs frequently made "snob zoning" even more stringent by requiring large minimum lot sizes and zoning for single-family housing only. The landmark U.S. Supreme Court case, *City of Euclid* v. *Ambler Realty Company* (1926), which established the constitutionality of zoning, involved a suburban Cleveland zoning law that set single-family housing as the preferred land use and barred all other types of development within those zones.

Middle-class protectionism left the bread-and-butter issues of social and economic reform to a new generation of leaders who were emerging within big-city ethnic communities, often people with prior training in the day-to-day tactics of successful machine politics. Their interests centered around pragmatic measures for improving the lives of the urban working class. Typical measures included factory safety laws, workers' compensation programs, widows' pensions, and child labor laws. In cases like that of New York City's Democratic boss Charles Murphy, or the Republican political organization run by the Vare brothers in Philadelphia, social reforms were another way to perpetuate the machine. Such leaders, points out historian Roger Lotchin, were power brokers who found that reform sometimes helped in maintaining control over their constituents and cities.

In other cases, however, these new ethnic politicians provided a preview of the social reforms associated with the New Deal of the 1930s and the Fair Deal of the 1940s. When Anton Cermak took office as mayor of Chicago in 1931, he symbolized entry into the American mainstream not only for his fellow Czechs, but for other Slavic Americans as well. He had spent thirty years learning the trade of politics within the Democratic party as a state representative, Chicago alderman, and president of the Cook County Board of Commissioners. He had the savvy to deal with such disparate groups as the hoodlums of the Prohibition era, professional politicians, businessmen, and ordinary voters who wanted a better chance in life. In the two years that he served as mayor before being killed by a bullet meant for Franklin D. Roosevelt, Cermak did the best he could to meet the needs of Chicago's poor and working class in the midst of national depression.

In New York, Irish-American Al Smith and German-American Robert Wagner both came from the poor side of Manhattan. They worked their way up through the ranks as loyal members of the New York Democratic machine. By the 1920s, however, Smith had risen to the job of governor of New York, where he promoted public health, accessible recreation, workers' compensation, and similar social improvements. As a U.S. senator, Wagner pioneered federal public works programs to fight the Great Depression and put his name on the landmark Labor Relations Act of 1935 and the Housing Act of 1937.

The most colorful of the entire new breed of reformers was Fiorello La Guardia, a "fighter against his times" (the phrase of his biographer Arthur Mann). With Jewish and Italian parents and a Protestant upbringing, La Guardia was a one-man balanced ticket. He accepted the urban political machine as the established way of doing things but used it with his own agenda for social change. After an ambitious start in Congress from 1916 to 1919, La Guardia succeeded

Al Smith as president of the New York Board of Aldermen. Over the next two years, he developed a progressive program including city control of mass transit, police reform, and taxation of unused property. Returning to Congress in the mid-1920s, he used all the skills of a professional politician to cultivate the Italian and Jewish communities of his East Harlem district. He also fought for tax reform and pushed through the Norris–La Guardia Act to assist labor unions at the onset of the depression. La Guardia's career continued from 1933 to 1945 with three terms as mayor of New York. He made headlines by riding along with fire engines and reading the comic strips over the radio during a newspaper strike. He also used his political skills to help a hard-hit city survive the depression. Like others of his political generation, he was an urban liberal who wanted newer Americans to share opportunities with the more established groups and communities. Men like La Guardia and Wagner were a mirror image of the Ku Klux Klan, looking to a better future rather than longing for a better past. They also prepared the nation for the fundamental social changes that were to come in the middle decades of the century.

Making the African American Ghettos

European ethnic neighborhoods and ethnic politics were the backdrop for the urban migration of more than 2 million African Americans between 1910 and 1940. A boom in factory jobs, as the United States became the arsenal for the Allies in World War I, triggered the "Great Migration" from South to North between 1916 and 1919, but the movement was more than a temporary response to labor shortages. Long-term social and economic trends simultaneously pushed blacks out of the rural South and attracted them to northern cities. In the first decades of the twentieth century, the number of agricultural jobs available to southern blacks fell steadily as landowners consolidated their farm holdings and replaced tenant farmers with machinery. After 1924, the decline in European immigration made poor southerners the most readily available labor force for northeastern and midwestern cities. Paralleling this development, race relations in the South reached a low point in the 1910s with the entrenchment of Jim Crow segregation and the relegation of African Americans to second-class citizenship through political disenfranchisement.

Within the context of the 1910s and 1920s, northern cities offered African Americans the best combination of social and economic
opportunity. In 1910, 90 percent of black Americans lived in the South.
The figure dropped to 85 percent by 1920 and 77 percent by 1930.
For the first decade of the century, the net result of migration among
the country's four major regions was a loss of 555,000 African Americans to the South balanced by gains of 242,000 in the Northeast,
281,000 in the Middle West, and 32,000 in the West. The South's net
outmigration was 903,000 for the 1920s and 480,000 for the 1930s.
The 1930s figure is especially telling since the Great Depression of
the 1930s made the familiar farms of the rural South seem relatively
attractive. Blacks from Florida, Georgia, and the Carolinas followed
coastal rail routes to the Middle Atlantic states and New England.
The great trunk lines of the Illinois Central and the Gulf, Mobile, and
Ohio railroads brought African American Alabamians, Mississippi-
ans, and Tennesseans to Chicago and the Middle West. Louisiana,
Arkansas, and Texas were the major source of black migrants to the
West.

The new northern blacks settled overwhelmingly in cities. African American populations doubled in Detroit, Buffalo, Chicago, and
Cleveland during the 1910s and grew by 50 percent in at least eight
other cities. New York's African American community totaled 92,000
in 1910, 152,000 in 1920, and 328,000 in 1930. The figures for Pittsburgh, which had one-tenth of New York's population, were 25,000 in
1910, 38,000 in 1920, and 55,000 in 1930. Nearly 90 percent of all
blacks in the North and West were city dwellers by the onset of the
depression.

Like their counterparts from Europe, African American newcomers chose large cities because urban life promised a wider scope for
their ambitions. A recent study of Pittsburgh has shown that participants in this first wave of black migration moved as family units or
maintained family ties and placed heavy emphasis on education as
the best means for advancement. In 1920, the rate of school atten-
dance for African Americans in Pittsburgh exceeded that among foreign-born and second-generation whites. Prosperous cities offered
immediate job opportunities. Black newspapers with national circu-

lation like the *Chicago Defender* kept hopes up by publishing want ads from northern factories and success stories of migrants like Robert A. Wilson. According to historian William Tuttle's summary of the newspaper's account, Wilson arrived in Chicago from Atlanta with a nickel and a penny.

> He spent the nickel for streetcar fare to the *Defender*'s offices and the penny for a bag of peanuts "to satisfy that pang of hunger." The newspaper directed him to the Urban League, which found him work at a foundry. Since that happy day, the *Defender* added, Wilson had acquired an automobile, house, and bank account, and had brought his family from the South; and "thus ends the romance of the lone nickel, the Lincoln penny, and the man who made opportunity a realization."

What African Americans found, however, was not so much the promise of the American dream as a series of roadblocks on every path to success. Tentatively in the 1910s and almost uniformly in the 1920s, white Americans constructed and patrolled institutional barricades that excluded blacks from the mainstream of urban life. Far too many African Americans found that virtue and ambition were not rewarded. By the end of the 1920s, major cities were split between a white and a black metropolis—separate and unequal communities divided by a few streets and invisible but real color lines.

The heart of the problem in northern cities was that African American migrants had to make room for themselves within functioning economic and social systems. From the point of view of working-class whites, the new arrivals competed for a limited supply of good jobs and affordable housing. They were viewed not as neighbors and co-workers, but as identifiable intruders whose every success threatened someone else's opportunities. The increasing strength of labor unions, for example, gave white workers an important tool for advancement but worked against African Americans. In the 1900s and 1910s, many black workers had naively arrived in northern cities as scabs (strikebreakers). Chicago packinghouse owners and East St. Louis factory managers recruited blacks directly in the South for the purpose of undermining growing union movements. Unionists held onto their resentment long after the use of African American strikebreakers stopped. Chicago unions were open to blacks officially but closed to them in practice. In Pittsburgh, another strong union town, only five of fifty-three labor organizations had African American members as late as 1940. Fifteen unions admitted to explicit discriminatory policies and the rest claimed that no African Americans had ever applied for membership. The result was the exclusion of blacks from skilled factory jobs and trades that paid well enough for families to put away savings, and exclusion from jobs that allowed fathers to pass on improved occupational status to their sons. In his detailed study of Boston, Stephen Thernstrom has concluded that there was "virtually no improvement" in the economic position of African American men between 1890 and 1940. "At least until World War II," he concludes, "blacks simply did not experience the same process of assimilation to urban life and consequent mobility" that European immigrants used to the advantage of their families.

Public facilities also shut their doors to African Americans as whites tried to erect barriers between white and black spheres. Northern cities failed to enforce civil rights laws that had been adopted after the Civil War to ensure equal access to public facilities. Some cities deliberately segregated their parks and beaches. In other cases, consensus within the white community blocked African Americans from their use. Many settlement houses—private centers for recreation, community education, and social services—closed their doors to blacks or offered segregated programs.

The climate of exclusion prevailed in small as well as large cities. Denver drew a careful line around its 7,000 black residents. Hence, African American workers in the 1920s and 1930s found nearly all their jobs in traditionally "black" trades: janitor, railroad porter, waiter, unskilled laborer, or servant. Private businessmen and public officials excluded African Americans from facilities considered outside their neighborhoods or beyond their social status. The city's best hotels refused service to both local and out-of-town blacks. The Denver Parks Department banned African Americans from swimming pools in neighborhood parks and allowed them swimming privileges on Wednesdays only at a downtown pool. Four-fifths of all Denver's black children went to five elementary schools, one junior high, and one senior high.

The most blatant segregation and the greatest number of conflicts involved housing. City officials could somewhat convincingly argue that segregation of parks and schools simply reflected neighborhood patterns. No one, however, could seriously maintain that the tight concentration of African Americans in a few core neighborhoods was the result of free choice in an open housing market.

As late as 1900, African American residential patterns resembled those of European immigrant groups. Most blacks lived in a few neighborhoods or sections of a city, but in no place were they the exclusive tenants of more than a small cluster of blocks. In Chicago, for example, most blacks lived on the south side of the city but were interspersed with whites in integrated neighborhoods. Only 25 percent of the city's African Americans lived in precincts that were 50 percent or more black, and 30 percent lived in precincts that were 95 percent white. Chicago's black population was, in fact, less segregated than its Italian population. A study of Philadelphia by the pioneering African American sociologist W. E. B. Dubois found the same pattern.

Nearly total residential segregation came as a response to the accelerating migration of the 1910s and 1920s. The process had two components. First, white residents defined a section of their city as suitable for African Americans. The choice was usually an old, deteriorating area that already had a substantial black population and that whites were willing to discard. African Americans found it extremely difficult to buy or rent outside the tacit boundaries of such an area. Second, whites began moving out of the "black" neighborhood and other whites refused to replace them. Even without a conscious white outflow, the normal turnover of an urban population is enough to create an all-black district within five to ten years. The boundaries of Chicago's black metropolis were clear by 1915 and the district was fully established by the early 1920s. New York's Harlem had 73,000 African Americans by 1920. Blacks in northern cities were more residentially segregated than foreign-born immigrants had been at the start of the decade, and the degree of this residential segregation increased over the next thirty years.

Urban America enforced neighborhood segregation through real-estate practices, public policy, and open violence. The housing mar-

covenants

ket was open to whites but not to blacks. Nothing prevented building managers and homeowners from refusing to rent or sell to blacks. New subdivisions were frequently protected by deed restrictions that prevented sale or rental to "persons of African descent." Although the U.S. Supreme Court declared in 1917 that cities could not legally use their land-use zoning power to enforce racial segregation, a number of southern cities tried to maneuver around the decision. Richmond, Virginia, passed a redesigned residential segregation ordinance in the mid-1920s that it tied to the state's 1924 "racial integrity" law forbidding miscegenation. Atlanta's 1922 zoning ordinance contained neighborhood categories of "R1 or White District," "R2 or Colored District," and "R3 or Undetermined." Both the Atlanta and Richmond laws were struck down by the federal courts, but the pattern they attempted to impose was maintained informally.

In the worst cases, violence and riot "enforced" residential segregation. The Chicago race riot of 1919, which left thirty-eight people dead after four days of violence between July 27 and July 30, was a confrontation over urban "turf." The trigger was the accidental encroachment on a white beach by African American children whose homemade raft had been caught and carried out of control by Lake Michigan currents. White bathers stoned the raft and killed one youth, enraged blacks confronted the white crowd, and the violence began. The tragedy followed a fifteen-month period in which at least twenty-five African American homes and real estate offices were bombed by whites trying to force scattered blacks into "their own" neighborhood. Most of the violence took place on the borders of the black neighborhood, and the favorite targets for white mobs were African American workers caught returning from jobs outside the black territory.

Similar tensions mounted in Detroit in the early 1920s. The city had historically been relatively open to African Americans, with strong civil-rights laws and a tradition of black employment in city government. When the 6,000 African Americans of 1910 became the 41,000 of 1920 and the 120,000 of 1930, however, public attitudes hardened. Nasty racial incidents plagued the city as black citizens tried to find housing outside their circumscribed neighborhoods, but neither the mayor nor the city council took any action. When an African American physician, Dr. Ossian Sweet, moved into an all-white neighborhood in 1925, a white mob assembled to drive him out. Within days after his move, one member of the mob had been shot to death and Sweet and two companions charged with murder. As in Chicago after 1919, the chief response of the city's establishment was a massive report on the situation of the city's African American population. The twelve volumes suggested improvements in social services and urged blacks to be less of an irritant by blending into the city's background. Particularly ironic, in view of white Detroit's demonstrated willingness to defend the integrity of all-white neighborhoods, was a suggestion that blacks try to live closer to their places of work so that they would make less use of public transit.

A race riot in Tulsa that killed between fifty and seventy-five people on May 31 and June 1, 1921, was less a battle over territory than an attempt to force a successful African American community into a subordinate role in the city. The "Magic City" of the Oklahoma oil business had grown from a country town of 1,300 in 1900 to a metropolis of 90,000 at the start of the 1920s. The new Tulsans included 11,000 African Americans who had moved from Arkansas, Louisiana, and Texas in search of "the big chance." In the new city, African Americans were able to carve out a neighborhood and a business district on the north side of town. "Deep Greenwood" was the center for a thriving minority community with two newspapers, thirteen churches, fraternal lodges, a hospital, theaters, and stores. The corollary of black prosperity was that racial lines were not clearly drawn in a city that was still in the process of defining itself.

Those lines were unmistakable after June 1. Violence erupted when several dozen African Americans armed themselves and congregated near the downtown jail to forestall a threatened lynching. After one white was shot in an exchange of gunfire, blacks withdrew to Greenwood. A growing white mob attacked the edges of the district in the early morning hours and invaded with daylight. While the police and National Guard disarmed African Americans and interned 6,000 at the fairgrounds and convention hall, the white mob had an increasingly free hand to loot, burn, or ransack a thousand black homes and businesses. Amid a great bustle of superficial concern and desultory relief efforts, the Tulsa establishment effectively forced the African American neighborhood away from the center of town to make room for a railroad terminal. About a thousand black Tulsans spent the winter of 1921–22 in tents and then rebuilt in a city where the lines of racial division had been burned into the map.

Beyond the individual tragedies of riot, enforced poverty, and blocked ambition, the disaster of the 1920s and early 1930s was the transformation of ghettos—segregated neighborhoods defined and imposed by the dominant society—into slums. There is no inherent reason why segregated housing must be poor housing. Harlem, for example, which developed before the turn of the century as a middle-class neighborhood, had become a middle-class African American neighborhood in 1920, with attractive apartments, wide streets, and an active community life. However, the same processes that produced segregation in the 1910s turned ghettos into slums in the years between the world wars. As a rough generalization, each step—from neighborhood to ghetto and from ghetto to slum—took about ten years in a typical city.

Half the problem was the externally imposed decline of neighborhood standards. White officials neglected public services in minority neighborhoods. When budgets were tight they deferred maintenance of African American neighborhood playgrounds, cut back on street cleaning, and let the garbage pile up for a week rather than three days. The law enforcement system tended to tolerate gambling and prostitution as a necessary evil as long as the business was confined to black neighborhoods. The Chicago police deliberately forced the vice district into the south-side ghetto so that it would not bother the white majority. White real estate agents who took pride in maintaining the stability of middle-class white neighborhoods were unable to recognize enclaves of middle-class African Americans, and thus placed an extra burden on families struggling to repeat the American success story.

The solidity of ghetto boundaries compounded the problems of African American neighborhoods. Landlords had a captive market that allowed them to milk their properties by neglecting upkeep and inflating rents. Housing prices in Harlem doubled between 1919 and 1927. The average African American family in a large city paid 50 percent more than a white family for comparable housing. Families coped with rising rents by accepting smaller quarters, sharing apartments, or taking in lodgers, with all the consequent pressures on family life. Outside the apartment building, neglected services and crowded neighborhoods meant old, overburdened schools and parks that turned into overused patches of packed dirt.

Without minimizing the economic and political limits on African American communities, it is important to note that African Americans were not passive victims. Black populations in New York and Chicago were large enough to support a vital cultural life of music and the arts. Jazz artists, painters, and writers in New York created the Harlem Renaissance of the 1920s. Chicago's South Side was another "Black Metropolis" that nurtured writer Richard Wright, painter Archibald Motley, and many other important figures. African American neighborhoods developed prosperous commercial districts— Atlanta's Auburn Avenue and Washington's Sixteenth Street, for two examples. High schools that served the black middle class were important centers of community life that trained future community leaders, many of whom continued their education at Washington's Howard University, Nashville's Fisk University, and Atlanta's set of colleges on the heavily African American west side.

The 1920s and 1930s also planted the roots of the postwar civil rights movement. American race relations had reached their low point in the early twentieth century with the legalization of racial discrimination in Jim Crow laws, an epidemic of lynching across the South, and the exclusion of many African Americans from federal jobs. Black communities fought back through political organization. Newspapers like the *Pittsburgh Courier* and *Norfolk Journal and Guide* as well as the *Chicago Defender* urged their readers to organize in their own interests. In Norfolk, neighborhood associations and civic leagues lobbied the city for practical improvements such as street paving and new schools. Some of that city's African American workers joined interracial labor unions such as the Amalgamated Clothing Workers. In 1939–40, future Supreme Court Justice Thurgood Marshall and the National Association for the Advancement of Colored People (NAACP) helped Norfolk's black school teachers win equal pay with white teachers, one of many court cases that chipped away at racial discrimination and set the stage for the monumental *Brown* v. *Board of Education* decision in 1954.

Model T Suburbs

For the majority of Americans, the 1920s were a time of increasing freedom rather than confinement. The automobile was the great liberator. In 1920, automobiles were still something extra on the urban scene. National registration of 8 million vehicles worked out to one car for every thirteen Americans; your family may not have had a car but one of your neighbors did. By 1930, the automobile had become a household appliance, with one car for every five people. Its spread was fastest in the country's newer cities. There was one car for every twelve New Yorkers in 1930, one for every eight Bostonians, and one for every six occupants of Pittsburgh. However, there was one for every four Detroiters and one for every three residents of Los Angeles.

In the eyes of many, the automobile was a positive development. It freed city dwellers of dependence on the grasping streetcar monopoly; it granted the freedom of personal mobility to millions of ordinary citizens; and it opened large territories on the edge of the city and promised to lower land and housing costs. The result, many Americans hoped, would be the end of unhealthy housing congestion and reduced pressure on crowded slums.

mentioned in class

When they could, Americans in the 1920s celebrated their expanded choice of residential locations by purchasing rather than renting a new house. The impulse to home ownership of many ethnic neighborhoods was repeated and multiplied among the growing American middle class. The federal Departments of Labor and Commerce cooperated in an "Own Your Home" campaign in 1920–21. U.S. Secretary of Commerce Herbert Hoover encouraged the real estate business to standardize building codes and develop uniform grading for construction materials. The YMCA offered courses for would-be homeowners. Better Homes in America, Inc., sponsored conferences, publications, and thousands of local committees that organized "Better Homes Week" activities each April. The results were impressive: the increase from 41 percent to 46 percent home ownership for non-farm dwellings meant 3.5 million new homeowning households for the decade.

Many of these new homeowners located in the bungalow belts that developed between two and six miles from the center of numerous cities. On the West Coast, "bungalow" meant a specific style of housing with wide overhanging eaves, an unpretentious exterior, and an open floor plan to meet the needs of the modern family. Many of the silent movie comedies of the early 1920s were filmed in the bungalow neighborhoods of Los Angeles, with their streets of single-family houses set behind occasional palm trees. In other parts of the country, the term covered an even wider range of housing styles that tended to share the moderate price and the five to eight rooms required by a middle-class family. The focal points of the new neighborhoods were their elementary schools and their comprehensive high school, the latter housed in a resplendent two-or three-story building that was the major community landmark.

The lifestyles in bungalow neighborhoods became increasingly "modern" as the 1920s wore on. Many residents still took the streetcar to work, but more and more demanded that their 50 by 100-foot lot include both a house and a garage. New houses were wired to allow the enjoyment of electric vacuum cleaners, irons, refrigerators, fans, and toasters. Consumers could visit "all-electric" homes like the Denver model built in 1922 that showed off all the conveniences but omitted "freakish or unusual innovations" that might put consumers off. The value of electrical household appliances produced in the United States grew from $23 million in 1915 to $180 million in 1929. By the end of the 1920s, two-thirds of all Americans could light their dwellings with the flick of a switch. Most of the remaining nonelectric homes were buried deep in the country. Sophisticated householders began to use home-heating fuels such as natural gas that eliminated the drudgery and dirt of the hand-stoked coal furnace. Conversion to gas or fuel oil had the side benefit of reducing the pall of grey smoke that blocked the winter sun.

The upper crust in the 1920s leapfrogged the ordinary middle class for stylish new suburbs on the urban fringe. Ever since the railroad and horse-drawn streetcar made commuting possible in the 1840s, the rich had been moving out to the urban fringe. The automobile, however, gave even greater flexibility and independence to the well off. As they moved outward after World War I, the rich, who comprised the top tenth on the economic scale, found that developers were eager to lay out new communities that reflected their social status. Shaker Heights, on 1,400 acres east of Cleveland, was one of the most successful. Developer-tycoons Oris and Mantis Van Sweringen planned the new town with rigorous internal controls to separate houses by price level. They also separated the major automobile arteries from the tastefully curving residential streets, set aside parklands, prohibited duplexes, and imposed strict architectural controls. Three hundred houses were added to the suburb each year from 1919 to 1929; its population jumped from 1,700 to 15,000, and the price of choice lots reached $20,000.

The Country Club District in Kansas City attracted international attention. Jesse C. Nichols began to market lots in 1922 for what grew to a 6,000-acre community with four golf clubs, thirty-three distinct subdivisions, and 6,000 homes. Nichols provided parks, a quarter million dollars in artworks to enliven the street corners, and Country Club Plaza, the nation's first large shopping center planned around and for the automobile. The quality of the district was maintained by comprehensive deed restrictions that mandated the minimum cost of buildings and aesthetic standards. Residents in each neighborhood elected board members for homes associations that enforced the development's regulations, maintained parks and playgrounds, and promoted community spirit within the context of comprehensive controls on individual use of property.

Other cities had comparable developments. Palos Verdes Estates draped over a rocky peninsula that juts into the Pacific, south of Los Angeles. Its art jury had to approve every house plan for architectural compatibility, while the developer provided schools, a golf course, a swimming club, and a riding academy. Sequoyah Hills in Knoxville was laid out in 1925 for lawyers and businessowners. Druid Hills in Atlanta was developed in the 1910s and filled by new suburbanites in the 1920s. The string of suburbs along Chicago's North Shore or Philadelphia's Main Line provided the same environment of Georgian revival and "stockbroker Tudor" houses for successful business or professional people.

Not every suburb, of course, was gracious and spacious. Many cities had outlying industrial zones along waterways or railroads that attracted working-class families looking for a cheap alternative to the center-city tenements. Residents in these districts—places like Compton, Belvedere, and South Gate in Los Angeles—often bought very small houses on large lots. Unlike Druid Hills or Palos Verdes, building regulations were slack. While they supplemented the family's food budget with backyard vegetable gardens, fruit trees, chicken coops, and rabbit hutches, residents slowly added additional rooms. Sometimes the housing was entirely self-built, with the whole family living in tents until they could pitch in to nail up walls of second-hand lumber and finish off the roof.

Most Americans in the 1920s applauded the suburban trend, which was making attractive, low-density neighborhoods available to millions of affluent and ordinary citizens. Historian Gwendolyn Wright has found that "most popular middle-class literature, housing guides, and even architects' manuals and government documents praised the suburbs as the haven of 'normalcy' in the twenties." Planners and reformers had battled the congestion of the industrial city for decades. They now looked to carefully controlled suburban growth as a sovereign remedy for urban ills. The alternative to "Dinosaur Cities," said Clarence Stein, was "a beautiful environment, a home for children, an opportunity to enjoy the day's leisure" in a new community. Harlan Douglass examined *The Suburban Trend* in 1925 and concluded that "a crowded world must be either suburban or savage."

Many of the nation's leading planners worked together as the informal Regional Planning Association of America (RPAA) to promote the development of a "middle landscape" that combined the creative energies of the city and the residential environment of the country or small town. Lewis Mumford, the RPAA's best-known spokesman, called for "a more satisfactory layout, region by region, with countryside and city developed together for the purpose of promoting and enhancing the good life." In Henry Wrights's *Report* on the work of the New York State Commission of Housing and Regional Planning in 1926, the prescription was for the dispersed and balanced development of an entire state, with power delivered by an electric grid and transportation over modern roads.

On a smaller scale, the same reform impulse looked to the creation of model suburbs that provided high-quality, low-density housing for a broad range of incomes. Radburn, New Jersey, was located just across the new George Washington Bridge that connected New York City and New Jersey. It was planned under the direct influence of RPAA members. Radburn's design called for housing built on 40- to 60-acre super-blocks, with front doors turned toward interior parks and pedestrians separated from automobile traffic. Unfortunately, the work began on Radburn in 1928 and its full financing was blocked by the depression. Even so, 1,200 residents (rather than the expected 25,000) found a superior community. Internationally known planner John Nolen had similar goals for Mariemont near Cincinnati, which he called "A New Town Built to Produce Local Happiness." Although the town was funded by a "public-spirited lady of large means" to give industrial workers homes away from the looming shadows of the factory district, the end result was closer to a well-designed, middle-class suburb.

There were costs as well as benefits associated with the boom in new neighborhoods. Residents of new towns and subdivisions increasingly fought for political independence from the central city. The 1920s were the first decade in which American suburbs as a whole (defined as the rings of land outside the boundaries of core cities but within the larger metropolitan areas) grew at a faster pace than the nation's central cities. Residents of the new communities increasingly resisted annexation to the central city and often incorporated to provide their own public services.

Some cities witnessed the wholesale exodus of their civic leaders to new suburban towns. The local elite still owned real estate, operated factories, and commuted to downtown offices in the central city, but their homes and families were now separated from their economic interests. They wanted to maintain low city taxes and a stable work environment for their businesses. However, they were increasingly indifferent to the quality of central-city schools, parks, and social services. In Detroit, for example, 1,800 out of a sample of 2,000 leading families lived within the city limits in 1910. By the early 1930s, the growth of Grosse Pointe and other suburban towns had cut the city's share of the elite to 50 percent. Cleveland experienced the same shift. "A close reading of the material from Chambers of Commerce and other such groups," reports historian James Richardson, "indicates a greater distancing of

Cleveland's economic and professional leaders from the 'cosmopolitan' population of the city than had been the case before 1915."

Indeed, if ghettoization walled African Americans into inner-city neighborhoods, suburbanization during the 1920s simultaneously walled them out of the pleasant new suburban communities. Deed restrictions in new subdivisions frequently prohibited rental or sale to "persons of African descent." Even enlightened developers like Jesse Nichols prohibited black residents as a matter of course. In the western states, the restrictions were often extended to Asians and Mexicans as well. Restrictive covenants, which were enforced as private contracts among individuals, were justified as a means of assuring stable communities by limiting them to "the better class of citizens." Not until 1948 did the U.S. Supreme Court overturn the practice in *Shelley v. Kraemer*, which declared that racially restrictive covenants were unenforceable. When African Americans did live in suburban rings, it was either in poorly served working-class neighborhoods or distinct, self-contained enclaves.

Suburbanization and the spread of the automobile not only changed the living environment for millions of Americans, but also forced cities to make transportation choices that have shaped our metropolitan areas to the present. Public transit, largely meaning the electric-powered streetcar or trolley, enjoyed increasing ridership in the early 1920s. Nationwide streetcar use peaked in 1923. When auto sales declined in 1927–28, many transit executives convinced themselves that the automobile market was saturated; they believed that downtown congestion would soon force drivers back to trolleys.

In fact, automobility undermined public transit throughout the 1920s. Auto commuting became not just a convenience, but a status symbol. George Babbitt enjoyed swooping up to streetcar stops on his way to the office and shouting "Have a lift?" As the victim of his benevolence climbed in, Babbitt was likely to add that "whenever I see a fellow waiting for a trolley, I always make it a practice to give him a lift—unless, of course, he looks like a bum." Suburbanization spread the population thinly over the landscape and made it difficult to generate enough ridership to support trolley or bus service to new areas.

Several cities made key decisions against major spending on public transit during the 1920s. The years from 1900 to 1915 had seen massive investment in rail and subway facilities for urban transit. Rapid transit construction in the 1920s, however, was largely confined to extensions of existing systems. Detroit voters in 1929 rejected a $280 million proposal that would have resulted in subways, sixty-five miles of surface rapid transit, and 560 miles of trolley lines. Transit companies shortsightedly opposed the plan because they feared the investment would force a politically unpopular fare increase to 15 cents. Los Angeles, the capital of the new automobile lifestyle, never even bothered to vote on a 1925 plan calling for $133 million for twenty-six miles of subway and eighty-five miles of elevated track.

Public funds went instead for thousands of smaller-scale improvements that were necessary to make cities compatible with the motor car. The twenties were the decade when American cities accepted modern traffic regulations. Police departments implemented traffic patrols, cities experimented with one-way streets, banned curbside parking in downtown districts, and installed the first automatic traffic signals. Philadelphia tried to control traffic on Broad Street with a single huge light hung on the City Hall tower but soon switched to "wooden policemen" at street corners. The parking meter made its appearance in Oklahoma City in 1935.

Because rubber automobile tires create strong suction on street surfaces, they tore up gravel and macadamized pavements that had been sufficient for iron-tired wagons and horses. Every major city invested millions in street paving, bridges, viaducts, and new streets. The central concern was to get cars into and then through the narrow downtown streets. Pittsburgh put $20 million into street widening, tunnels, and boulevards, and still remained trapped amid its rivers and steep hills. The double-decked Wacker Drive opened in 1926 along the Chicago River, with the upper level for general traffic and the lower for trucks serving downtown warehouses and terminals.

A related response was the development of suburban park systems that were accessible by automobile. Sunday drivers wanted destinations more accessible than the city parks designed for horse-drawn carriages. The answer was rings of public parks located 10 to 30 miles from the city's center. For New York, Robert Moses built a magnificent system of public parks along the south shore of Long Island. Cleveland developed a distinguished metropolitan park system. The Cook County Forest Preserves embraced 35,000 acres in a "green border" outside Chicago. They were intended "neither for show nor for tree cultivation as such, but for the use of the people, for park and picnic grounds, if you will. On Sundays and holidays hundreds of thousands of people swarm there."

The ultimate response to the automobile by the end of 1930s was the invention of a new type of transportation system—the automobile freeway. Benton MacKaye, a member of the RPAA who thought up the Appalachian Trail, introduced the concept of the "Townless Highway." As described by MacKaye and Lewis Mumford in 1931, such roads would have separate rights-of-way through lesser developed country between cities and controlled access from feeder roads, with the consequent separation of local and intercity traffic. The "townless highway" would allow planners to "recognize the motor revolution and attempt at every point to meet the new situation it has raised," rather than struggling to adapt nineteenth-century roads built for wagons and carriages.

Traffic engineers agreed. By the late 1930s, the professionals had concluded that new highways should be designed for in-town speeds of 50 miles an hour and intercity speeds of 70. Those standards meant that autos should move on controlled access roads with multiple lanes, sweeping banked curbs, wide median strips, and cloverleaf intersections. In 1939, a report by the U.S. Bureau of Public Roads on *Toll Roads and Free Roads* set out the design criteria that led directly to the interstate highway program. Visitors to the General Motors' Futurama exhibit at the 1939 New York World's Fair could marvel over a huge three-dimensional model of the future American landscape knit together by sweeping multilane freeways.

Early efforts to build the highways of the future included the Pennsylvania Turnpike from Philadelphia to Pittsburgh and a number of New York–area parkways on Long Island, in Westchester County, and in Connecticut. The future really opened, however, on December 30, 1940. The Rose Bowl queen and her court helped Governor Culbert Olson of California dedicate the new six-mile Arroyo Seco Freeway from Los Angeles to Pasadena, which was the first step toward the full automobilization of Southern California and the direct ancestor of the modern freeway system.

Urban Survival in the Great Depression

Freeway planning in 1939–40 was a symbol of new optimism for American cities after ten years of economic depression. Sharp observers should have known that something was wrong even before the stock market crash of October 1929. The nation had suffered from chronic unemployment in coal mining and textile manufacturing through the 1920s. Farm income had also showed a steady decline. A short recession in 1927 interrupted the booming sales of new cars and new houses, and the leading automotive and construction industries scrimped through 1928 and 1929 with flat markets.

The clearest preview of future problems was the popping of the Florida land bubble in 1926. Completion of good highways into South Florida and the construction of luxury hotels triggered intense interest in property in Miami and Miami Beach, Fort Lauderdale, Boca Raton, and a number of other towns that existed only in the imagination of promoters. The result was a classic land boom where everyone hoped to get rich by selling to someone else. One estimate counted 25,000 real estate agents operating out of 2,000 southern Florida offices at the peak of the boom. The trick was to buy with only a deposit and resell within thirty days before the first payment was due. The pyramid collapsed in 1926 when the land sharks ran out of suckers. There was real growth in the midst of the real estate mania, as Miami grew from a town of 30,000 to a city of 110,000, but swampland subdivisions were more common. The most telling sign of the impending depression was the increasing number of bank failures in 1928 and 1929 as buyers defaulted on speculative loans.

No other city approached the Miami frenzy, but real estate was overbuilt nationwide by the end of the decade. Developers had platted land far in advance of demand on the suburban fringe of most cities. Speculators subdivided land, ran utility lines, and poured concrete for curbs and sidewalks, but throngs of buyers failed to materialize. Even though the population of suburban Skokie, ten miles northwest of Chicago, jumped from 700 to 5,000, 30,000 lots still remained to be sold. Atlanta's entrepreneurs put up more than a dozen major office buildings in the 1920s but found it difficult to fill the hundreds of thousands of square feet of new office space. Even the Empire State Building earned the nickname of the "Empty State Building" in the early 1930s.

The most direct measure of the building economic disaster after 1929 was the unemployment rate. National unemployment climbed from 3 percent in 1929 to 9 percent in 1930, 16 percent in 1931, 24 percent in 1932, and 25 percent in 1933. Mining towns and cities built around heavy industry felt the impact worst. More than 75 percent of the families in Butte, Montana, were on relief by the early 1930s. Steel mills in Gary, Indiana, laid off 90 percent of their workers. Cleveland's machine tool industry shut down completely for lack of factory expansion. Cities like Toledo, which supplied parts for automobiles, virtually collapsed. The unemployment figures for individual cities were little more than guesses, for even a person with a job might work short hours and two-day weeks. Estimates for late 1931 and early 1932 put Philadelphia's army of unemployed at more than 250,000, Chicago's at 600,000 to 700,000, and New York's at 800,000 to 1 million.

The depression brought a housing crisis to the middle class and poor alike. Most home mortgages during the 1920s required that the borrower pay simple interest, with the full face value of the loan coming due at the end of five or ten years. When times were good, it was easy to refinance when the loan was up, but when times were bad, it was virtually impossible. Banks that had been drained of savings had no capital to back new loans. Unemployed home buyers had no way to make payments. The nation's banks reached 1,000 foreclosures a day. Many people had no homes at all. Every city had a Hooverville, a shantytown of shacks made from old crates, abandoned building materials, and tar paper. On crisp nights during the fall of 1931, the lower level of Chicago's Michigan Avenue bridge sheltered up to 1,500 men who wrapped themselves in multiple layers of the *Chicago Tribune* and the *Chicago Daily News*.

The physical deterioration of urban America matched the misery of millions of its residents. Between 1929 and 1933, the physical plant of the United States wore out faster than it could be replaced. Industrialists saw no reason to replace old machinery that was standing idle. Construction of new housing fell by 95 percent. Homeowners put off repairs in the hope of making their monthly payment. In sixteen Illinois cities, people spent 6¢ on home maintenance and improvements in 1933 for every dollar they had spent during an average year in the 1920s. City governments let roads, schools, and fire engines run down because they had no money for repairs or replacement. Urban America was cannibalizing itself, consuming its physical facilities without the ability to rebuild for the future.

The Great Depression was a special nightmare for city officials. Exploding demands collided with shrinking resources. During the prosperous twenties, many cities had gone deeply into debt to pay for new sewers, schools, roads, and bridges. As revenues shrank in the thirties, debt payments took up an increasing proportion of public spending. At the same time, more and more property owners failed to pay their taxes. Unmarketable subdivisions, which many cities had served with expensive roads and utility systems, were often the first to be delinquent. By 1932, Birmingham counted 12,000 delinquent properties. Detroit owed $27 million per year to its creditors; its total budget was $76 million, of which only $57 million was actually collectible. Cities and school boards laid off staff and sometimes paid their employees in *scrip*, funny money that the governments promised to exchange for cash at some point in the future and that local merchants took at a discount. By the time the 1932 presidential campaign was in full swing, 600 urban centers had defaulted on some sort of financial obligation.

Relief for the unemployed during the first two winters of the depression came from improvised partnerships of private charities and local welfare offices. Little Rock, Arkansas, combined an emergency appropriation of $20,000 in January 1931 with $25,000 from private sources to provide emergency jobs. The money was gone within three months. Proper Philadelphians organized a Committee on Unemployment Relief in November 1930. They raised nearly $4 million for free food and make-work jobs for 14,000 destitute heads of families. By June 1931, this ad hoc group evolved into the Bureau of Unemployment Relief within the city's Public Welfare department and distributed $3 million in city funds in the form of food, fuel, and clothing. The Community Chest campaign raised millions more, but all available money had been tapped and dispensed by June 1932, when organized relief in Philadelphia stopped.

Other communities tried to deal with economic disaster without involving local government at all. Residents of Fort Wayne, Indiana, organized the Allen County Unemployment Association to provide opportunities for self-help. The group ran a fleet of trucks that took jobless city workers to Allen County farms, where they traded their work for tons of meat and truckloads of vegetables. Association members refurbished sixty rundown houses in return for free accommodations. With about 500 members, the Unemployment Association was able to find regular work for about 150 people, while constantly stressing "patriotism," "patience," and opposition to "un-American ideologies" that advocated government charity.

In fact, by 1932 most city officials were desperately pleading for federal assistance. The situation in Cincinnati as described in the *National Municipal Review* summed up the disparity between needs and resources.

> Standards of relief have been radically reduced so that the average relief given is only about $5.00 per week per family. In April the city had over 700 evictions. The May census shows that only one half of the working population is employed on a full-time basis. Some idea in the decline of living standards can be guessed by the fact that payrolls declined about $96,000,000 during the last year and only about $2,000,000 was given for relief.

In response, Mayor Frank Murphy of Detroit organized the mayors of dozens of large cities into an informal group that drafted an appeal for federal help. "We've done everything humanly possible to do," he told the group, "and it has not been enough. The hour is at hand for the federal government to cooperate." The best that the Hoover administration would do was to give $300 million in loans from the Reconstruction Finance Corporation to be shared by all units of local government.

The inauguration of Franklin Roosevelt after the fourth long winter of discontent initiated a "new deal" for the new urban poor. The Federal Emergency Relief Administration (FERA) and the Civil Works Administration put millions of people back to work within months. FERA money in New Orleans put 20,000 men back to work on public construction projects. Robert and Helen Lynd described the impacts of the new programs on Muncie, Indiana—population 37,000.

> When, on November 15, 1933, the blessed rain of Federal CWA funds began to fall upon the parched taxpayers, the straining city brought out projects big and little to catch the golden flood. "County Rushes Projects to Place Unemployed Persons on Government Payrolls" shouted the headlines. It was too good to be true! Thirty hours a week at fifty cents an hour. . . . Nobody was talking then about the unbridled waste of Washington spending in the hands of "brainless bureaucrats[.]" . . . By mid-January 1934, $33,500 of Federal funds were pouring in each week to 1,840 workers. . . . Then after $350,000 of CWA funds had been expended locally, the FERA took up the load, and . . . paid in sums ranging up to $16,000 to $17,000 a week.

Longer-term public construction efforts under the Public Works Administration (PWA) and the Works Progress Administration (WPA) followed the first emergency jobs programs. The PWA funded "heavy" projects that would help resuscitate the construction industry. The WPA concentrated on jobs that mainly required picks and shovels. Cities that had supported active planning efforts during the 1920s took the plans and blueprints off the shelf, updated the engineering specifications, and mailed their application to Washington. New York developed beaches, swimming pools, baseball diamonds, tennis courts, and more than 200 new playgrounds. Muncie obtained an arts building with the help of the PWA and built a new sewer system with WPA workers. Overall, more than half of the WPA's grants went to the fifty largest cities. The program built or paved more than 500,000 miles of roads and streets, allowed 500,000 sewer connections, and constructed more than 100,000 public buildings before the decade was over.

In the later 1930s, as workers struggled to exercise their rights to collective bargaining under the Wagner Act, cities were the sites of bitter strikes and job actions that recalled the abysmal labor relations of a generation earlier. When General Motors refused to recognize and bargain with the United Auto Workers, union members staged a sit-down strike at the company's Flint, Michigan, factories. Workers refused to leave the factories and subsisted on food smuggled in by the Women's Emergency Brigade. Ford Motor Company hired thugs to beat up union officials such as Walter Reuther until it finally caved in 1941. In Chicago, police fired on strikers and family members demonstrating at a Republic Steel Company plant on Memorial Day, 1937, killing ten and injuring dozens of others.

Labor conflict rocked even the smaller, nonindustrial city of San Antonio. The city had long been marked by low wages, poor housing, and inadequate public services, especially for the Mexican Americans who made up one-third of its population. The depression hit Mexican American women especially hard. Anglo American women might have to take pay cuts to keep their clerical jobs, but the service sector survived the depression relatively well. Mexican Americans, who depended on factory jobs, faced layoffs and exploitative wages. In 1938, the men and women who worked in San Antonio's pecan shelling plants for $2.00 per week walked off the job. Led by the fiery Emma Tenayuca, more than a thousand workers were jailed because of their demonstrations and picketing. By calling embarrassing national attention to San Antonio poverty, the strike helped pave the way for a reform mayor in 1939.

One of the few cities that actually thrived during the depression was Washington, D.C. As in other white-collar cities, unemployment came gradually rather than catastrophically during the early 1930s. The beginning of the New Deal revived the economy and charged the atmosphere with a sense of new possibilities. By 1940 Washington had more than 150,000 federal workers and posted a population gain of 36 percent for the decade, making it one of the few cities with inflationary pressures on housing costs. White Washingtonians moved into new suburbs in Maryland and Virginia and displaced African Americans from the old Georgetown neighborhood forty years before neighborhood gentrification became apparent in most other cities. Black residents in turn pushed into older areas in the northeast quarter of the city.

The federal programs to assist and rehire city dwellers were both a cause and a consequence of a political revolution in American cities. As late as 1924, the Republican party had expected to capture the majority of urban votes. By 1932, the situation had reversed. The nation's twelve largest cities were New York, Chicago, Philadelphia, Los Angeles, Detroit, Baltimore, Cleveland, Boston, St. Louis, Milwaukee, Pittsburgh, and San Francisco. The net Republican plurality of 1,252,000 votes from these cities in the 1924 presidential election became a net Democratic plurality of 38,000 in 1928, 1,910,000 in 1932, and 3,608,000 in 1936. The shift toward Democratic cities started with the unsuccessful presidential campaign of New York Democrat Al Smith against Republican Herbert Hoover in 1928. Topped with a derby hat, speaking with the unmistakable accent of Manhattan's Lower East Side, and professing the Roman Catholic faith, Smith had a natural appeal to second-generation Americans—the children of the great migration of 1890 to 1915—as they came of age and voted for the first time. Franklin Delano Roosevelt capitalized on the new allegiance in 1932, when a dozen leading cities went Democratic for the first time in decades. In ten of them, the Democratic margin was enough to carry the entire state for the Roosevelt-Gamer ticket.

FDR and his advisers knew how to count. New Deal agencies such as the Home Owners Loan Corporation and the Federal Housing Administration aided the struggling urban middle class. While the FERA and WPA provided immediate help for the unemployed, the Social Security Act and the Wagner Labor Relations Act promised longer lasting security as the economy recovered. Mayor La Guardia of New York and other spokesmen for the United States Conference of Mayors (organized in 1933 out of Frank Murphy's informal group) received a respectful and attentive hearing from the new administration.

The result in 1936 was the consolidation and strengthening of the Democratic hold on city voters. The 1928 and 1932 campaigns had shown the Democratic appeal to Catholic and Jewish voters, particularly in the Northeast. In 1936, Roosevelt picked up a net of 1.7 million additional votes in southern, western, and midwestern cities populated largely by native-born Americans. White Protestant workers decided to vote their pocketbooks rather than their prejudices, joining in common cause with big city Catholics. At the same time, African American voters decided that they could no longer support the party of Abraham Lincoln when it had become the party of Alf Landon. Roosevelt's 25 percent of the black vote in 1932 grew to 75 percent in 1936. The national political calculus was set for a generation, with racial minorities, ethnic groups, and industrial workers providing the electoral support for the city-oriented programs of Roosevelt's New Deal, Harry Truman's Fair Deal, and Lyndon Johnson's Great Society.

City Problems and Possibilities

One document and one movie documentary from the end of the 1930s summed up thinking about American cities after a decade of exuberant growth in the 1920s followed by the crushed expectations that resulted from the depression.

The City is a classic film from the first great era of documentary cinema. A grant of $50,000 from the Carnegie Foundation enabled the American Institute of Planners to hire the best talent available. Lewis Mumford and filmmaker Pare Lorentz worked on the script, Aaron Copland helped with the music, and William Van Dyke was the cinematographer. When the film was first shown in 1938 and again at the World's Fair the next year, audiences saw a dramatic indictment of the state of American cities. The film takes viewers on a full circle, starting with idyllic scenes of a New England village that existed only in our national nostalgia. In shocking contrast to the rolling landscape of rural New England are the slum-covered hills of a Pennsylvania mill town, with grubby children playing beneath wooden shanties perched on bare slopes overlooking grey, smoky factories. The film follows with hectic scenes of the New York lunch hour and jammed weekend traffic on a two-lane road to the beach, with crying children and overheated radiators. The final segment shows a scrubbed and sparkling suburb as the alternative to the congested city. The urban landscape, says the film, can be made as peaceful, clean, and open as the New England village with properly planned decentralization and the construction of a new type of environment—the suburb. The film's message was a justification for the suburbanization of the 1920s and a rationale for the sprawl of the postwar decades.

Where Mumford, Lorentz, and their co-workers catered to Americans' antiurban prejudices, a 1937 report to the federal government's National Resources Committee presented a more balanced and thoughtful view. *Our Cities—Their Role in the National Economy* was prepared by a committee that included several of the country's leading specialists on urban government and society. They placed the blame for many urban problems squarely on public neglect, pointing out that "although the United States has been a predominantly urban nation for more than two decades, this report . . . is the first inquiry of national, official, and comprehensive scale into the problems of the American urban community." The report explored the dynamics of urban growth and forthrightly examined thirty-two separately identified problems of urban areas, starting with poverty and unemployment and ending with governmental disorganization and lack of municipal cooperation. Along the way, readers learned about pollution, community disorganization, slums, and crime. The report concluded with wide-ranging recommendations for federal studies, federal policies, and federal programs to address the needs of cities, many of which have been implemented in the nearly fifty years since its publication.

Just as important is the fundamental optimism of *Our Cities*, in contrast to the bleak view of the AIP film. The report's authors argued against wholesale decentralization and abandonment of core areas. They asserted that the many defects of cities "are but blemishes or infections which an otherwise healthy organism can check," in this case through "judicious reshaping of the urban community and region by systematic development and redevelopment in accordance with forward-looking and intelligent plans." The goals of planning and public policy could and should be to extend and increase "the benefits of modern civilization which the great city has brought to an ever-increasing proportion of our people."

CHAPTER TWO

Building and Rebuilding

Mayor Frank Skeffington lost the election because his city was working too well. Frank O'Connor's best-selling 1956 novel, *The Last
Hurrah*, detailed the final campaign of a traditional urban politician
in a city that is instantly recognizable as Boston. Amid a discussion of
the nuts and bolts of a mayoral campaign, *The Last Hurrah* portrayed
a city that was giving its residents a shot at personal success during
the prosperous years after 1940.

The Ninth Ward Democratic Club's spring dance took place as
scheduled on the same day that Skeffington announced his drive for
reelection. Ward boss John Gorman knew the importance of giving
newer immigrant groups a place next to those longer established groups
in American cities. For the Ninth Ward, this meant that Irish American Jack Shea and Italian American Eddie Maculuso split the cater-
ing business for the dance. The whole affair was intended to unite the
party.

The bar was open; the buffet was formidable. At the end of the great
hall sat the orchestra. It was large, it was expert, it was expensive[.] . . .
Music strengthened fraternity; in the benign solvent of song, traditional

animosities faded. Dr. Joseph Brady sang "My Wild Irish Rose"; Mr. Arthur Piccione sang "O Sole Mio"; the applause for the latter nearly equaled that for the former. It was evidence of the growing tolerance of the Irish; it was even greater evidence of the growing numbers of Italians.

By mid-campaign, impartial observers knew that Skeffington was in trouble. His crowds were largest in the older neighborhoods, and his grey-haired supporters wanted to talk about the old days. Their children and grandchildren stayed home. The new generation who had ridden the GI bill and good times to white-collar jobs and a house in the suburbs swung the election to Skeffington's young opponent. Political novice Kevin McCluskey didn't defeat the old pro because of his own abilities. In fact, one of his supporters admitted he had "nothing upstairs but a mass of floating custard." He won because his credentials represented the culmination of the tenement trail—Holy Cross College '40, a law degree from Georgetown University, service in the navy, a new house, and five well-scrubbed children.

A city that was willing to trade a Frank Skeffington for a Kevin McCluskey was a city that had outgrown many of the issues that dominated urban affairs in the first half of the twentieth century. The problems of urban America in the 1940s and 1950s centered on rapid growth. Total metropolitan population surged from 63 million to 120 million. Businessmen, experts, mayors, and federal officials turned their attention to the needs of expanding downtowns, the quantity and quality of housing, and the explosive growth of suburban rings. When John F. Kennedy called on Congress to create a federal Department of Urban Affairs and Housing in January 1962, his list of problems summed up the postwar agenda for building and rebuilding American cities.

There must be expansion: but orderly and planned expansion, not explosion and sprawl. Basic public facilities must be extended ever further into the areas surrounding our urban centers[.] . . . The scourge of blight must be overcome, and the central core areas of our cities, with all their great richness of economic and cultural wealth, must be restored to lasting vitality. . . . Sound old housing must be conserved and improved, and new housing created.

Cities at War

John Kennedy's analysis of the needs of urban America came during the twenty-second year of sustained urban growth after the long pause of the depression. The onset of World War II changed the lives of the fictional Kevin McCluskey and tens of millions of other Americans. It also transformed the face of urban America. Defense production expanded in 1940 and 1941 as the United States made itself the "arsenal of democracy" for embattled Britain, and hastily built up its own armaments. The months after Japan attacked Pearl Harbor and conquered the Philippines brought national mobilization for war production and military service. Organization of an immense military enterprise tilted the economic balance toward the South Atlantic, Gulf, and Pacific coasts.

Americans became a nation in transit during the early 1940s. Military personnel followed their orders and went to training and staging bases. Civilians followed the new defense jobs. When the war boom peaked in 1943, 81 of the 137 metropolitan areas in the United States had larger civilian populations than in 1940. In the West, thirteen of fifteen metropolitan areas recorded gains. In the South, forty-three of forty-nine increased in population. For the Northeast and Middle West, in contrast, the figures were only twenty-five of seventy-four. Detroit automakers retooled to produce tanks and military vehicles. Aircraft manufacturing or air bases brought tens of thousands of newcomers to Atlanta, St. Louis, and most of the cities of the Southwest. Shipbuilding and naval bases brought extraordinary growth to nearly every major port. Even the sleepy town of Seneca, Illinois, found itself transformed by the construction of a shipyard for landing ships. "You would wake up in the morning and someone would be rolled up in a blanket on your front porch," one resident remembered. "The taverns were the ones who did really well."

War-boom towns had to act fast and think big. The first problem on everyone's list was the shortage of decent housing for war workers and their families. Close behind was the problem of overburdened public transportation. Increased population compounded the problems of wartime gasoline and tire rationing. Workers in Seattle's shipyards and Boeing plants scrounged for space in offices, tents, and chicken coops. A well-publicized visit by the U.S. House Committee on National Defense Migration in the summer of 1941 found San Diego swamped by 90,000 defense industry workers and 35,000 military personnel. *Life, Business Week, Fortune,* and the *Saturday Evening Post* all described the crowded schools, overpacked hotels, makeshift trailer parks, and raucous nightlife in the "rip-roaringest coast boom town." Inadequate and poorly located housing, said one expert, was the "core of every problem and controversy." The story was the same in southeastern Michigan. The Ford Motor Company began hiring the first of 42,000 workers to build B-24 bombers at its immense new Willow Run bomber plant one week before the United States entered the war in December 1941. Set in flat farmlands twenty-eight miles from Detroit, the plant had no high-capacity highway to the metropolis until late in 1942. There was no convenient emergency housing until 1943, leaving migrants to bed down in tarpaper shacks, barns, trailers, and spare rooms in every town from Ypsilanti to Flat Rock.

Sudden growth triggered social tensions. A majority of the newcomers were unattached young men, whether in the armed forces or working in defense jobs. They crowded longtime residents in the stores, claimed seats on the streetcars, and filled downtown restaurants and movie houses to overflowing. Their need for recreation, and the prostitution and crime that went with it, became interrelated problems. Norfolk, Virginia, suffered especially bad publicity because it was convenient to journalists from New York and government officials from Washington. Magazine stories with titles like "Norfolk Nights" and "Growing Pains of Defense" detailed Norfolk's sleazy trailer camps, its rampant prostitution, and its hotels where "hot beds" were rented in twelve-hour shifts.

Mobile, Alabama, fared even worse. An air base, army supply depot, aluminum plant, and two major shipyards made it the fastest growing city in the country by 1943, with a 67 percent population increase since 1940. Mobile's mayor threw up his hands at the city's inability to supply adequate housing or clean water, reduce traffic jams, or even enforce the law. Writer John Dos Passos reported from the town in the spring of 1943:

> Sidewalks are crowded. Gutters are stacked with litter that drifts back and forth in the brisk spring wind. Garbage cans are overflowing. Frame houses on tree-shaded streets bulge with men in shirtsleeves who spill

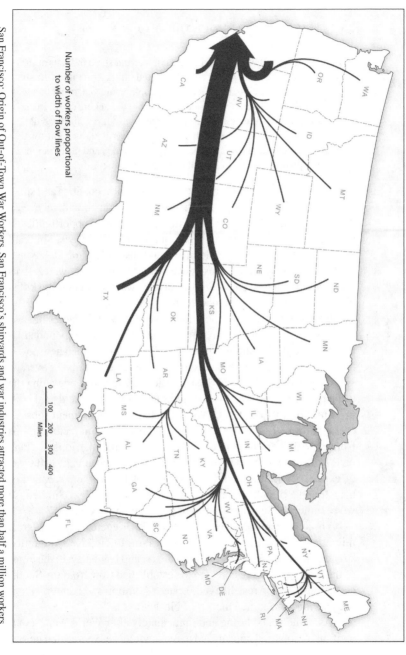

Number of workers proportional
to width of flow lines

0 100 200 300 400
Miles

San Francisco: Origin of Out-of-Town War Workers. San Francisco's shipyards and war industries attracted more than half a million workers from all parts of the United States. Adapted from President's Committee for Congested Production Areas: Final Report, December 1944.

out onto the porches and trampled grassplots and stand in knots at the streetcorners. . . . The trailer army has filled all the open lots with its regular ranks. In cluttered backyards people camp out in tents and chickenhouses and shelters tacked together out of packing cases. In the outskirts in every direction you find acres and acres raw with new building, open fields skinned to the bare clay. . . . Over it all the Gulf mist, heavy with the smoke of soft coal, hangs in streaks, and glittering the training planes endlessly circle above the airfields.

Wartime booms in the big cities emptied farm counties and small towns of their unemployed and their men and women with an eye on "the main chance." Women in particular found new opportunities in the war boom. They made up one-quarter of West Coast shipyard workers at the peak of employment and nearly half of Dallas and Seattle aircraft workers. Most women in the shipyards were clerks and general helpers. The acute shortage of welders and other skilled workers, however, opened thousands of journeyman positions to them as well, work that was far more lucrative than waiting tables or sewing in a clothing factory. Aircraft companies, which compounded labor shortages by stubborn "whites only" hiring, developed new power tools and production techniques to accommodate the smaller average size of women workers, increasing efficiency for everyone along the production line. By July 1944, fully 19 million women held paid jobs, up 6 million in four years. Women's share of government jobs increased from 19 to 38 percent and their share of manufacturing jobs from 22 to 33 percent. Some women worked out of patriotism. Many others, however, needed to support their families and already had years of experience in the work force. As one of the workers recalled of herself and a friend, "We both had to work, we both had children, so we became welders, and if I might say so, damn good ones."

The labor demands of defense plants also triggered a second "great migration" of African Americans from farm to city. New migration streams from Texas, Oklahoma, Arkansas, and Louisiana to the cities of the West Coast were added to the established flow from the Southeast to the North. Areas like the Western Addition and Hunter's Point in San Francisco joined the list of black ghettos.

As in the years during and immediately after World War I, competition for jobs and housing led to racial violence. Segregated unions excluded African Americans from shipyard jobs (although Higgins Industries in New Orleans was an exception to this rule). When the Alabama Dry Dock Company in Mobile responded to pressure from Washington by integrating its work force at the end of May 1943, white workers reacted with two days of violence. Tensions in Detroit focused on competition for scarce housing. The opening of a new public housing project that was intended for blacks but located in a white neighborhood had nearly touched off uncontrolled violence in 1942. On June 20, 1943, an argument over the use of Belle Isle Park did set off a three-day race riot in which thirty-four people died.

Tensions between Hispanics and Anglo Americans in Los Angeles paralleled black-white conflicts in eastern cities. During the 1930s, tens of thousands of Mexican Americans had settled permanently in western cities when their rural jobs as railroad hands and farm laborers disappeared. New migration in the early 1940s swelled the Mexican community in Los Angeles to an estimated 400,000, prompting discrimination and a steady stream of anti-Mexican articles in Los Angeles newspapers. On June 6, 1943, two weeks before the Detroit riots, several thousand Anglos, including off-duty sailors and soldiers, attacked Mexicans on downtown streets and invaded Mexican neighborhoods. African Americans and Filipinos were incidental targets. The "zoot suit" riots, named for the flamboyant attire of some young Hispanics, dragged out for a week of sporadic violence.

The Mobile, Detroit, and Los Angeles riots marked the end rather than the beginning of the wartime crisis for defense cities. The pace of growth slackened in 1943 at the same time as emergency civilian housing became available in large quantity. Under the Lanham Act and related programs, the federal government financed approximately 1 million temporary housing units for wartime use. The largest single project was the instant "city" of Vanport, built on the flood plain of the Columbia River between huge Kaiser Corporation shipyards in Portland, Oregon, and Vancouver, Washington. Working under federal direction, Edgar Kaiser's bulldozers broke ground in September 1942, and the first tenants arrived on December 12. By 1944 over 40,000 residents lived in 9,000 apartments in 600 wooden buildings whose dull gray paint blended into the cool winter rains of the Pacific Northwest. Vanport had its own schools, community centers, day-care program, post office, cafeterias, fire district, playgrounds, shops, 150-bed hospital, and 750-seat theater that offered three double features each week.

As a victory in the war looked increasingly probable in 1943, civic leaders turned their attention to the expected problems of reconverting to a civilian economy and absorbing returning veterans. Postwar planning typically involved appointment of an ad hoc committee to devise a list of public works projects that could relieve expected unemployment and equip the metropolis for further growth. When mayors or city councils were slow to act on this, businessmen worked through their Chamber of Commerce or a local affiliate of the Committee for Economic Development, a national organization representing major corporations interested in rational growth. Independent city planning consultants did their briskest business since the 1920s. New Yorker Robert Moses received $100,000 for a report on *Portland Improvement* that proposed $60 million in highway, sewer, park, and port investments. Day and Zimmerman, Inc., provided San Diego with a 1,300-page blueprint for postwar public works and economic diversification. Harland Bartholomew prepared a fifteen-part report on the future of Dallas and delivered Richmond's first master plan in 1946. Dozens of other cities also worked on schemes for carrying wartime prosperity into the coming years of peace.

The tone of American politics in the last years of the war was eminently practical. An increasingly conservative Congress used the excuse of the war emergency to kill a number of New Deal programs in 1943 and 1944. Politicians and civic leaders at the local level carefully tailored wartime housing for minimum impact on the value of existing property. At the same time, they defined postwar readjustment as a problem of industrial salesmanship. The predominantly "businesslike" approach to wartime services and postwar planning previewed what would be the dominant theme for the next twenty years in city politics.

The Landscape of Prosperity

In 1944–45, many civic leaders expected the economy to react as it had following World War I. In their darkest moments, they feared that a reduction of military spending would cause another Great Depression. In fact, victory in the Pacific war in August 1945 ushered in a great boom—a full generation of economic growth interrupted only by relatively minor recessions.

Even though federal spending dropped by $90 billion from 1945 to 1946, consumers took up the slack as they rushed to use their savings for new vacuum cleaners, washing machines, and automobiles. Few of the war years' boomtowns suffered the feared reconversion crisis. Sunshine cities in the Southwest enjoyed a GI boom as veterans returned to settle in communities they had first visited on weekend passes from nearby military bases. The onset of the Cold War brought continued business to military cities like Norfolk, Mobile, San Antonio, and El Paso. California and Texas attracted disproportionate shares of new investment in manufacturing as national companies opened new plants to serve growing southwestern and western markets.

A middle-sized city like Dayton, Ohio, also illustrates the postwar boom. Expansion of air power in the new era of nuclear deterrence meant military and civilian jobs for the Wright-Patterson Air Force Base. Major industries were ready to meet the needs of a consumer society. The Delco and Inland divisions of General Motors fed parts into GM assembly lines; Dayton Tire kept the new cars rolling; and Frigidaire turned out appliances for new homes. Housing values shot up as the metropolitan population grew from 331,000 in 1940 to 457,000 in 1950, and 695,000 in 1960. As new subdivisions sprawled north and south of the city, glossy supplements to the *Daily News* chronicled the frantic efforts of public officials to build new schools to keep pace with the growing numbers of young families.

Over the long term, the seemingly endless repetition of suburban development like that in Dayton redrew the map of urban America and fueled the prosperity of the 1950s. Suburbanization meant new houses, appliances and furniture to fill the new rooms, automobiles to connect the new subdivision to jobs and shopping, and roads, sewers, and schools to make the new settlements livable. Public and private investment in new residential areas required expanded production from basic industries—steel, lumber, glass, textiles. During the 1930s, the aggregate value of all urban houses and apartments had *declined* because of deferred maintenance and limited replacement. From 1945 to 1960, however, the total value of the American housing stock increased by 65 percent (adjusted for inflation). The total value of consumer durables tripled as annual spending on household goods climbed from $6 billion to more than $20 billion.

Immediately after the war, returning veterans and families who had been crowded into small apartments waited impatiently for the construction industry to develop the capacity for large-scale production. An estimated 2.5 million families lived with relatives in 1945–46. Thousands of others found space in defense housing projects that were temporarily spared from the wrecking ball. One response from Washington was the Veterans Administration (VA) mortgage program, which guaranteed loans by private lenders and allowed veterans to buy with no downpayment. The number of loans given under the parallel mortgage insurance program of the Federal Housing Administration (FHA), which began in 1934, roughly doubled wartime and prewar levels.

Large-scale "industrial" land developers made the most effective response to the housing demand. With a few exceptions like Jesse Nichols, developers before 1930 had cleared land, laid out streets, and made their profits by selling lots. Individual households and small builders who operated out of their hip pockets had then filled in the new neighborhoods one or two houses at a time. By the late 1940s, in contrast, the successful developer sold the complete package—a mass-produced house on a mass-produced lot. Developers bought fifty or a hundred acres, put in basic utilities for the entire tract, purchased materials in carload lots, and kept a specialized labor force busy on scores of identical houses. In total, large-scale developers accounted for more than 60 percent of new housing in 1959, compared to 5 percent before World War II.

The results were obvious on both sides of the country. Outside New York, Arthur Levitt and Sons specialized in the efficient production of affordable housing. Their first Levittown in Nassau County, Long Island, east of New York, was empty land at the start of 1947. It counted 51,000 residents in 15,000 identical houses by the end of 1950. For $8,000 (later $9,000), a young family got a basic 800-square-foot home that could be expanded as their family increased, neighborhood parks, and the sites on which new schools would be built. A second Levittown outside Philadelphia sold 3,500 houses in ten weeks, with prices ranging from $9,000 for the smaller "rancher" model to $17,500 for the expensive "country club" style. The "jubilee," at $10,900, came with two full baths, push-button ranges, all-steel kitchen cabinets, and twenty-three pieces of shrubbery. On the other coast, Lakewood covered 3,000 acres in Los Angeles County. Historian Remi Nadeau described mass production without an assembly line:

> While the farmers were harvesting the last crop from the land . . . construction crews were starting to lay down 133 miles of paved streets. Small teams of specialists moved down one side of each street with fantastic new machinery. Great power diggers gouged out a foundation trench for each house in fifteen minutes. Lumber arrived precut. . . . Expediters with radio cars moved from one home to another looking for bottlenecks. On some days as many as 100 new homes were started; 10,000 were finished in the first two years.

The new suburbs confirmed the American taste for detached, single-family homes. We built 14 million of them from 1946 through 1960, compared to approximately 2 million new apartment units over the same time span. Massive postwar construction reduced the average age of urban housing from twenty-six years to nineteen. Adaptations of the one-story western ranch house, one-and-a-half-story Cape Cod, and the stylish split level replaced potato fields on Long Island, truck farms and fields around Indianapolis, and citrus groves in the San Fernando Valley. Tract housing climbed over the brush-covered hills south of San Francisco and pushed aside the pines around Atlanta and Washington. In its January 4, 1954, issue, *Life* magazine reported on the fruits of the new boom. In Marietta, Georgia, the Perryman family paid $748 per year for a five-room house out of the $5,850 salary of a Lockheed draftsman. In Denver, the Waidmanns enjoyed "a pleasant, secure life on what to many Americans seems like the ultimate economic goal—a five-figure income." An annual income of $12,291 supported payments on a six-room house (with do-it-yourself additions) and allowed one great splurge—a television set bought for $389 in cash. The Rector family of Little Rock, buoyed by an extraordinary year in the insurance business, used part of their $49,000 income to expand their already impressive house. They had $3,744.06 left over for a new plastic-top Mercury sedan.

As the *Life* profiles indicate, the 1940s and 1950s brought a "home-ownership revolution." The proportion of urban householders who owned or were buying their own homes rose from 44 percent in 1944 to 62 percent in 1960. One of the keys was the nearly universal use of the self-amortizing mortgage, another innovation of the depression decade whose full impact was felt after 1945. Under previous banking practice, home buyers put down 40 percent or 50 percent of the purchase price up front and paid annual interest on the balance. At the end of eight or ten years, the buyer had to either refinance or pay the full principle balance. The self-amortizing mortgage, in contrast, acts like an automatic savings account. Each monthly payment covers interest and a small fraction of the principle balance. Over the twenty-to-thirty-year life of the loan, the monthly payments gradually eliminate the entire debt. With the built-in repayment factor, banks and savings and loans were willing to loan 80 percent or 90 percent of the value of the house; they went even higher with the added protection of FHA insurance or VA guarantees.

The new suburbs of the 1950s did their booming business despite a bad press. As the chance for suburban living opened to the majority of Americans for the first time, popular writers reacted with sharp criticisms. The pop sociology of the fifties described a tawdry physical environment that fostered false values and social disorganization. There was a common indictment behind terms like "slurb" and "sloburb" and titles like *The Suburban Sadness, The Split Level Trap,* and *The Crack in the Picture Window.* Suburbs were accused of being transient, conservative, conformist, materialistic, and superficial. Their houses and shopping centers were described as monotonous ticky-tack. Even serious journalists and scholars tended to accept this "suburban myth," concentrating on family relationships, the supposed trend toward Republican voting, and the problems of the "other-directed life," in which people paid more attention to what others thought than to their own values.

One of the prime exhibits was Park Forest, Illinois, started in 1947 on nearly four square miles of land thirty miles south of the center of Chicago. Park Forest included rental row houses for new families seeking their first home, and single-family dwellings for established households. Ads developed after consultation with psychologists announced that "coffeepots bubble all day long in Park Forest. This sign of friendliness tells you how much neighbors enjoy each other's company." A few years after the bulldozers arrived, William H. Whyte's best-seller, *The Organization Man* (1956), used Park Forest to illustrate the lifestyle of the growing white-collar middle class. He thought the ads were right and used the hypothetical example of Dot and Charlie Adams.

> Charlie, a corporate trainee, is uprooted from the Newark office, arrives at Apartment 8, Court-12, it's a hell of a day—the kids are crying, Dot is half sick with exhaustion, and the movers won't be finished till late. But soon . . . the neighbors will be over to introduce themselves. In an almost inordinate display of decency, some will help them unpack, and around suppertime two of the girls will come over with a hot casserole and another with a percolator full of coffee. Within a few days the children will have found playmates, Dot will be Kaffeeklatsching . . . like an old-timer, and Charlie . . . will be enrolled in the Court Poker Club.

In fact, the new suburbanites were very much like the friends and neighbors they had left behind. They didn't drop their ties to ethnic organizations or abandon the Democratic party (although millions of Democrats inside and outside the suburbs preferred Republican Dwight Eisenhower to Democrat Adlai Stevenson as president in 1952 and 1956). The suburb of Milpitas, California, near San Jose was a good example. Most of its new homeowners were families whose union workers labored in a Ford assembly plant that had opened in 1955. They preferred the better quality and more respectable addresses of their new homes, but these people showed no inclination to cut off ties to the city they had left behind.

Residents of the third Levittown, started in 1958 in southern New Jersey about fifteen miles from Philadelphia, felt much the same way. Herbert Gans, a professor of city planning and sociology at the University of Pennsylvania, astonished his urban colleagues by packing his family and belongings and joining the first wave of new Levittowners. He found that 85 percent of his new neighbors preferred the suburbs for the down-to-earth reason that they offered the best and biggest houses for the money. Good schools and convenient shopping ranked almost as high. Few Levittowners were changed by their new environment. Fewer still thought that there was any reason to feel embarrassed about a home in suburbia. For many of them, after all, the realistic alternative to Levittown was a crowded walk-up apartment or a South Philly row house shared with the in-laws.

Despite the generally positive attitudes, new suburbanites in the 1950s did notice serious problems with their surroundings. Subdivisions gobbled up the streams, woodlands, and open spaces that had made suburbia attractive in the first place. Builders often opted for septic tanks rather than more expensive sewer systems. As population grew and overburdened the soil, the septic systems' contamination bubbled up to the surface and polluted streams. These environmental problems helped to fuel the environmental movement, providing suburban foot soldiers for the conservation generals who had been focusing on protecting the western wilderness. Rachel Carson's best-selling *Silent Spring* (1962) documented the general effects of pesticides on wildlife, but it took its strongest image from the imagined disappearance of songbirds from suburban backyards. Landscape architect Ian McHarg articulated many of the growing worries in *Design with Nature* (1969). Earth Day, first observed in 1970, and the spate of antipollution legislation in the 1970s owed much to the quiet suburban crisis.

Another unanticipated product of the suburban movement was increasing prominence for women in electoral politics. Suburbs were communities filled with newcomers who often lacked ties and obligations to extended families, churches, and other community institutions. Women who had satisfied their responsibilities to their nuclear families were relatively free to give time and energy to political activity. At the same time, the spreading suburbs were "frontiers" that called for concerted action to solve immediate needs such as adequate schools and decent parks. Since pursuit of such services has often been viewed as women's work (in contrast to the men's work of economic development), burgeoning suburbs offered numerous chances to engage in civic work, to sharpen skills as political activists, and finally to run for local office. Women's campaigns were aided by the fact that the suburbs lacked the entrenched political machines of older cities. The results were seen first in local elections in the 1960s and 1970s (for one of many examples, women were a majority on the San Jose City

Council and Santa Clara County, California Board of Supervisors by 1980) and later in elections to governorships and to the U.S. Congress.

Neighborhood Change and the Northward Movement

The hidden problem of suburban growth was not what it did to the residents of the new communities, but what it did to the people and neighborhoods that were left behind. The rationale for suburban expansion was the belief that housing was a hand-me-down commodity—like old clothes. New housing on the suburban frontier was intended for the richest element of a city's population, and when the rich moved out, the now older neighborhoods were available for individuals and groups a step below them on the economic ladder. As everyone moved up in housing quality and out toward the edge of the city, even the poor found alternatives to the worst slums and were able to abandon their dilapidated shacks, cold-water flats, and windswept "workingman's cottages" by the hundreds of thousands.

If the "filter-down" system accurately described the postwar housing market, the unspoken corollary was that neighborhoods were perishable goods. Inner-city neighborhoods were passed successively from the rich or the middle class to the working class and then to the abject poor before being abandoned or razed. City governments that depended on property tax revenues found it increasingly difficult to finance public services. City residents who depended on viable, socially supportive communities found that older neighborhoods were no longer comfortable places to live. In 1958, journalist William H. Whyte, Jr., summarized the results of this process.

> More and more . . . the city is becoming a place of extremes—a place for the very poor, or the very rich, or the slightly odd. Here and there, in pleasant tree-shaded neighborhoods, there are still islands of middle class stability, but for young couples on the way up—most young couples, at any rate—those are neighborhoods of the past. They are often the last stand of an ethnic group, and the people in them are getting old. The once dominant white Protestant majority has long since dispersed, and among the Catholic[s] and the Jews who have been the heart of the city's middle class, the younger people are leaving as fast as they are able.

These effects were apparent on a grand scale in metropolitan New York. By the 1950s, four distinct residential rings surrounded the ten-square-mile retail-office core south of 61st Street in Manhattan. The first was an expanding zone of minority dominance that had spread from Harlem to the South Bronx, northern Brooklyn, and across the Hudson into Newark, New Jersey. The "grey areas" came next, mile after mile of predepression houses, duplexes, and apartments built on small lots behind heavily commercialized streets and street corners. Most of Brooklyn, the northern Bronx, and the blue-collar neighborhoods of Queens fell into this category of hand-me-down neighborhoods that young white families scorned and overcrowded minority families looked at with envy. The aging population and the abandoned multistory factory buildings of the grey areas reflected the migration of young families and businesses into the third ring of postwar suburbs on Staten Island, north into Westchester County, and east into Long Island. Even further out—thirty miles or more from the Macys and Gimbels department stores—was a fourth ring of old railroad commuter suburbs that would be reshaped by the suburban tide after 1960.

In Brooklyn and the Bronx, Germantown in Philadelphia, Compton in Los Angeles, and scores of similar communities across the country, the filter-down housing system had to accommodate the transition from one racial or ethnic group to another, in addition to changes in socioeconomic level. In the years around the middle of the century, the great northward movement of the American population compounded the problems of change in older neighborhoods. The same factors that had attracted rural southerners to northern cities in the 1920s operated even more strongly during the 1940s and 1950s. African American migrants from the South totaled 1.5 million in each decade; over the twenty-year span, the northeastern states gained 1,140,000 black residents, the Middle West gained 1,126,000, and the West gained 703,000. Virtually all of the migrants settled in inner-city neighborhoods. By 1960, two-thirds of all African Americans living outside the South could be found inside the city limits of the twelve largest American cities.

The mass migration of whites from the sun-starved hollows and coal-mining country of the central Appalachian Mountains was less noticeable but just as extraordinary. New outmigration from western

Virginia, Kentucky, and West Virginia was roughly 3 million between 1940 and 1970, taking one-third of the population of mountain Kentucky and one-fifth of all West Virginians. Like the renewed black migration, the flow was triggered by the wartime labor demand, especially in the cities of the Middle West. Harriet Arnow's novel *The Dollmaker* captured the disruption of rural culture and values in the story of a Kentucky mountain family who moved to Detroit for defense work. Even the sky looked different on the nights when the smoke cleared from the Detroit air, with the Big Dipper and the North Star shifted from their accustomed spots in the sky. To someone raised in the hills and hollows, "the black alleys were all exactly alike. All were bordered by the same low buildings, even the patterns of light on the snow from the government windows were always exactly the same."

Appalachian migration reached its peak in the 1950s when the total movement equaled that of southern blacks. These migrants settled particularly in Cincinnati, Cleveland, Detroit, Chicago, and smaller cities in the heart of the industrial belt. Following the pattern of European immigrants, they tended to fill up older low-rent neighborhoods such as Chicago's Uptown or Dayton's east side, and to depend heavily on networks of friends and extended families. Counting both migrants and their children, Cincinnati's Appalachian community may have reached 200,000 by the end of the 1960s, at which time the migration tapered off. In the 1970s, opportunities opened for middle-class migrants and skilled workers, but data from that decade show relatively little upward mobility within or between generations for unskilled workers and their families.

Puerto Ricans constituted yet another stream in the northward movement. A trickle of migration from the impoverished commonwealth of Puerto Rico in the 1930s became a flood after 1945. Puerto Ricans were American citizens who could travel freely between the island and the mainland. They quickly took advantage of expanding airline connections and fares that dropped as low as $5 down with easy monthly payments. The first Puerto Rican immigrants were ambitious members of the middle class, followed rapidly by men and women seeking industrial and service jobs. As with earlier transatlantic migrations, the average Puerto Ricans who left home were younger and better educated than those who stayed on the island. The peak year was 1953, when the demand for labor during the Korean War attracted 75,000 migrants.

Their preferred destination was New York, whose Puerto Rican community increased from 61,000 in 1940 to 613,000 in 1960. Second choices were Philadelphia, Chicago, and Cleveland because of jobs in heavy industry. Then came smaller cities in the shadow of New York such as Newark, Jersey City, Paterson, and Bridgeport. The center of Puerto Rican life in the 1950s was the 110th Street subway station of the Lexington Avenue line through East Harlem—the heart of El Barrio de Nueva York, which Puerto Ricans took over from an earlier generation of Italian immigrants. Puerto Ricans also concentrated in the South Bronx and in neighborhoods near the Brooklyn Navy Yard, where many found their first jobs.

Some members of other minority groups also benefitted in the 1950s from regular industrial and government jobs. Manufacturing cities with progressive labor unions, such as Detroit with the United Auto Workers, offered them factory jobs at wages that could support a family. African Americans worked through the Urban League, the National Association of Colored Women, and other race-oriented groups to secure fair employment laws and jobs with large corporations. Mexican American families in San Antonio benefitted from maintenance jobs available at the city's military bases. Steady employment allowed blacks and Latinos to build strong community institutions and vibrant neighborhood business districts

However, massive migration and even more massive suburban growth opened the way for rapid racial change in one neighborhood after another. Newcomers to the city were the logical people to inherit older neighborhoods as the filter-down process operated. When the new residents were members of an identifiable minority, however, the natural transition often turned into panicked "white flight." Real estate agents looking for a quick buck from the rapid sale and resale of properties sometimes practiced "block busting." Following an actual or rumored move of a black family onto a previously all-white block, realtors would work door-to-door, attempting to persuade homeowners to sell out at panic prices. Virtually every northern city had a list of neighborhoods that "changed" in the space of four or five years.

The responses to racial change varied. Hundreds of neighbor-hood associations and community leagues across the country worked hard to keep whites in changing neighborhoods. They lobbied city hall for zoning changes and community improvements, held block meetings to check the spread of rumors, and tried to maintain neighborhood cohesion. Despite their efforts, it was difficult to counter fears that integration would lower property values or to combat many whites' deep-seated unwillingness to share territory with blacks and Hispanics. As one Detroit realtor wrote to a neighborhood newspaper "The problem with neighborhoods becoming ghettos is due to the white buyers. They will not buy within three miles of mixed neighborhoods. When my company advertises a house in a mixed neighborhood, only Negro buyers inquire. If, by mistake, a white buyer calls on the property, he soon disappears when he finds the neighborhood is mixed."

With continuing pressures for black housing, white residents in some cities such as Chicago responded by harassing African American families and destroying properties. Historian Arnold Hirsch has called the late 1940s and early 1950s in Chicago an "era of hidden violence." Whites engaged in "chronic guerilla warfare" to preserve the racial homogeneity of their neighborhoods, with violence peaking in the spring and fall during the city's traditional moving seasons. Unlike the massive racial rioting after World War I, each Chicago disturbance was confined to a specific neighborhood and most participants were local residents "defending" their turf. The situation was similar in Detroit. White working-class families saw residential integration as a threat to property values and community identity and used political pressure and violence to try to contain African Americans in ghetto neighborhoods.

Federal policy encouraged tension and disequilibrium among the races and made the situation worse. Land clearance and highway construction, which targeted the most run-down neighborhoods, frequently set off a chain reaction. Displaced African Americans crowded into the remaining ghetto blocks and pushed middle-class blacks out the other side into previously white districts. The FHA played a direct role in racial segregation by promoting homogeneous neighborhoods. Its handbook, *Planning Profitable Neighborhoods*, advised develop-

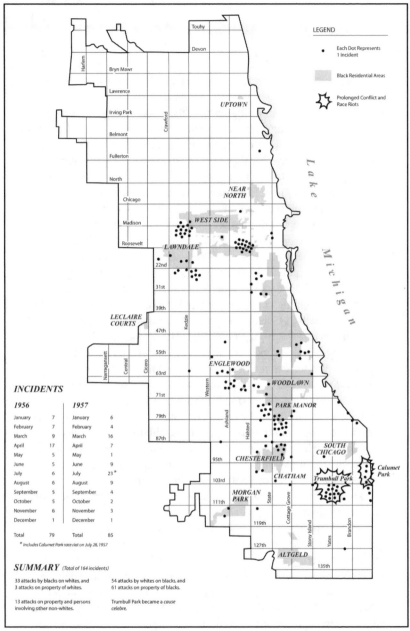

INCIDENTS

1956		1957	
January	7	January	6
February	7	February	4
March	9	March	16
April	17	April	7
May	5	May	1
June	5	June	9
July	6	July	23 *
August	6	August	9
September	5	September	4
October	5	October	2
November	6	November	3
December	1	December	1
Total	79	Total	85

* Includes Calumet Park race riot on July 28, 1957

SUMMARY (Total of 164 incidents)

33 attacks by blacks on whites, and 3 attacks on property of whites.

54 attacks by whites on blacks, and 61 attacks on property of blacks.

13 attacks on property and persons involving other non-whites.

Trumbull Park became a *cause célebre.*

Racial Violence in Chicago, 1956–57. Racial incidents in Chicago in the 1950s concentrated in white neighborhoods on the edges of the expanding black ghettos of the west and south sides. From *Black Metropolis*, copyright 1945 by St. Clair Drake and Horace R. Cayton; renewed 1973 by St. Clair Drake and Susan C. Wordson. Reprinted by permission of Harcourt, Brace, Jovanovich, Inc. and the Chicago Urban League.

ers to build for a single age group, income level, and race. In the new suburbs, FHA officials encouraged the use of racially restrictive covenants to prevent "undesirable" mixing of the races and assure "harmonious, attractive neighborhoods." The National Association of Real Estate Boards operated with an equally discriminatory code of ethics until 1950. Real estate agents tacitly ranked Germans more desirable than North Italians, Poles preferable to Greeks, and Mexicans and African Americans at the bottom. The FHA also wrote off huge tracts within city limits by "redlining"—refusing to guarantee mortgage loans for older housing and homes in areas threatened by "Negro invasion." When the leading federal housing agency announced that racially mixed neighborhoods were bad risks, private banks and savings and loans quickly adjusted their lending policies. Redlining created a self-fulfilling prophesy, as even stable working-class neighborhoods began to deteriorate when people found it was difficult to get home improvement loans and adequate insurance, and almost impossible to sell their houses—whether to black or white families.

Racial discrimination by the federal government was possible in part because of the political weakness of the country's minority groups in the 1940s and 1950s. Chicago elected the century's first African American congressman in 1928, establishing a permanent "black seat" on the city's South Side. A second black representative did not reach Congress until a New York district that included Harlem voted in Adam Clayton Powell, Jr., in 1944. In 1954, with a total of 531 U.S. senators and representatives, the election of Charles Diggs from Detroit gave the nation's 16.5 million black citizens their third black member of Congress.

African Americans were also underrepresented in local governments. In 1951, blacks constituted 29 percent of Detroit's population but held only 11 percent of the positions on the city council. Percentages compared to populations were similarly low in Philadelphia and New York. After a militant black was elected to the city council in the early 1950s, Cincinnatians rewrote their city charter to effectively eliminate African American representation. Congressman William Dawson and other black politicians in Chicago ran a South Side branch of the city's Democratic party machine, but men with names like

Quigley, Fratto, Girolami, and Bieszczat ran the black wards on the west side.

Oakland, California, shows how the two forces of suburbanization and redevelopment worked together to disadvantage African Americans. Following World War II, Oakland civic elite picked a strategy of industrial decentralization and residential segregation to undercut a nascent biracial coalition among the city's industrial workers. Factories were located or relocated in new suburbs such as San Leandro where housing markets were open to white workers but effectively closed to blacks. Meanwhile, the Oakland Planning Commission introduced a massive redevelopment plan in 1959 with the forecast that Oakland could become the metropolitan center for northern California. To accomplish this ambition, the city cleared much of heavily African American West Oakland for port expansion, highways, and rapid transit. Oakland fell short of matching San Francisco while its East Bay suburbs flourished and its marginalized African Americans turned to radical options that would include the Black Panther party in the 1960s.

The Politics of Growth

For most Americans in the 1940s and 1950s, the lurking problems of racism and neighborhood decline took a back seat to the opportunities offered by postwar prosperity. In city after city, the commercial-civic leadership encouraged "progressive" local government to direct growth and allow businesspeople to seize new opportunities. Professional administrators viewed defense housing and postwar planning efforts as dry runs for more ambitious civic improvement programs. For other citizens, the same programs demonstrated the ability of city governments to support the growth of private business.

The local businesspeople who dominated city politics in the postwar decades shared a common goal: the mobilization of public and private resources to provide the necessary physical facilities for commercial and industrial expansion. Each public shopping list included a mix of faster highways, larger airports, more modern docks, an expanded water supply, and cheaper electric power. The focal points for the urban strategies, however, were the nation's dingy city cores. Most downtowns in 1953 looked like they had in 1930. Depression, war, and the growing competition of new suburban shopping centers had put downtowns on hold. In many cases, no new buildings had been started since the Great Depression. Metropolitan residents were deserting downtown movie theaters and medical offices, drifting away from department stores, and complaining about the cost of parking. New programs for downtown renewal were designed to protect existing investments and preserve established businesses by making the areas clean and attractive, and by improving accessibility and upgrading parking.

Downtown revitalization also served as a competitive tool for rival cities. In the nineteenth century, cities had competed by acquiring, for example, the first canal or the best railroad connections. After World War II, civic leaders worked to attract white-collar managerial and professional jobs by supplying abundant new office space, convention-exhibition centers with accompanying hotels, and public universities to train technical and managerial staff for new white-color jobs. San Francisco's redevelopment plans were intended to convey a picture of that city as a national metropolis. Charlotte viewed urban redevelopment as a tool for establishing commercial primacy in the Carolinas and for competing with Richmond and Atlanta, while Atlantans looked on smugly as their city outdistanced its longtime rival Birmingham.

Some of the most impressive examples of postwar civic renewal came in the old industrial cities of Pennsylvania. The first step in the transformation of cramped and sooty Pittsburgh was to lift the thick pall of coal smoke that clung to the city's steep hills and filled its valleys. The effort started in 1940–41, when rising defense production added more smoke to an already serious problem. Borrowing from the experience of St. Louis's smoke control officer Raymond Tucker (who later became that city's reform mayor), Pittsburgh developed an air pollution control plan that was to go into effect immediately after the war. While the Democratic party and Mayor David Lawrence (1946–59) sold the program to Pittsburgh households, the city's business elite pressured the Pennsylvania Railroad into compliance.

As the skies lightened in the later forties, the Allegheny Conference on Community Development took the lead in community improvement. The Allegheny Conference evolved from a postwar plan-

ning committee. It linked the Democratic party with the city's investment and business community, especially Richard King Mellon from
the family of tycoons that controlled Gulf Oil, Alcoa, and a host of
other companies small only by comparison. The Allegheny Conference sponsored detailed redevelopment plans and helped to pass a
"Pittsburgh Package," legislation that included parking control, a mass-
transit study commission, and new taxes. That legislation paved the
way for insurance companies to invest in the first new downtown buildings in a generation as part of the Gateway Center redevelopment
project. The city's Urban Redevelopment Authority cleared land for
underground parking and a new park at the confluence of the Alleg-
eny and Monongahela rivers. Alcoa and U.S. Steel joined in by erect-
ing new downtown office towers around Mellon Square. City officials and journalists from all parts of the country flocked to inspect
the new Golden Triangle that had replaced the worn-out core of downtown Pittsburgh and created space for tens of thousands of new white-
collar workers.

The "Philadelphia Renaissance" required a resounding political
revolution. The war had brought business-backed efforts for systematic planning and a new city planning commission. The Better Philadelphia Exhibition in 1947 gave dramatic visual expression to ideas
for downtown reconstruction and expressways. An average of 6,500
people per day filed through the Gimbels Department Store audito-
rium to look at giant dioramas and exhibits. The "Time-Space Machine" was a series of edge-lit plastic maps showing the growth of the
city and its current blighted condition. It was designed by Edmund
Bacon (the city's future planning director) while he was en route to
Iwo Jima. The downtown model showed the city as it was in 1947 and
presented a thirty-year rebuilding plan. In the same year as the exhibition, young Democrats Richardson Dilworth and Joseph Clark began a concerted effort to reform a city government that was notorious
for what journalist Lincoln Steffans had once called its "corrupt and
contented" Republican party machine. Dilworth lost the 1947 mayoral election by a wide margin but brought to light a staggering network of embezzlers who had siphoned $40 million from the city trea-
sury. The scandals forced the adoption in 1951 of a new city charter
that centralized power in the mayor, blocked political appointments

to city jobs, and paved the way for Clark (1952–55) and Dilworth (1956–62) to lead the city as mayors.

The Clark and Dilworth administrations combined liberal social services and a commitment to the preservation of the city's center as the economic core for Philadelphia's 3 million residents. Under the direction of Edmund Bacon, Philadelphia's leadership built a new downtown on top of the old. The old Broad Street Station and the "Chinese Wall"—a railroad embankment that split the center of the city—came down in showers of rubble and dust. In their place came a subsurface commuter railroad station and private office buildings adjacent to city hall. Low-income residents and low-rent warehouses gave way to the University City Science Center near the University of Pennsylvania and a new mall around Independence Hall. Society Hill attracted trendy urban professionals to the same historic neighborhood in which Betsy Ross and Benjamin Franklin had lived. Downtown redevelopment and aggressive industrial promotion changed Philadelphia's image in the 1950s from "heavy, old-fashioned immobility" (in Joseph Clark's words) to that of a city winning its "race with time."

Cities across the country mirrored Philadelphia's pattern of political reform and municipal revitalization. A wave of "GI revolts" swept city politics in 1946 and 1947 as bright young veterans—the more competent versions of Kevin McCluskey from *The Last Hurrah*—marched against complacent civic leaders and self-satisfied politicians in towns from the South Atlantic coast to the Rockies. The common goal was to replace the small-time politics of cronyism with administrations comprised of growth-oriented business leaders and bureaucrats. The new politicians lambasted entrenched officeholders, promised to crack down on vice and clean up police departments, and argued for effective planning and efficient city bureaus.

Mayor Robert Maestri of New Orleans was a perfect target for the postwar reformers. An ally of the late Huey Long and leader of the regular Democratic organization, Maestri had governed through payroll padding and routinized graft. For his challenger in the 1946 election, a committee of business leaders chose thirty-four-year-old de Lesseps S. Morrison, a returning army officer and dynamic campaigner. Morrison's platform of civic reform and economic revital-

ization rallied businesspeople, women's organizations, and veterans
eager to see New Orleans and share in postwar prosperity. In his first
administration, he modernized city government and convinced *Time*
magazine that he "symbolized as well as anyone or anything the postwar energy of the nation's cities." During his sixteen years in office,
Morrison worked consistently for physical redevelopment and industrial growth.

Denver's "interminable Ben" Stapleton was another road-block
to change, governing in 1947 as he had twenty-four years earlier. If
the city's notoriously bumpy streets and illegible street signs failed to
tell newcomers they were unwelcome, Mayor Stapleton could be more
direct. "If all those people would only go back where they came from,"
he responded to complaints, "we wouldn't have a housing shortage."
His replacement in 1947 was James Quigg Newton, a navy veteran
who offered new leadership for a city fearful of losing out on the
national boom. In his eight years in office, Newton provided efficient,
professional municipal management and made Denver safe for ambitious entrepreneurs.

Business-oriented reform was similarly successful in several
southwestern cities. Phoenix department store executive Barry Goldwater was among the prominent business and professional people who
organized a Charter Government Committee in 1949 to fight blatant
corruption in city hall. They kicked the rascals out in their first campaign and swept every city election for the next twenty years. In Albuquerque, the immediate wave of postwar reform had ended the re-
gime of Clyde Tingley, an old-line politico who had made the position of city commission chair into that of partisan boss. Eight years of
fragmented politics persuaded middle-class reformers in Albuquerque's "Heights" neighborhoods to organize their own Albuquerque Citizens Committee. It acted as an informal political party to back
businesslike candidates. San Antonio went through precisely the same
process. Younger business leaders squeezed out an inept political boss
in 1949 and instituted city-manager government in 1951. They were
not able to give the city clear direction until they established a business-oriented political party under the guise of the Good Government
League in 1955.

Other cities ended the war with the local business establishment already in firm control. In Dallas and Dayton, in Charlotte and Seattle, the foreground of civic affairs was filled by the same people who could be found in the chamber of commerce boardrooms, the bar at the country club, and the monthly meetings of the Jaycees. Behind the scenes were the big executives who met for lunch at the exclusive male-only, white-only, and often Protestant-only downtown club. In Atlanta, the men who pulled the strings ran Southern Bell, Georgia Power, Citizens and Southern Bank, the Georgia Trust, the First National Bank, Rich's department store, and Coca-Cola. Seattle had its "big ten" businessmen. Bankers, builders, and big retailers ran Dallas through the elite Citizens Council—"a collection of dollars represented by men" according to journalist Warren Leslie.

Control was even more tightly concentrated in Houston. The "8F Crowd" was named for the Lamar Hotel suite of George Brown, cofounder of the engineering and construction firm of Brown and Root. Three or four other tycoons would join Brown for periodic nights of drinking, cards, storytelling, and decisionmaking. Jesse Jones owned the *Houston Chronicle* and huge chunks of downtown real estate. William Hobby was a former Texas governor and represented his family's *Houston Post*. Gus Worthman was the founder of American General Life Insurance and James Ellis ran the First National City Bank. Leon Jaworski, a protege who later became the Watergate prosecutor, recalled that an evening's talk in the late forties or early fifties could "pretty well determine what the course of events would be in Houston, politically, particularly, and economically to some degree."

The 8F Crowd illustrated the continuing importance of major metropolitan newspapers in middle-sized cities. In the last century, the newspaper was often a city's greatest cheerleader, booster, and advocate of rapid development. In the country's younger, fast-growing cities, that tradition continued into the postwar era. Until his death in 1955, newspaper publisher Amon Carter *was* Forth Worth. He pushed economic growth, dipped into the federal porkbarrel for West Texas, and denigrated Dallas. E. K. Gaylord controlled both of Oklahoma City's newspapers, its leading radio station, and its first TV station until he died in 1974 at age 101. In alliance with Kerr-McGee oil and the local banks and utilities, he made sure that Oklahoma City was safe for unrestricted business enterprise. Norman Chandler, publisher of the *Los Angeles Times*, picked Norris Poulson for that city's mayor in 1953 because the incumbent Fletcher Bowron favored federally subsidized housing. Council members during Poulson's term reportedly waited for a nod from a *Times* representative before casting votes on city business.

Whether they were canny professional politicians like David Lawrence in Pittsburgh, Richard Lee in New Haven, and Robert Wagner in New York, or committed amateurs like Raymond Tucker in St. Louis, Quigg Newton in Denver, and Richardson Dilworth in Philadelphia, the typical mayor of the 1950s gave his city the most efficient government it had ever enjoyed. A new breed of civic leaders recruited professional administrators from a national pool. These people upgraded city departments and persuaded voters to approve new taxes and bond issues for public improvements. When *Fortune* magazine surveyed municipal experts in 1956, it concluded that some of our largest cities were the best run. Cincinnati stood out as the country's best governed, with New York, Philadelphia, Detroit, Baltimore, San Francisco, Pittsburgh, and Milwaukee as runners-up.

Federal Housing and Federal Highways

The growth-oriented administrations that dominated American cities in the 1950s benefitted from federal programs that dealt directly and often exclusively with the physical problems of cities. When the major problems appeared to be building new suburbs and rebuilding older downtowns, it seemed appropriate that public money be spent on brick and mortar, asphalt pavement, and reinforced concrete.

Federal housing assistance for low-income families illustrates the focus of government policy. Public housing originated in the 1930s as one item on a long menu of social reforms. Advocates of federal low-rent apartments wanted to combine slum clearance with the creation of affordable, community-focused housing. Early efforts by the Public Works Administration (PWA), which built 22,000 apartments in fifty-nine projects from 1934 to 1937, emphasized common parks and malls, community recreation centers, and other neighborhood facilities as part of its overall design. The Housing Act of 1937, which substituted the United States Housing Authority (USHA) for the PWA as the federal low-income housing agency, committed the nation "to provide financial assistance to the States and political subdivisions thereof . . . for the provision of decent, safe, and sanitary dwellings for families of low income." Before World War II ended, USHA provided 90 percent of the construction costs for 168,000 housing units. Local housing authorities put up the matching 10 percent, picked the sites, constructed the apartments, selected the tenants, and managed the complexes. The underlying idea was slum clearance, with one-for-one replacement of substandard tenements and shacks by inexpensive but decent apartments. As historian Gail Radford has documented, however, the legislation was too limited to live up to its promise, creating a dual housing system of directly subsidized, minimal quality housing for the poor while indirectly subsidizing private market housing for everyone else.

The federal government reaffirmed its concern about housing for families who were priced out of the private market with the Housing Act of 1949. Passed with the remarkable backing of Ohio's extremely conservative Senator Robert Taft, the act provided $500 million in federal aid. Local redevelopment agencies were to use the money to assemble, clear, and then sell or lease land for "predominantly residential uses" to private developers or housing authorities. Congress also put housing development in a broad context by declaring in the same law that "the general welfare and security of the Nation and the health and living standards of its people require . . . the elimination of substandard and blighted areas, and the realization as soon as feasible of the goal of a decent home and a suitable living environment for every American family."

The practice of the 1950s was far from the promise of the 1930s and 1940s. The 1949 legislation authorized 135,000 units of public housing per year, but the Korean War diverted tax money to the Defense Department. Construction after 1954 was cut to fewer than 50,000 units annually. The country lost an estimated 2.5 million housing units to abandonment, freeway construction, and slum clearance during the 1950s, regaining only a fraction in new low-rent apartments. With public housing decisions in the hands of local housing authorities, new projects tended to perpetuate racial segregation. Many of the public housing projects of the depression decade had been attractively landscaped, low-density communities designed as sets of row houses or low-rise apartments with ground-floor entrances for every unit. In the 1950s and early 1960s, agencies and their architects turned to ten- or twelve-story slabs set in paved superblocks. Each massive project was an island in its city, cut off from cross traffic and isolated from neighborhood stores and streetcorners. Interior-design standards forbade large bedrooms and prohibited closet doors (to encourage neatness). In a project like the Robert Taylor Homes in Chicago, whose two-mile row of sixteen-story high-rises once loomed over the Dan Ryan freeway like a sort of modern Stonehenge, the ideal of community building through public housing turned into a program for storing the urban poor in vertical warehouses.

Congress also transformed the redevelopment and housing program of 1949 into the urban renewal program of the 1950s and 1960s. Amendments in 1954 allowed 10 percent of federal capital-grant funds to be used for nonresidential projects. Additional amendments in 1959 expanded the nonresidential allocation to 20 percent and removed a previous requirement that projects include the demolition of large numbers of substandard buildings.

Under the amendments of the 1950s, urban renewal became the central program by which businessmen's governments could revitalize their downtowns. The typical urban renewal project was planned in the late 1950s and implemented in the 1960s. The site was a shabby tract of rundown housing and marginal businesses on the edge of the active business district. Urban renewal was a systematic way to hasten the outward expansion of the central business district and its related uses into its surrounding "zone of transition." In one case after another, the available land was used for public institutions that would help to anchor and sanitize the downtown. The favorites were state university campuses, hospitals, civic centers, and coliseum/convention center complexes, with the choicest land reserved for private offices and hotels. Until the right investors could be found, the renewal agencies were content to hold block after block of cleared land for cheap downtown parking ("flexible planning" is what one agency called its holding of acres of empty land). The quality of local planning determined whether the redeveloped district meshed with the fabric of the central business district or turned its back on the downtown it was designed to save.

In the renewal process, most cities sacrificed low-income neighborhoods of varying social quality for the office buildings, luxury apartments, and public facilities needed to serve a growing white-collar economy. Pittsburgh removed the homes and relocated 8,000 people for its downtown projects in the 1950s. Los Angeles bulldozed the seedy Victorian mansions of Bunker Hill, just northwest of downtown, for a music center, bank towers, and costly high-rise apartments. The fate of Chavez Ravine, a mile to the north, illustrates the changing goals of renewal programs. The ravine itself was a 315-acre tract of hilly, wooded land that had managed to escape intense urban development. Its Mexican American population lived in substandard houses and shacks but maintained a lively sense of pride and identity with their community. Plans from the 1940s for a major public housing project collapsed in 1953 in the face of conservative political opposition. The alternative was to use the site as a major-league baseball stadium for the new Los Angeles Dodgers. The city "traded" the ravine, which had already been cleared of its residents, for other property owned by the Dodgers. Dodgers owner Walter O'Malley broke ground for Dodger Stadium in 1959. It's a fine place to watch a ball game, and it has economically benefitted recreation and tourism in Los Angeles, but the stadium hardly serves the social purpose of housing low-income families that Robert Taft had in mind a decade earlier.

The growing metropolitan system of booming suburbs and revitalized downtowns was to be tied together by a massive federal freeway system. The Federal Aid Highway Act of 1956 committed the nation to the largest building program in its history. Construction of 41,000 miles of interstate and defense highways was the rough equivalent of digging sixty Panama Canals. The system would connect nine out of ten American cities of 50,000 or more residents with multilane, limited-access freeways. Half of the estimated cost of $27.5 billion (actually more than $100 billion by 1980) would go toward 5,500 miles of high-speed freeways that would cut directly through urban areas.

The Interstate Highway System implemented a decision that had been made in 1944 when Congress approved the principle of a national freeway system. In the early 1950s, the question was whether the system would be financed by tolls, (like the turnpikes already built or under construction in eleven states from Connecticut to Kansas) or by a gasoline tax. In its 1954 report, a special advisory committee to President Eisenhower took the position that automobiles were the superior form of transportation within cities as well as between them, asserting that family cars had "restored a way of life in which the individual may live in a friendly neighborhood" by allowing cities to spread into suburbs.

Politicians and highway industry lobbyists reflected a decision that the American public had already made. Transit ridership in U.S. cities had peaked in 1946, when new autos were still difficult to acquire. A dozen years later, the use of buses, streetcars, and subways was less than it had been since the first years of the century. Passenger-car registration leapt from 26 million in 1946 to 62 million in 1960. Only eight years later, the United States would reach the twentieth-century milestone of one registered motor vehicle for every two people—an achievement that would allow every American man, woman, and child to ride in the front seat at the same time.

Like urban renewal projects, most urban freeways were planned in the 1950s but built in the 1960s. Freeways were intended both to increase the value and accessibility of suburban land and to shore up the downtown core. The typical result was a hub-spoke-rim pattern. An inner freeway loop distributed traffic to the central business district while relieving congestion on its narrow streets, a series of radial routes connected the inner ring to the suburbs, and an outer circumferential loop diverted long-distance traffic around the city and brought the different parts of suburbia together. What historian Sam B. Warner, Jr., has called the "interstate wheel" now leaps out at us from highway maps of cities from "A"—Atlanta—to "W"—Washington and Wichita. In the morning, if civic leaders' plans went right, suburbanites would speed over the new freeway system to their work in banks and insurance company towers built on urban renewal land. In the evening, they would return to enjoy the symphony in the civic center theater, finish a degree at the public university, or cheer their professional basketball or hockey team at the new coliseum.

One man whose career epitomized this era of public construction was Robert Moses, whose influence on New York and the nation spanned five decades from the 1920s to the 1960s. His biographer, Robert Caro, has called him "America's greatest builder," a formative influence on parks, highways, and urban renewal. Moses suffered an embarrassing defeat the only time he ran for public office. Thus, he built his career by pyramiding a set of interrelated appointive positions as the head of the Long Island Parks Commission, the Triborough Bridge Authority, the New York City Planning Commission, the mayor's Slum Clearance Committee, and many more. Even as he gladly took credit for his work, however, he operated with the tacit approval of New York's liberal business elite, who saw top-down redevelopment as the best way to help the city and their own bank accounts.

Robert Moses's power in New York reached its apex after 1946 when Mayor O'Dwyer appointed him city construction coordinator. That position made him the sole intermediary between the city and the federal agencies that helped to fund many of its major projects. Moses decided which projects to build and to whom contracts would be awarded. In the late 1940s, he often visited Mayor Impellitteri before breakfast with a briefcase full of orders and papers for the mayor to sign. Between 1945 and 1960, when age and public resistance began to erode his power, Moses controlled the expenditure of roughly $4 billion through the various commissions and agencies that he ran. That sum was greater than what all of the city's elected officials spent during the same years. He guided the construction of 145,000 units of public housing with more than half a million tenants, and he facilitated private housing projects for the middle class that were nearly as massive. Moses helped put together the deals that built the United Nations headquarters, Lincoln Center, and Shea Stadium. He was responsible for the Verrazano Narrows Bridge, the Long Island Expressway, and nearly every other freeway in New York City—even though he was so busy he never learned to drive.

Robert Moses was equally important to the nation as its most prominent advocate of "practical" city planning. In a report for the city of Portland, he proclaimed himself the opponent of "ivory-tower planners who will accept nothing short of a revolution in urban life." In place of social change, he set the much simpler goal of building physical improvements that worked. Engineers and planners trained by Moses spread the same ideas to other cities during the 1940s and 1950s. His New York projects in the early fifties helped to give the new urban renewal program its direction, and he played a hidden role in shaping the Interstate Highway Act. The first federal highway administrator had trained under Moses and learned from his example how to push expressways through the heart of great cities. In a nation that wanted to get on with the job of solving the physical problems of its cities, Moses set an example that was imitated by highway and renewal officials from coast to coast.

He also showed how new highways could be used as a tool of a social engineering. The routes of urban interstates could be carefully chosen to disrupt minority neighborhoods and to erect physical barriers between minority and majority populations. Gary, Indiana, located its freeways to act as a Chinese Wall between its black north side and white south side. Atlanta did the same with I-20 and Orlando with I-4. In Miami, I-95 cleared African Americans from the Overtown neighborhood, adjacent to downtown, and pushed them further away from the city center. Richmond, Virginia, and Nashville ran freeways through black business districts. In St. Paul, an urban interstate displaced one-seventh of the city's African American residents. One critic commented bitterly that "very few blacks lived in Minnesota, but the road builders found them."

Metropolitan Governments

New automobiles and new highways helped the postwar metropolis leap beyond the political boundaries of central cities. By the 1950s, most experts agreed that public services and government coordination within metropolitan areas were lagging far behind the spread of population. Thus, residents of new communities were turning to a confusing jumble of small governments, many of them created piecemeal to meet specific needs. Cities found themselves surrounded by ring after ring of independent suburban municipalities and overlapping special districts that provided one service at a time—parks, water, fire protection, drainage. The result was hundreds of government units in each metropolitan area, each with the power to levy taxes. In

1954, there were 402 such governments in the St. Louis area, 702 in greater Philadelphia, and 960 in metropolitan Chicago. The situation was the same in New York, where political scientist Robert Wood counted 1,467 distinct political entities. Wood concluded that the New York area governments constituted "one of the great unnatural wonders of the world: that is, a governmental arrangement perhaps more complicated than any other that mankind has yet contrived or allowed to happen."

Specialists on urban affairs agreed about the problem of metropolitan fragmentation. In many urban areas, small towns and service districts duplicated specialized city services and expensive facilities. Lack of coordination meant spillovers from one jurisdiction to another. More often than not, the local government system proved ineffective because the plans of one unit tended to cancel out those of another. Confusion was an equally prevalent problem. Citizens found it difficult to know which official to call about stray dogs, where to report a broken traffic light, and who was responsible for plans to build a supermarket at the end of their street. In the familiar case of Park Forest, a single citizen might live within the jurisdiction of Cook County, Bloom Township, the village of Park Forest, the Cook County Forest Preserve District, the Bloom Township Sanitary District, the Suburban Tuberculosis Sanitarium District, and the South Cook County Mosquito Abatement District.

The traditional response of central cities to the outward movement of population had been annexation, the legal extension of city boundaries to include urbanized areas within a single city government. Chicago, Los Angeles, and most of the nation's other great cities had grown through annexation from the early nineteenth century to the early twentieth century. After World War II, annexation remained a viable option for many southern and western cities. The addition of new subdivisions and shopping centers to the core city was an important part of the growth strategy of postwar reform governments. Part of the motivation was the booster's pure joy in numbers; the other part was the reformers' desire to ensure that new growth enhanced the interest of the central city and its central business district.

The dozen cities that annexed more than fifty square miles of suburban land during the 1950s were all located in a band of states from Florida to southern California. Atlanta's "Plan of Improvement," which added 100,000 residents to the city in 1952, met the goal of its chamber of commerce. Mayor William Hartsfield spelled out the goal when he said that annexation would decide "whether Atlanta is to be an expanding progressive unit of government, or whether it is to be condemned to slow deterioration, surrounded by suburbs which are themselves unable to do those large things that must be undertaken if a metropolitan area is to grow." Similar reasons lay behind the annexation campaign that increased the area of Phoenix from 17 to 187 square miles. Civic leaders hoped to attract new industry by reducing the confusion of rapid suburbanization. Said one of the leaders of the annexation movement: "We wanted Phoenix to be the economic center of the Southwest."

Many northern cities, however, found that changes in attitudes and state laws had eliminated the annexation option. Historian Kenneth Jackson has argued that the increasing size and wealth of suburban areas made it possible for them to provide their own services without joining the city. Political independence also allowed suburbanites to maintain their social distance from urban minorities. Once established, most suburban municipalities became as permanent as the core city. Indeed, most of the annexation activity in the Northeast and Middle West after World War II involved expansion by suburbs, not central cities.

The most widely acceptable alternative to annexation was voluntary cooperation through regional planning. The urban renewal amendments of 1954 committed the federal government to help with the physical problems of burgeoning suburbs. Under Section 701, the government made funds available for comprehensive planning by suburban counties, smaller suburban cities, and metropolitan planning agencies. By the end of the decade, more than 1,000 towns and nearly 100 metropolitan areas were involved in planning for basic physical facilities. Councils of Government (COGs) also began to appear in major metropolitan areas such as Detroit and Washington. Often arising out of efforts to develop regional transportation plans, COGs were voluntary associations of elected county and municipal officials. They often provided basic research data and allowed politicians to talk out regional issues face to face.

Creation of new metropolitan supergovernments, in contrast, was the subject of much talk but little action. Miami-Dade Metro in Florida, established in 1957, is the nation's first and only example of a two-tier metropolitan federation. It was developed and sold to the voters by a Miami business community that was fed up with traffic tie-ups, the pollution of Biscayne Bay, and squabbling among twenty-six separate cities. A modernized Dade County government took responsibility for area-wide functions such as mass transit, public health, planning, and central police and fire services. Other functions were left to the local municipalities and service districts. After political squabbling in its first years, Metro began to fulfill its expectations in the mid-1960s.

Consolidation of a city and its surrounding county into a single new government unit has a history dating back to the nineteenth century, with Philadelphia, New York, and Denver as examples. However, the 1947 decision to consolidate Baton Rouge and Baton Rouge Parish (the parish is the equivalent of a county in the Louisiana system) was the first use of the procedure in forty years. City-county consolidations followed by Hampton, Virginia, in 1952, Newport News, Virginia, in 1955, Nashville, Tennessee, in 1962, and more than a dozen other communities since 1962. Overall, however, voters rejected three city-county consolidation proposals for every one they accepted. Major defeats included St. Louis, Cleveland, and Louisville. Advocates tended to be central-city commercial interests, major newspapers and television stations, banks, utilities, and civic organizations. Opposition came from suburban real estate developers, suburban government officials and employees, and racial minorities concerned about dilution of their voting power.

Passage of consolidation proposals usually required special circumstances. In suburban Davidson County outside Nashville, public services were so limited that many homeowners relied on private companies for fire and police protection. Suburbanites also saw consolidation as a way to strike back at Nashville Mayor Ben West, who had forced commuters to buy and display green stickers on their windshields when they used city streets. Jacksonville, Florida, made the change in 1967 after twelve public officials were indicted for bribery and larceny. Creation of a new government through consolidation with

Duvall County seemed the best way to wipe the slate clean. "Things seem to have sunk so low," said one observer, "that almost any change would have been welcome."

Evaluating the Great Cities

After two decades of impressive growth and new government programs to deal with the most obvious needs of housing, highways, and urban redevelopment, American cities at the end of the 1950s seemed to present enormous opportunities in the midst of real but solvable problems. Two books that came out in 1961 summarized the positive view. Jean Gottmann's *Megalopolis* and Jane Jacobs's *The Death and Life of Great American Cities* found specific problems, but they also described city systems with extraordinary possibilities for economic growth and social improvement.

Gottmann believed that American metropolitan growth was creating an entirely new form of settlement. The string of cities along the eastern seaboard from Washington to Boston had the world's greatest concentration of industry, commercial activity, and wealth. It was also Megalopolis, a supermetropolis that extended outward "on a rapidly expanding scale . . . mixing uses of land that look either rural or urban, encircling vast areas which remain 'green' . . . creating a completely new pattern of living and of regional interdependence between communities."

The East Coast Megalopolis was the "hinge" of the American economy—its gateway to the world and the focus of its intellectual life. As a European geographer, Gottmann brought new perspectives to the analysis of the American scene. Where American planners saw particular problems with traffic or transportation, Gottmann found an interlocking set of commercial facilities that functioned as a single entity stretching over 250 miles. Where critics saw blighted neighborhoods and disadvantaged populations, Gottmann found the world's greatest complex of cultural activities and facilities—research laboratories, universities, libraries, charitable foundations, communication networks, and national newspapers and magazines.

The point, of course, was not that the problems of slums, transportation, water supply, and ineffective local government should be ignored, but that American urban development was generating the resources with which to build a more equitable society. The Megalopolis in the Bos-Wash corridor was the most fully developed in 1960, but similar patterns were appearing in southern California, around San Francisco Bay, in Florida, on the Gulf coast, from Milwaukee through Chicago to Detroit, from Cleveland to Pittsburgh, and from Cincinnati to Columbus. In each case, Gottmann argued, individual cities retained their particular identities and functions, but the supermetropolis provided a new level of support for societal growth and change and a forecast for the world's urban future.

Jane Jacobs looked inside the same booming metropolitan areas and found a sense of excitement and possibility in cities as economic and social communities. *The Death and Life of Great American Cities* attacked many of the specifics of recent city planning and redevelopment. It also celebrated the vitality of New York, Boston, Philadelphia, San Francisco, and the other centers of the national economy and culture. "Cities are fantastically dynamic places," she told readers, "that offer fertile ground for the plans of thousands of people."

The life of Jacobs' great city lay in its diversity. Like the fictional Frank Skeffington, who could blend the diverse interests of Irish, Italians, Jews, and Portuguese fishermen into a single political coalition, Jacobs found that the variety of economic classes and ethnic groups was a source of energy and ideas that could be tapped for the development of the larger community. Equally important was the "intricate and close-grained diversity of uses that give each other constant mutual support, both economically and socially."

Paralleling the way in which Gottmann described the benefits of diversity through decentralization, Jacobs looked at the very heart of big cities and found the same virtues in the density of core neighborhoods. With an eye trained by a background in architectural journalism, she analyzed how the apparent chaos of a crowded city was actually an example of "organized complexity" that functioned effectively at the human level. Brooklyn Heights and Greenwich Village in New York, Rittenhouse Square in Philadelphia, and Back-of-the-Yards in Chicago—all these big city neighborhoods, she argued—had *enough* residents and a sufficient variety of activities to generate opportunities for individuals and to sustain networks of social support.

Despite their contrasting subject matter, both authors caught and reinforced the feeling that American cities were creative economic and social systems. It was certainly flattering to be told that American urbanization was pioneering new institutions and forms of settlement and that the suburbs of New Jersey or the sprawl outside San Jose could be viewed as laboratories "where much of what may well be accepted as the 'normalcies' of the advanced civilization of the latter part of the twentieth century is slowly shaping." When the problems of physical development and congestion that had haunted industrial cities for a century seemed on the way to being solved, it was also easy to agree with Jacobs that "vital cities have marvelous innate abilities for understanding, communicating, contriving and inventing what is required to combat their difficulties. . . . The surplus wealth, the productivity, the close-grained juxtaposition of talents that permit societies to support advances . . . are themselves products of our organization into cities."

CHAPTER THREE

A New Urban America

Harry Angstrom has lived all his life in the small metropolis of "Brewer," Pennsylvania, fifty miles or so northwest of Philadelphia. An outstanding career as a high school basketball player in the early 1950s earned him the nickname Rabbit. It stuck with him in the years after his graduation when he followed in his father's footsteps and went to work as a linotype operator in a downtown shop. Novelist John Updike has chronicled the life of Rabbit Angstrom and the evolution of his community at ten-year intervals in *Rabbit, Run* (published in 1960), *Rabbit Redux* (1971), *Rabbit is Rich* (1981), and *Rabbit at Rest* (1990).

The fictional Brewer is a stand-in for Reading, Updike's home community, with 79,000 residents inside the city limits and 313,000 in the metropolitan area. In July, 1969, at the end of a long working day in *Rabbit Redux*, Harry Angstrom takes the bus to his suburban tract house. Where George F. Babbitt drove triumphantly from the edge to the center of the thriving city of Zenith, Rabbit's bus takes him outward through rings of decay, starting in a declining business district with "its tired five and dimes . . . Kroll's Department Store . . . and its flowerpotted traffic circle where the trolley tracks used to make a clanging star of intersection." A few blocks farther out are "empty dusty windows where stores have been starved by the suburban shopping malls and the sad narrow places that come and go called Go-Go or Boutique . . . and the surplus outlets and a shoe parlor that sells hot roasted peanuts and Afro newspapers printed in Philly." Although Brewer's black residents number only a few thousand, they puzzle Rabbit and set the entire city on edge as Brewerites remember the explosive race riots of recent years in every major American city.

Beyond the city limits, Rabbit's bus deposits its last African American passengers. The landscape is now suburban, with "the twirlers of a car lot, the pumps and blazoned overhang of a gas station, the lakelike depth of a supermarket parking lot crammed with shimmering fins." Rabbit's destination is 26 Vista Crescent, a house faced with apple-green aluminum siding and "flagstone porchlet." "Hey Dad," his son calls as he steps into the living room, "They've left earth's orbit! They're forty-three thousand miles away."

Ten years later, the forty-six-year-old Rabbit has arrived at a successful middle age. When electronic typesetting ended his job as a mechanical linotypist, he took over part interest in his father-in-law's car dealership and found his talent in selling Toyotas along a wide suburban highway. Brewer, in contrast, is still in trouble, having lost 10,000 residents during the decade.

> Railroads and coal made Brewer. Everywhere in this city, once the fourth largest in Pennsylvania but now slipped to seventh, structures speak of expended energy. Great shapely stacks that have not issued smoke for half a century. Scrolling cast-iron light stanchions not lit since World War II. . . . The old textile plants given over to discount clothing outlets teeming with a gimcrack cheer of banners FACTORY FAIR and slogans Where a Dollar Is Still a Dollar. . . . All this had been cast up in the last century by what now seem giants, in an explosion of iron and brick still preserved intact in this city where the sole new buildings are funeral parlors and government offices, Unemployment and Join the Army.

Brewer represents scores of specialized industrial cities that fell behind in the changing economic world of the 1960s and 1970s. Cities whose businesses and workers had learned to produce particular commodities in high volume for mass markets found that technological revolutions were making them obsolete. Automakers and consumers decided they preferred radial tires to the old bias-ply tires that Akron turned out so efficiently from the 1910s to the 1960s. Japanese steel makers undercut the mills of Gary, Pittsburgh, Birmingham, and Bethlehem. The railroad bridge over the Delaware River between Morristown, Pennsylvania, and Trenton, New Jersey, had long displayed the motto "Trenton Makes, the World Takes" to motorists crossing the river on Route 1. In the 1920s or 1940s, the slogan had made perfect sense, but it was an ironic comment on industrial decline by 1980.

From New England to the Mississippi River, the result of the eroding northeastern manufacturing base could be read in population statistics. During the 1970s, two dozen metropolitan areas lost population, including eight of the twenty largest. The sharpest declines included Pittsburgh (5.7 percent), Buffalo (7.9 percent), and New York (8.6 percent). New York's loss of 850,000 people was equal to the entire metropolitan populations of thriving cities like Nashville or Greensboro. Smaller cities such as Pittsfield, Massachusetts, and Utica and Elmira, New York, shared the declines. Springfield, Ohio, a metropolitan area with a population of 180,000, was typical. It lost 10,000 industrial jobs and 4,000 people during the decade, suffered unemployment of 17 percent in the early 1980s, and needed $30 million in subsidies to keep its largest manufacturing employer from closing down in 1982. Journalists began to use the term *Rustbelt* to refer to this region of shuttered factories and idled machinery.

For many Americans, the symbol of industrial decline was Cleveland. A manufacturing city that had built a century of prosperity on oil refining, and steel- and metalworking, metropolitan Cleveland had grown from 1.3 million in 1940 to 2.1 million in 1970. In the 1970s, however, its population loss of 165,000 was second only to that of New York. As high-paying jobs in unionized industries disappeared, sagging per capita income cut retail sales and damaged both the downtown and neighborhood shopping districts. In 1978–79, a political deadlock and fiscal crisis that brought the city of Cleveland into technical default on a set of bonds focused national attention on its problems. The financial solution forced by the city's bankers included service cuts and income tax increases, the effects of which have been the further erosion of local jobs.

Paradoxically, Cleveland retained major strengths in the midst of economic crisis. It boasts one of the largest and best-funded public library systems in the country, the excellent Case-Western Reserve University, and a world-class art museum and symphony. It houses nationally prominent accounting and law firms, a federal reserve bank, and as many corporate headquarters as San Francisco. The challenge left by the 1960s and 1970s was to make the transition from the economy and society of the mid-twentieth century to the information-based economy of the twenty-first. Even in Brewer, Rabbit Angstrom looked askance at "the lean new race of downtown office workers" whose patronage has turned an old German restaurant into the Crepe House. While he may not feel comfortable with the new office workers and their new lifestyle, he sees nothing wrong with selling them Toyotas rather than cars made in Detroit.

Meanwhile, Rustbelt images increasingly found their way into popular culture. The movie *Slapshot* (1977) was set in a thinly disguised Johnstown, Pennsylvania, following a minor league hockey team whose problems are paralleled by those of laid-off steelworkers. *Flashdance* (1983) romanticized the landscape of the "world made of steel," but the TV situation comedy "Roseanne" (1988–97) took the problems of industrial transition seriously. Living in an industrial satellite of Chicago, Roseanne and Dan Conner struggled to raise a family in a world where the lifelong unionized factory job was a thing of the past. Billy Joel sang about the decline of Allentown, Bruce Springsteen about Youngstown, and Bob Seger about the days back in '55 when Detroit's workers still made Thunderbirds.

Discovering the Sunbelt

"Brewer," Cleveland, and Springfield, with their problems of urban decline, represent only half the story of urban America in the 1960s and 1970s. Journalists and scholars found their opposite in the headlong prosperity of cities like Orlando, Atlanta, and Phoenix. Houston in particular emerged as a symbol of a new Sunbelt America that was replacing the old industrial belt as the focus of national growth. At the start of the 1970s, when space-age corporations discovered Houston's possibilities as a location for business headquarters, *Business Week* and *Fortune* gave top billing to its management boom. By the middle of the decade, its free-form growth, its political conservatism, its business spin-offs from the NASA space center, and its purring air conditioners in the steamy nights all seemed to epitomize the booming metropolitan areas of the South and West. It was, wrote Ada Louise Huxtable of the *New York Times*, "the place that scholars flock to for the purpose of seeing what modern civilization has wrought."

The rise of the American Sunbelt is one of the most obvious and important changes in the country's national population pattern and economic activity. The westward and southward tilt can be traced to the mobilization for World War II, but its identification as the Sunbelt dates to Kevin Phillips's book *The Emerging Republican Majority* (1969). In his discussion of the South and West, Phillips used the terms *Sun Belt* and *Sun Country* to describe a region of conservative voting habits where Republicans might expect to solidify their status as a majority party. The term *Sunbelt* caught on in 1975 and 1976, when the *New York Times, Business Week, Saturday Review, National Journal,* and other magazines deluged the reading public with discussions of its impacts on the national balance of power. A natural corollary was the invention of the terms *Snowbelt* and *Frostbelt* (as well as Rustbelt) to describe the former core region, with its troubled manufacturing industries.

The Sunbelt's development was essentially a process of urban growth. Journalists tried to capture the essence of the emerging region by describing "an incredible urban explosion" or "booming cities" or "new urban complexes," all of which add up to what Phillips called a "new urban America." The public image of the Sunbelt centered on the rise of a new set of metropolises that aspire to national leadership—from Miami to Houston to Dallas to Los Angeles. The South and West accounted for 62 percent of the nation's metropolitan growth in the 1960s and for an astonishing 96 percent in the 1970s. In total, the metropolitan population of the South and West grew by roughly 40 million persons during the two decades compared to 17 million in the Northeast and Middle West.

The Sunbelt is not simply a new name for the South and West. Only parts of those traditional regions experienced consistently rapid growth and urbanization after 1940. At a bare minimum, the Sunbelt is anchored by the boom states of Florida, Texas, and California. The most common definition sets the regional boundary at the continuous line of state borders that run along the northern edges of North Carolina, Tennessee, Arkansas, Oklahoma, New Mexico, and Arizona, with an extension to include greater Los Angeles. However, at least three other areas have shared the same underlying patterns of economic change and metropolitan growth. The first is the northern Pacific coast from Monterey north to Seattle; the second is the central Rocky Mountains of Colorado and Utah; and the third is the Chesapeake Bay region. All of these are areas that enjoy at least one of the three big S's—sun, sea, and skiing. At the same time, the central South—Alabama, Mississippi, Tennessee, and Arkansas—participated only marginally in the rapid economic changes that occurred at the heart of the Sunbelt.

The regional pattern could be seen in the locations of boom cities during the 1970s. Growth can be measured either by absolute increments or percentage changes. By both standards, the focal points of Sunbelt growth have been at the southeastern and southwestern corners of the country. In the Southeast, Florida accounted for six of the twenty metropolitan areas that added 180,000 or more residents and Georgia for one more. Further West, Houston and Dallas–Fort Worth had the largest absolute gains of the nation's top twenty metro areas. The list included six more entries from California and single metropolitan areas from Arizona, Colorado, Utah, Nevada, Oregon, and Washington. The list of fastest-growing metropolitan areas during the 1970s started with Fort Myers, Florida (95 percent growth), Ocala, Florida (77 percent), and Las Vegas, Nevada (69 percent).

Sunbelt cities in the 1960s and 1970s benefitted from four major shifts in the character of the American economy and society. They enjoyed disproportionate economic benefits from (1) the aging of the national population, (2) the development of a permanent military-defense industry, (3) the evolution of an information-based economy, and (4) the growing importance of foreign trade.

During the 1960s and 1970s, the number of Americans over age sixty-five increased from 16.6 million to 25.5 million. With improved medical care, better private pensions, and the federal social security/medicare system, many retired Americans have moved to warm climates and attractive Sunbelt communities. A significant portion of southern and southwestern growth has been financed by money earned in the Frostbelt and transferred to the Sunbelt by its new elderly migrants. A Harvard-MIT research team described the "enormous, unprecedented shift of retirement age population to the South Atlantic states." Florida, of course, has been the prime destination, accounting for eight of the ten metropolitan areas with the highest proportion of residents aged sixty-five or older. Other Sunbelt cities that have felt the impact of new retirees from the North include Asheville, in the North Carolina mountains; Joplin, Fort Smith, and Fayetteville on the edges of the Ozarks; Medford in southern Oregon; Tucson and Phoenix in sunny Arizona; and the urban complex of southern California.

The steady expansion of the American defense industry also favored the Sunbelt, with its mild winters for training bases, clear skies for flight schools, and ice-free harbors for the navy. The frontrunners among the nation's military cities were Norfolk, San Antonio, San Diego, and Honolulu. The housing market, job picture, and local politics were all affected by the plethora of retired army colonels and navy captains looking for second careers—"geranium growers" in the jargon of old San Diego. Major military installations also dominated smaller Sunbelt cities such as Colorado Springs (Air Force Academy and Fort Carson) and Fayetteville, North Carolina (Fort Bragg).

In raising and spending a defense budget that reached $200 billion per year by the end of the 1970s, the federal government massively redistributed resources among the nation's regions and cities. Taken together, the South and West received 78 percent of military payrolls in 1976. Southern and western companies received 56 percent of all prime defense contracts in the same year, more than double their share twenty-five years earlier. The net impact of the defense budget on specific cities can be calculated by subtracting the tax burden for defense from the amount spent in each community for defense personnel and supplies. Using this formula, approximately two-thirds of American metropolitan areas came up losers and one-third winners in the late 1970s. The ten biggest gainers included one northeastern Standard Metropolitan Statistical Area or SMSA (Hartford), one midwestern SMSA (St. Louis), and eight from the Sunbelt. The cities that lost the most were New York, Chicago, and Detroit.

The rise of an information economy was, in many ways, the most significant and complex economic trend of the 1960s and 1970s. High-growth information-producing and manipulating activities include education, research and development, government, data processing and transmission, advertising, mass communications, and professional consulting. They are essentially the activities that add to national wealth by directly or indirectly creating and applying new ideas, rather than by supplying standardized products and services.

Other indicators of the geographic concentration of information industries are fragmentary but suggestive. A rigorous definition of "high-technology" industries includes those in which the ratio of research and development expenditures to net sales is at least twice the average for all industries. The industries that qualify are drugs, computing equipment, communication equipment, electronic components, and aerospace manufacturing. Employment in these industries grew by 40 percent from 1972 to 1982. In relation to local economies, high-tech employment was most important in New England and the West. Metropolitan areas with more than 100,000 high-tech employees in 1982 were San Jose, Los Angeles, Dallas, Boston, and New York.

Research and development can be conducted within manufacturing corporations or at independent federal or university research centers. Stanford University pioneered the "city of knowledge" in the 1940s and 1950s by encouraging its scientists and engineers to develop marketable products and establishing Stanford Research Park to house new electronics firms. Boston benefitted from the presence of Harvard, MIT, and other universities that helped to nurture an electronics industry along its Route 128 beltway. The University of Pennsylvania tried to emulate the Stanford Model for Philadelphia and Georgia Tech for Atlanta, but their efforts were overshadowed by the success of North Carolina's Research Triangle Park, drawing on the proximity of the University of North Carolina, North Carolina State

University, and Duke University. By the 1980s, expanded research activities transformed the small cities of Chapel Hill, Raleigh, and Durham into a major metropolitan complex. Hundreds of high-technology, defense, and biomedical firms located in the suburbs west and southwest of Washington in order to be near the federal science agencies and the Pentagon. Bright new headquarters for companies dealing in computers, biotechnology, communications, and aerospace systems lined the I-270 corridor through Bethesda and Rockville, Maryland.

A fourth trend was the increasing importance of international connections for the United States and its cities. Foreign trade roughly doubled its share of the gross national product from the early 1960s to the end of the 1970s. New York remained the nation's number one port, but the biggest gains in foreign trade came from ports on the Gulf of Mexico and the Pacific coast. Between 1971 and 1983, Houston, Galveston, and other southern ports increased their share from 19 percent to 27 percent. West Coast ports moved from 15 percent to 23 percent. At the start of the 1980s, the United States shifted from a predominantly Atlantic trading nation to one whose economy is oriented toward the Pacific. By 1982, the total value of trade with the Pacific Rim nations reached $121 billion compared to $116 billion for trade across the Atlantic, confirming that the nation had a bi-coastal economy.

New Americans

The increased importance of America's southern and western port cities and their international trade went hand in hand with a surge of foreign immigration into the United States. From 1961 through 1965, 1,450,000 documented immigrants entered the country. In the latter year, Congress abolished the national quota system that had been in effect since 1924. It substituted overall limits of 170,000 immigrants per year from the eastern hemisphere and 120,000 from the western hemisphere, with special provisions available to political refugees. Legal immigration jumped to 1,871,000 for 1966–70, to 1,936,000 for 1971–75, and to an imposing 2,899,000 for 1976–80. Illegal immigrants may have doubled the total number of newcomers in the 1970s. Not since the 1910s had the United States absorbed so many new residents from Europe, Asia, and Latin America.

In large part, the new migration was an amplification of the internal "northward movement" that brought millions of southern whites, southern blacks, and Puerto Ricans to northern cities in the 1940s and 1950s. In addition to a renewed westward flow of Europeans and eastward flow of Chinese and Koreans, the new migrants moved northwestward from the Caribbean, north from Mexico, and northeastward from the islands and the mainland of southern Asia. About 40 percent of the migrants in the 1970s originated in Latin America, 40 percent in Asia, and 20 percent in Canada and Europe.

Fidel Castro's Cuban revolution sent 250,000 Cuban businessmen and white-collar workers and their families into exile in the United States between 1959 and 1962. As many as six planeloads per day touched down in Miami. Another round of "freedom flights" brought 150,000 additional Cubans to the United States from 1966 to 1973, and a third round of immigration added 125,000 people in 1980. Most settled in Miami and adjacent Florida cities, and in New York, Chicago, and Los Angeles. Other West Indian and Caribbean nations sent hundreds of thousands of additional migrants. Particularly large contingents have come from Haiti, the Dominican Republic, Guatemala, Honduras, Nicaragua, Costa Rica, El Salvador, Colombia, and Jamaica. In an age of ubiquitous air travel, many came as tourists and stayed to live and work in the anonymity of greater New York or Los Angeles.

Mexico was the greatest single source of new Americans. Legal migration was 442,000 for 1961–70 and 584,000 for 1971–79. However, the porousness of the U.S.-Mexican border has made it impossible to sort out temporary workers, shoppers, visitors, legal migrants, and illegal migrants in the border cities of Texas and California. One specific estimate for San Diego found about 50,000 illegal immigrants living among its 275,000 recorded Hispanics (who include both Latin American immigrants and native-born Americans of Hispanic background). The country's total Mexican American population at the start of the 1980s included somewhere between 1 and 3 million illegal immigrants. Hispanics from Mexico and Central America have partially reclaimed the border provinces that Mexico lost to the United States in 1848.

By the late 1970s Asians accounted for two of every five legal immigrants to the United States. The most publicized were the approximately 600,000 refugees from communist victories in Vietnam, Cambodia, and Laos who arrived in 1979, 1980, and 1981. Residents of West Coast cities were also aware of heavy immigration from Taiwan, China, Korea, Japan, the Philippines, Thailand, and Samoa. These new arrivals concentrated in major ports from Seattle to Los Angeles and in eastern supercities.

In the late 1970s and early 1980s, international migration streams were supplemented by new waves of refugees. There were Lebanese uprooted by protracted civil war and invasion, Iranians escaping revolution and reigns of terror, and Guatemalans and Salvadorians in flight from violently repressive right-wing regimes. Ethiopians fled an economy shattered by drought, civil war, and doctrinaire Marxism. Soviet Jews and Armenians sought the religious and economic freedom of the West.

Just as they did three generations earlier, foreign immigrants settled overwhelmingly in cities because of the capacity of urban areas to deal with their specific needs. Large cities have been able to offer special social services for refugees, classes in English as a second language, and bilingual instruction in the elementary grades for Hispanic children. Concentrations of particular groups provide customers for new ethnic businesses, support for established churches and social networks, and reassurance to many immigrants who settled here in previous years. In total, the United States counted only fourteen metropolitan areas in 1970 in which more than one-tenth of residents were foreign born. By 1980, there were thirty-two such SMSAs, including Miami, Jersey City, Los Angeles, El Paso, Monterey, and New Bedford. Thirty-six other SMSAs fell between 6.2 percent foreign born (the overall figure for the United States) and 10 percent.

The new immigration spectacularly transformed the city of Miami, about which historian Raymond Mohl has noted that "issues of ethnicity, race, and culture have dominated politics and public discussion" since the start of the 1960s. Hispanics in 1980 constituted 55 percent of the population within Miami's city limits and 35 percent in the metropolitan area. The city's American-born black population was supplemented by the arrival of tens of thousands of Haitian refugees, while non-Hispanic whites are now a minority in the Miami-area population. One result in the 1970s was a three-way ethnic tension in local politics as Cubans asserted political leverage in Miami and adjacent communities like Hialeah, frequently at the perceived expense of African Americans. An illustration of Miami's new ethnic character was the 1985 election in which the city's first Cuban-born mayor won his job at the expense of a Puerto Rican incumbent.

The new immigration also revived New York's role as the melting pot of the American population. Between 1965 and 1980, it received a million legal immigrants and between 500,000 and 750,000 illegal newcomers. Counting the undocumented migrants, Louis Winnick of the Ford Foundation estimated in 1983 that 36 percent of the population in the five boroughs of New York City were born in other countries, compared to 42 percent at the height of European immigration in 1910. About 60 percent of the new New Yorkers are Latin Americans and 40 percent are from Europe and Asia. The largest numbers in the 1970s came from the Dominican Republic, China, and Italy. Journalist Andy Logan described their impact by the early 1970s.

> The new immigrants are working at jobs that most American-born residents do not want, but they are also busy at enterprises they have invented for themselves—such as the Korean fruit markets that now crowd the city, where there were no such markets before. Other newcomers take over from representatives of previous migrations—as in the case of the Indians and the Pakistanis who have replaced many now elderly Jewish newsstand proprietors. Recently arrived Filipinos are seen in all segments of the medical field. Peruvians make use of welding skills they learned in the old country. A third of the children now in the city's public schools are said to be the children of parents who were born in other countries. . . . Whole areas of the city, such as Washington Heights, in Manhattan, and Elmhurst, in Queens, would be half empty without the new arrivals.

With almost half of the new Americans arriving in the western and southwestern states, Los Angeles by the late 1970s had become "the new Ellis Island." As *Time* magazine put it in 1983, the arrival of more than 2 million immigrants in greater Los Angeles altered "the collective beat and bop of L.A., the city's smells and colors." In 1960,

1 percent of the 6 million people in Los Angeles County were Asian and 11 percent Hispanic. The approximate figures for a population of 7.5 million by the early 1980s were 10 percent Asian and 32 percent Hispanic, making L.A. the second-largest Mexican city in the world. There were vast new ethnic neighborhoods—Iranians in Beverly Hills; Vietnamese in Westminster; Chinese in Monterey Park; Japanese in Gardena; Koreans along Olympic Boulevard; Samoans in Carson. Mexicans occupied a huge city within a city that stretched from Boyle Heights (near downtown) eastward for twenty miles. Two-fifths of the schoolchildren in Los Angeles County were Hispanic in 1979–80; a quarter were less fluent in English than in one of a hundred other languages.

The new immigration has brought infusions of entrepreneurial talent and ambition to urban America. Vietnamese, Koreans, and Mexicans have all shown an inclination to own and/or operate small businesses. In a middle-sized western city like Portland, these peoples have followed the pattern of earlier European immigrants by starting with food stores, restaurants, and other businesses that serve needs of their own groups before expanding into larger markets. In the early 1980s Asians constituted 20 percent of the students in California's leading public universities and were moving into the professions. More than half the Cubans in Miami were homeowners, and substantial proportions of West Indian blacks, Asians, and second-generation Mexicans had become comfortable members of the middle class in New York, Los Angeles, Denver, and scores of other cities.

The Exploded Metropolis

The growth of the Sunbelt was essentially the growth of sunbelt sub-urbs. Between 1960 and 1980, California added 4.3 million suburbanites, Florida added 3.1 million, Texas added 1.8 million, and Arizona, Colorado, Georgia, and Virginia together added another 2.5 million. California and Florida joined nine northeastern states in which a majority of the total state population lived in suburban rings.

In the Frostbelt as well as the Sunbelt, the same decades brought basic changes in the character of American suburbs. In the first years after World War II, most of the new suburbs were bedroom communi-

ties for the "man in the grey flannel suit" and his working-class companions. They were residential communities that still depended on
the established central city for jobs, services, and shopping. By the
end of the 1960s, signs pointed to the evolution of suburbia into the
"alternate city" or "outer city," a new urban world whose inhabitants
had less and less need for the central city and less and less interest in
it. A poll conducted by the *New York Times* in 1978 found that 40
percent of New York's Long Islanders and New Jersey's suburbanites
visited the city fewer than three times a year and more than half de-
nied that they were part of greater New York. The *Times* concluded
that "the suburbs have become a multicentered urban chain with sur-
prisingly limited ties to the metropolitan core. . . . Suburban residents
have established their own institutions and go about their lives in an
increasingly separate world."

One key to this fundamental change in the character of the suburbs was a shift in the sources of suburban populations. In the first
decades after the war, hundreds of thousands of young white families
moved out of old walk-up apartments and row houses and into bright
new tract houses. After the mid-1960s, however, new residents in a
suburban ring were most likely to be migrants from the suburbs of
another metropolis. By 1980, fewer than 10 percent of suburban residents in the typical metropolis had moved from the central city within
the previous five years.

The 1960s brought increasing choice to suburban housing. Developers doubled the number of suburban apartments, adding millions of low-rise units along suburban arterial highways. Garden apartment complexes with swimming pools and parking lots were designed
to house the children of the postwar baby boom as they left home for
college and jobs. The suburban condominium boom of the 1970s catered to the same men and women as their salaries increased and/or
they married. By the end of the 1970s, the outer city provided housing for every phase and style of life, from traditional single-family
houses to suburban retirement villages.

Retailers followed their customers. Developers experimented with
the large regional mall during the Eisenhower years. Lakewood in
Los Angeles and Northgate in Seattle were prototypes built in the
early 1950s, while the two-level, climate-controlled Southdale center

that opened near Minneapolis in 1956 signaled what the future would be like. By the 1970s, superregional centers with more than a million square feet of shopping area were the catalysts for further suburban growth. For example, the Cherry Hill center in the flatlands east of Philadelphia sparked suburban sprawl and prompted the surrounding community to rename itself Cherry Hill, New Jersey, to capitalize on the notoriety. The Galleria in Houston became not only a retail center but a tourist attraction with hotels, restaurants, movies, and night-clubs. The largest superregionals in the 1970s cost $100 million to build and became instant main streets for large sectors of the outer city.

Suburbs also captured the bulk of new jobs. In the country's fifteen largest SMSAs, the number of central city jobs fell from 12 million to 11.2 million in the 1960s, while the number of suburban jobs rose from 7 million to 10.2 million. Nationwide, only 28 percent of employed suburbanites in 1970 commuted to jobs in the central city. Ten years later, St. Louis, with two-thirds of its metropolitan labor force working in the suburban ring, provided an example of decentralized employment.

The turning point in terms of suburban self-sufficiency in a middle-sized metropolis like Atlanta can be dated precisely to the end of the 1960s. During that city's building boom of the 1960s and early 1970s, national attention was focused on the central business district, but the suburbs were the real beneficiaries. Atlanta itself gained only 10,000 residents from 1960 to 1970 and lost 70,000 from 1970 to 1980. Its suburban ring more than doubled from 1960 to 1980. Atlanta's share of retail sales in the metropolitan area dropped from 66 percent in 1963 to 28 percent in 1977. Lenox Square and Cumberland Mall on the city's north side both surpassed the downtown area in sales volume in the late 1970s.

The shift in retailing was only one facet of the massive suburbanization of employment in Atlanta. Between 1960 and 1975, total metropolitan employment in the central business district fell from 20 percent to 12 percent. Government agencies, major utilities, and the largest corporations remained in the new downtown office towers, but branch operations of national corporations and business services such as data processing filled dozens of suburban office parks. By the 1980s, each sector of Atlanta's suburban ring—northwest, north, east, and south—was independent of the others, with residents living, working, and shopping in the same suburban quadrant.

Where the identity of an old core city was weak or its resources and leadership limited, public facilities to serve the entire metropolis were increasingly moved to the suburban ring. Pioneered in California in the 1960s, the community college served the maturing suburban children of the baby boom. Many of the new four-year colleges that were added to state university systems in the 1960s and early 1970s were built for suburbanites as well. For example, Towson State University lies on the far side of the Baltimore beltway, George Mason University among the suburbanizing fields of northern Virginia, Wright State University in the suburbs of Dayton, and the University of Texas at San Antonio on a limestone ridge twenty miles outside the city. The University of Texas at Arlington serves the supersuburbs of Dallas–Fort Worth. New sports complexes in the 1970s were as apt to be situated in suburbs as in cities. Both the New York Giants and New York Jets moved to New Jersey, the Detroit Lions to Pontiac, and the L.A. Rams to Anaheim. The Washington Bullets entertained visiting National Basketball Association teams in Landover, Maryland. The New York Islanders gave suburban Nassau County its own major league sports franchise. The Dallas Cowboys and Texas Rangers played in stadiums between Dallas and Fort Worth.

The prototype for the outer city may well be Orange County, California, which originated without the counterbalance of an inner city. Orange County residents can choose between the two suburban universities of California State-Fullerton and the University of California-Irvine. The California Angels made Orange County the first suburban area with its own major league team. One Orange County resident described her life in what technical jargon calls the "widely dispersed multi-nodal metropolis." "I live in Garden Grove," she told an interviewer in 1971, "work in Irvine, shop in Santa Ana, go to the dentist in Anaheim . . . and used to be president of the League of Women Voters in Fullerton."

Orange County's conservative politics gave support to Kevin Phillips's projection of a Republican Sunbelt. The county drew many of its new residents directly from the relatively conservative South and Middle West rather than older Los Angeles neighborhoods. Many of their jobs depended on the defense industry, a connection that helped to nurture strong anticommunism. Orange County was fertile ground for radical rightwing organizations like the John Birch Society, for Barry Goldwater's presidential campaign in 1964, and for Ronald Reagan's election as California governor in 1966. The county's most prominent feature—Disneyland—reinforced the county's conservative image. Opened in 1955, it expressed a nostalgic vision of a well-ordered society in which white middle class values were the norm and the increasing racial variety of Los Angeles was kept at a distance.

By the 1970s, the shock wave of the metropolitan explosion had carried beyond even the boundaries of metropolitan areas, which are explicitly defined to include suburbanizing populations. Interim census data in 1974 surprised the experts by showing that nonmetropolitan areas in the United States were growing faster than areas inside SMSAs. Although the new trend, quickly dubbed counterurbanization, was not measurable until the mid-1970s, it probably began in 1967 or 1968. The decade's growth rate was 17 percent for nonmetropolitan areas compared to 10 percent for all SMSAs combined. During each decade from 1940 to 1970, about half of the nation's 3,100 counties lost population as small town and country people moved to the cities. From 1970 to 1980, in contrast, the census takers found declines in only 545 counties, including many that contained large cities.

"Nonmetropolitan" is a catchall word that includes everything from the cotton counties of the South to the potato country of Idaho and northern Maine. One of the common forces behind the counterurban trend, however, was the completion of the interstate highway system, which enabled light industry and distributing to disperse into smaller communities where inexpensive land, low taxes, and nonunion labor are still available. The Federal Reserve Bank of Philadelphia described the situation: "The very kinds of forces which gave rise to suburbanization have also made rural locations economically attractive. Technical innovations in information storage, retrieval, and transmission have reduced the economic advantage of locating closely related activities near one another." Thus, with the advantages of mobility dispersed throughout American society, businesses that were previously tied to urban labor supplies were able to take their factory and warehouse jobs to underemployed farmers.

This outward movement of employment also brought immense new areas within commuting range of suburban rings. In the 1970s, 60 percent of nonmetropolitan growth was comprised of suburban spillover from counties adjacent to existing metropolitan areas. Millions of Americans grew accustomed to commuting an hour from a suburban home to a downtown office. Thus, it should be no surprise that millions more chose to drive to a factory or office from a house and five acres located thirty or forty miles out. In an area like central North Carolina, many workers were able to commute to jobs in cities like Winston-Salem or High Point while maintaining the family farm through evening and weekend work. Rapid nonmetropolitan growth actually extended the social and economic range of cities. Since the 1970s, more than nine out of every ten Americans has lived within the "daily urban system" or long-range commuting shed of metropolitan areas, including central cities, suburban rings, and the "exurbs" or "rurburbs" beyond official metropolitan-area boundaries.

The Urban Crisis

In the years after World War II, big cities enjoyed an upbeat image in the popular media. The typical movie filmed in New York opened with a shot of the magnificent Manhattan skyline, then plunged into the island's bustling business or theater districts with their promise of success. As Richard Eder remarked: "When *My Sister Eileen* was made [in the 1950s], it was taken for granted that two pretty sisters could come to New York from Columbus, Ohio, and get into only minor trouble. Nobody expected them to be robbed, raped, polluted, or driven to hang out in singles bars." Even gang wars and slums were viewed with hope in *West Side Story* (1961), whose Puerto Rican immigrants sang about the opportunities to be found: "I want to be in America, Okay by me in America."

A decade later, slums and squalid back streets dominated the popular image. In the world of television cop and car-chase shows, New York, Miami, and Los Angeles were environments of random and frequent violence. The film *The French Connection* (1971) followed a drug dealer from Fifth Avenue to dark and empty warehouse districts. *Klute* (1971) and *Taxi Driver* (1976) took moviegoers through the twilight world of prostitution.

The popular media reflected a decline of American confidence in their central cities. The nation entered the 1960s with the assumption that urban problems were essentially those of rapid growth. Exploding metropolitan areas needed money for streets, schools, and sewers and procedures for ensuring orderly expansion. The problems of the central cities were viewed as the byproducts of exuberant suburban growth, which left outmoded cores in need of redevelopment and physical refurbishing. By the end of the decade, however, TV networks and news magazines had served the public a massive helping of documentaries and articles such as "Urban Unrest," "Battlefield, USA," "Slums: Cancer in the Heart of Our Cities," and "Crisis in the Cities." The same public was convinced that American cities were sinking under a crisis comprised of racial violence, crime, unemployment, and economic obsolescence.

The key to the growing concern about the social pathology of big cities was the rediscovery of poverty as an ineradicable American problem. The recession of 1957–58 was a painful reminder that black ghettos had missed out on the postwar boom. In response, federal agencies and major private foundations funded New York's Mobilization for Youth and other innovative programs to break the cycle of poverty through concentrated education. President Kennedy's Committee on Juvenile Delinquency and Youth Crime (1962) offered grants for the politically popular goal of fighting delinquency, but its broader concern was to alter the basic conditions of family life, poor schooling, and unemployment that presumably bred criminals.

General awareness of poverty as a continuing national problem came with an unexpected best seller by social activist Michael Harrington. *The Other America* (1962) was an uncomfortable reminder that the United States contained a nearly invisible "underdeveloped nation" of 40 to 50 million poor people, living "beyond history, beyond progress, sunk in a paralyzing, maiming routine." The American poor were invisible during the affluent 1950s because they had been walled off physically from the American mainstream. "The very development of the American city," Harrington wrote, "has removed poverty from the living, emotional experience of millions upon millions of Americans. Living out in the suburbs, it is easy to assume that ours is, indeed, an affluent society."

Harrington's analysis was part of a larger challenge to the urban policies of the 1950s. Federal housing and transportation programs had tended to assist places rather than people, creating the new physical facilities that delight local politicians. At the same time, as Jane Jacobs pointed out, well-photographed ribbon-cutting ceremonies were often the last stage in the disruption of natural city neighborhoods through sudden and "cataclysmic" infusions of federal funds.

Urban renewal was a special target for critics. In many cities, renewal agencies had ambitiously cleared more downtown land than the private market could absorb. The rubble-strewn lots and parking fields, complained a president of the U.S. Chamber of Commerce, made the Housing and Home Finance Agency the country's largest grower of ragweed. From the political right, Martin Anderson's *The Federal Bulldozer* claimed that urban renewal short circuited the private market, added to the net cost of new development, and destroyed scores or hundreds of small businesses. A series of studies by Herbert Gans, Marc Fried, and Chester Hartman arrived at even more striking conclusions about the urban renewal of Boston's West End—a working-class, Italian-American neighborhood of forty-eight acres that was demolished in 1958–59 to make room for luxury apartments. Described as a slum in official reports, the West End was actually a stable ethnic neighborhood. Demolition destroyed a viable community and forced residents into more expensive housing in unfamiliar neighborhoods.

An alternative to the urban renewal strategy was to focus on the direct needs of people. In 1964, President Lyndon Johnson reformulated and expanded some of John Kennedy's ideas into a nationwide War on Poverty. For urban America, the core of Johnson's program was the Office of Economic Opportunity (OEO). Under the direction of R. Sargent Shriver, the OEO operated a Job Corps for school dropouts, a Neighborhood Youth Corps for unemployed teenagers, Head Start and Upward Bound programs to supplement overburdened public school systems, and VISTA (Volunteers in Service to America), a domestic equivalent of the politically popular Peace Corps. The OEO's biggest program was the establishment and funding of Community Action Agencies (CAA), to operate with "maximum feasible participation" of the poor. By 1968 more than 500 Community Action Agencies provided services through at least 800 neighborhood service centers. In some cases such as San Francisco, the local CAA turned into the equivalent of the old ward-based political machine for minority politicians. In the intensely poor Brownsville neighborhood in Brooklyn, in contrast, the CAA provided real assistance in consumer education, recreation programs, health services, and a neighborhood credit union.

Almost before it began, the federal War on Poverty was upstaged by an unexpected war in the streets of American cities. Riots in Harlem, the Bedford-Stuyvesant section of Brooklyn, and Rochester in mid-July 1964 opened four years of racial violence unmatched since the World War I era. Before it subsided, the violence would cause nearly 200 deaths (most of them African Americans), 20,000 arrests, and hundreds of millions of dollars in property damage.

Although rioting also erupted in Chicago and Philadelphia before the end of the summer of 1964, the new danger of racial violence was fixed firmly in the public mind in 1965 by events in Watts, a black neighborhood on the south side of Los Angeles. Trouble started on the evening of August 11, when a white highway patrolman arrested a young African American for drunken driving. The mother of the arrested youth protested loudly. A crowd assembled and a scuffle ensued with the arresting officers. The arrival of the Los Angeles police incited the crowd, which turned into an angry mob that stoned passing cars and threatened the police. Rioting, looting, and arson spread through the entire Watts community the following day, with the police powerless to intervene. The California National Guard arrived on the evening of August 13, two days after the trouble started, and effectively laid siege to Watts. By August 15, the Guard occupied a quiet and pacified neighborhood.

The Watts riot resulted in thirty-four deaths, 1,000 injuries, and 4,000 arrests, with damage to at least six hundred buildings. It also frightened white Americans by turning the tables of racial violence. In Chicago and Tulsa forty-five years earlier, African Americans had been the victims and whites the instigators who used collective violence to keep the newcomers in their place. In Watts, however, blacks were the aggressors, while white "civilians" who were unlucky enough to be in the wrong place at the wrong time found themselves victims. The real targets, however, were two symbols of white authority—the police and ghetto businesses with reputations for exploiting black consumers. As the National Advisory Commission on Civil Disorders concluded in 1968, most property damage was the "result of deliberate attacks on white-owned businesses characterized in the Negro community as unfair or disrespectful toward Negroes." In short, the riots in Watts and other cities were protests—attempts by frustrated members of the African American community to call attention to the problems and disabilities of ghetto life.

In the two years after Watts, Americans expected "long hot summers" and got them. The summer of 1966 brought disturbances to a score of major cities. Racial rioting began again in the South during the spring of 1967 and spread north with the warm weather. The worst violence was in Detroit, where forty-three deaths and block after block of gutted and burning buildings along 12th Street made an unforgettable impression. April 1968 brought yet another wave of riots in reaction to the assassination of Martin Luther King, Jr. Mayor Richard J. Daley of Chicago flew over the city's burning West Side and ordered his police to "shoot to kill" arsonists. The United States Army mounted machine guns on the steps of the Capitol in case the disorder spilled out of downtown Washington.

The riots followed a remarkably consistent scenario. The triggering incident was often a routine police action that sparked rumors and drew a crowd. Rioting erupted in Jersey City in 1964 after police tried to break up a fight, in Omaha when police stopped illegal Fourth of July fireworks, and in Detroit when police raided a "blind pig" or illegal bar. Angry bystanders turned into rioters when it became apparent that the police lacked the power to disperse large crowds, enforce curfews, protect stores, or, even protect themselves. After the police withdrew and sealed off the violence-ridden area, the random looting that took place on the first night usually became a serious assault on property during the second day, with scattered arson and systematic looting of food, clothing, liquor, furniture, and appliance stores. Rioting continued until the National Guard or the regular army arrived in sufficient strength to scare the crowds off the streets and reoccupy the neighborhood. Many of the deaths came on the last day when heavily armed and fearful white soldiers opened fire on phantom snipers.

Few politicians wanted to admit that the residents of black ghettos might indeed have serious grievances. The initial impulse of mayors and governors was to blame the riff-raff, fringe groups, outside agitators, or, to quote future California Governor Ronald Reagan, "lawbreakers and mad dogs." In fact, the riff-raff theory was wrong. Average participation in the rioting ran between 10 percent and 20 percent of people aged fouteen to fifty-nine living in the area. Almost all participants were neighborhood residents and were representative of the general black population.

There is little doubt that the violence came from the frustration of rising expectations. The civil rights revolution of the early 1960s brought real gains in political rights for African Americans but little improvement in the day-to-day lives of younger ghetto dwellers. Unemployment and underemployment remained high, ghetto merchants continued to sell shoddy goods at exorbitant prices, and police persisted in treating all African Americans as potential criminals. Local officials often compounded the frustrations by ignoring real problems. Los Angeles's Mayor Sam Yorty, for one, refused to appoint a human relations commission and maintained, almost to the day of the Watts riot, that L.A. had the country's most harmonious race relations. Its police chief, William Parker, was notorious for his racial prejudice. In this context, the riots can be seen as political actions to force the problems of urban black America into the national consciousness. "What are these people rioting about?" asked one resident. "They want recognition and the only way they're going to get it is to riot."

Even when the riots subsided at the end of the 1960s, the shells of burned-out buildings and memories of armored personnel carriers in city parks contributed to a pervasive sense of fear in American society. Many urban Americans ended the decade with a deep sense of unease compounded from fears of race, civil disorder, and crime. An upturn in reported property crimes (burglary, larceny, auto theft) began in 1961. Rates of violent crime against individuals (robbery, aggravated assault, rape, homicide) began to rise around 1963. Explanations for this phenomenon include a greater willingness on the part of the public to report crimes because of improved police departments and the growing proportion of Americans in the crime-prone years between ages fifteen and thirty—an unanticipated consequence of the postwar baby boom. A more obvious contributing problem was the growing use of addictive drugs such as heroin, whose spread was connected to the nation's military involvement in the opium-producing regions of Southeast Asia.

Crime statistics showed some obvious and some not-so-obvious patterns. Rates of reported crime increased with a city's size, confirming the perception that the country's Detroits and New Yorks were especially dangerous. Within the large cities, the incidence of crime was greatest in the old slums around central business cores. Despite whites' fears of racially motivated crime, black criminals preyed predominantly on other blacks—their available targets. According to a 1972 survey, African Americans were more fearful than whites and the poor more fearful than the middle class, reflecting the ability of Americans with money to escape to the relatively safe suburbs.

Federal programs to deal with the social and economic problems of American cities expanded against this backdrop of gnawing fear. Congress created the new Department of Housing and Urban Development (HUD) in 1965 to provide better coordination of federal housing and urban renewal programs. The following year, the Model Cities program emerged out of efforts to find new strategies to deal with the problems of impoverished communities. It was intended as a demonstration program that would use public resources to improve selected target neighborhoods and was expected to have a substantial spillover effect on the larger urban areas. By the time Congress finished with President Johnson's proposal, an appropriation that was originally intended for thirty-six cities had been stretched to cover 148. In order to preserve the program's intention of focused impact, the size of each model-city neighborhood was limited to 15,000 in smaller cities and to 10 percent of total population in larger cities.

Although the Model Cities program has often been cited as proof of the failure of the national initiative to deal with urban problems, the truth is that it never had a fair chance. Model Cities was always a small program, with a budget averaging $390 million per year—only 15 percent of all urban assistance funds coming out of HUD and 1 percent of all direct or indirect federal aid to cities. Funding levels were adequate to improve education, child care, health care, and other social services but far too small to permanently assist communities enmeshed in the poverty cycle. Other federal agencies such as OEO, and the Departments of Labor and Transportation, which were supposed to cooperate by concentrating their own programs on the Model Cities neighborhoods, showed no interest in the necessary coordination. Few cities were able to get their programs in operation before 1968. By February 1971, President Nixon had decided to terminate Model Cities, leaving two years to wind down an orphaned program. As funded and administered, the Model Cities program did not demonstrate that it is futile to "throw money" at social problems. Rather, the program revealed the political problems of attempting to invest sufficient resources to meet the needs of those Americans most in need of help. Detroit's Mayor Jerome Cavanaugh expressed the frustration of many city officials when he complained in 1970 that "some academics now find it stylish to deny that there is an urban crisis at all, let alone one that money can solve. But once just once—I'd like to try money."

The unpleasant reality was as evident in 1970 as it had been when Michael Harrington published *The Other America* in 1962. American cities had substantial numbers of residents who had been permanently bypassed by the prosperity of the private market. The majority of Americans had benefitted since the 1940s from the simultaneous suburbanization and upgrading of housing, jobs, and community facilities. Millions of others, however, had been left behind by the growth of booming suburbs. Ghetto blacks, impoverished elderly, unemployable school dropouts, neighborhood businesspeople, and physically and mentally handicapped persons were proportionally overrepresented in the old neighborhoods of old cities. Despite the sincere goals of the War on Poverty, in 1970 there were few signs that the chasm that divided the winners and losers in urban America was narrowing.

The Decline of Public Policy

In the 1970s, policymakers at the highest levels effectively abandoned federal efforts to deal with cities as social problems. As historian Richard Wade pointed out in 1976, spokespeople for the Republican administrations of Richard Nixon and Gerald Ford "simply announced that 'the urban crisis' was over and then systematically dismantled or bureaucratically crippled" the urban initiatives of Lyndon Johnson's Great Society. The decision was made in part because of the frustrations of trying to break the poverty cycle with short-term programs. The other motivation was the obvious political attractiveness of redirecting federal resources to those needs of growing cities that could be easily met, as had been done in the 1950s.

One complaint about the urban programs that emerged from the ferment of the 1960s was their lack of consistent direction. Daniel Moynihan, a Harvard professor and adviser to President Nixon, pointed out that hundreds of pilot projects, grant authorizations, and evaluative studies amounted to considerably less than a coherent urban policy with clear goals. The Department of Housing and Urban Development (HUD) administered only a fraction of the government's urban programs, many of which were run by the Departments of Transportation, Labor, Commerce, and Health, Education, and Welfare. A real try at a comprehensive urban strategy did not come until President Carter's first national Urban Policy Report in 1978.

A second complaint about the failures of Johnson's Great Society was based on a more radical analysis of the urban future. Edward Banfield's *The Unheavenly City* (1968) represented an emerging set of "neoconservative" statements from people who questioned the very premise of government solutions for urban social problems. Banfield argued that the Great Society failed because social inequity was rooted in human character and built into the spatial and economic structure of cities. Government action could solve only those problems that required better engineering, whether pollution control, sanitation, or transportation. When government tried to deal with social problems, the almost inevitable result was to make things worse due to unexpected consequences. In cities whose basic geography and institutions had derived from the contrast between rich and poor, Banfield concluded, efforts to do good were likely to do harm or to do nothing at all.

Unfortunately, HUD's experience during the 1970s gave support to the neoconservative position. In 1969, HUD had set up what was known as the Section 235 program to help low-income families become homeowners by guaranteeing their mortgages and paying the difference between a fixed percentage of household income and the necessary monthly mortgage payments. By the early 1970s, the program had become a nightmare in which unscrupulous speculators sold fourth-rate houses to poor families at inflated prices with either the unknowing acquiescence or open cooperation of HUD officials. When the families proved unable or unwilling to keep up payments on shoddy property, the federal government found itself the unhappy owner of tens of thousands of houses in dozens of ruined neighborhoods.

In the short run, the Section 235 scandal helped to force HUD Secretary George Romney out of public life and triggered a moratorium on federal low-income housing assistance in 1973–74. In the longer run, it shaped the housing programs of the Housing and Community Development Act of 1974. The new Section 8 program allowed low-income households to find rental housing on the open market and then paid the difference between 25 percent of their income and the market rent. The program worked smoothly for preexisting houses and apartments, with more than 800,000 occupied under Section 8 by 1981. A portion of the program that guaranteed subsidized tenants for new or substantially rehabilitated housing, however, sparked complaints that the federal government was supporting the construction of luxury housing that was actually priced above the fair market rents. In response, the Reagan administration sharply limited the program in the early 1980s.

The federal experience in helping to develop "new towns" in the 1970s was even less successful. The concept of relieving the congestion of central cities via self-sufficient satellite communities derived from British planning theory at the beginning of the twentieth century, when Ebenezer Howard proposed the creation of "Garden Cities of Tomorrow." The new town idea was implemented in Britain and other parts of Europe on a large scale after World War II. Approximately 1.6 million Britons lived in dozens of new towns around London, Glasgow, and other major cities by the early 1970s.

Two private developers introduced the American public to new towns in the mid-1960s. Robert Simon planned Reston, Virginia, as a set of villages and employment centers that would be a self-contained satellite of Washington. Its accessible location and innovative town-

house architecture in the first village center around Lake Anne attracted national attention in 1965–66. Columbia, Maryland, between
Washington and Baltimore, was an even larger undertaking built to
house more than 100,000 residents and to have all necessary services
and employment centers. Builder James Rouse, who had made a fortune in shopping center development, had a deep-seated and conta-
gious belief that carefully planned new towns could provide high-
quality environments and still turn a profit. By 1980, Columbia housed
53,000 residents and Reston 37,000 in attractive, racially integrated
communities.

With the "New Communities Act" (officially part of the Housing
and Urban Development Act of 1968), the federal government joined
the new-towns movement. It offered to guarantee bonds issued by
private developers who agreed to build genuine new towns, communities that would have people of mixed incomes, social services, and
a balance in jobs and housing. Most of the new towns begun enthusi-
astically in the years around 1970 crashed to a halt during the 1974
recession, when federal assistance proved far too limited to overcome
rising costs and interest rates and a sagging real estate market. Some
new-town plans were left on the drawing board. Others, caught half-
built (like Jonathan, Minnesota, and Newfields, Ohio) survived at reduced scale as straightforward suburbs. Their wide access roads and
bike paths serve as reminders of the greater ambitions once held for
them. Those new towns that survived as planned had the advantages
of Sunbelt locations and hot real estate markets. The Woodlands, thirty
miles north of Houston, housed 10,000 people on 17,000 meticulously
planned and controlled acres. Irvine, California, on a single, privately
owned tract of 83,000 acres between Los Angeles and San Diego,
adapted the concept of neighborhood clusters and employment nodes
to the automobile culture of the West.

Whether compact Reston or sprawling Irvine, private new towns
were no solution to the ongoing financial crises of older cities. Even
the most socially conscious new-town developer skimmed off the relatively successful central-city residents and ignored the poor. During
the first half of the 1970s, the average family moving out of America's
central cities had an annual income of $14,169; the average house-
hold moving into central cities earned only $12,864. Central cities

continued to bear a special burden for the nation by supporting the domestic poor and acculturating new foreign immigrants, with necessarily higher costs for public education, public health, and welfare. In 1970, the twelve largest central cities had 12 percent of the country's population but accounted for 40 percent of its locally financed health and welfare payments. Baltimore had 27 percent of the Maryland population but 66 percent of the state's welfare recipients. Boston had 14 percent of the Massachusetts population but 32 percent of its welfare clients.

Central cities faced additional financial problems not found in the suburbs. Many of their roads, bridges, fire stations, and water mains, which dated from the nineteenth or early twentieth centuries, were wearing out by the 1960s and 1970s. Closure of the elevated West Side Highway along Manhattan's Hudson River shore due to the collapse of huge chunks of roadway was symbolic of a spreading urban problem. Replacement costs for utilities or transportation systems are inevitably higher than new construction because of the expense of demolition and the need to maintain traffic and/or service while rebuilding. Personnel costs in older central cities tended to be higher than those in new communities because of the expense of long-established pension systems for public employees.

One result was high local taxes. By the early 1970s, the average central-city resident paid roughly twice the state and local taxes per $1,000 of income that the average suburbanite paid. For 1980, the Joint Economic Committee of Congress calculated local taxes based on an average family of four who owned their home, lived inside the city limits, and had one wage-earning spouse and two school-aged children. Such a family would have paid more than 10 percent of its income in local taxes in Boston, New York, Philadelphia, Milwaukee, Detroit, Baltimore, and Chicago. As Mayor Moon Landrieu of New Orleans commented: "We've taxed everything that moves and everything that stands still; and if anything moves again, we tax that, too."

The fiscal collapse and subsequent rescue of New York City in 1975 brought home the magnitude of city budget problems. New York's problems were the result of ten years of rising costs and lagging revenues compounded by political sleight of hand. Like every other municipal government, New York borrowed funds to pay for capital projects. It also borrowed on short-term notes to raise necessary cash while waiting for periodic tax and grant payments. Unfortunately, anticipated revenues often fell short of the amount borrowed, leaving the city with a steadily accumulating deficit that it dealt with by further borrowing. By 1975, bankers and bond brokers were frightened by the city's $2.6 billion debt and refused to allow New York to continue to refinance. The state of New York generated stopgap funding in return for a city wage freeze that abrogated its union contracts, as well as drastic cuts in public education, the public university system, libraries, parks, police and fire departments, sanitation, and virtually every other city service. A financial emergency control board dominated by state appointees administered city finances. With great reluctance, Congress agreed in December to provide loans of $2.3 billion a year for three years, followed by a federal guarantee for new city bonds in 1978.

Although the federal treasury ended up making money on its loans to New York, the preferred policy of the Nixon and Ford administrations was to tilt federal assistance toward the suburbs. The cornerstone of the New Federalism, proposed by President Nixon and cheerfully accepted by congressional Democrats in 1972, was general revenue sharing. By 1980, the federal government had transferred more than $18 billion from the federal treasury to the states and more than $36 billion to thousands of local governments. Revenue sharing was preeminently a suburban aid program. Its grants were allocated with no strings attached to supplement the general funds of every full-service government, whether a city of 2 million or a suburban town of 500. Another $40 billion in sewer construction grants during the 1970s paid for one of the major costs of suburban sprawl. The Housing and Community Development program (HCD) of 1974, which consolidated federal funds for the Model Cities program, urban renewal, neighborhood facilities, housing code enforcement, and similar programs into single "block grants," was considered a central-city assistance program. However, the federal government also sent HCD funds automatically to more than eighty "urban counties" with populations of 200,000 or more and to all cities of 50,000 or more within metropolitan areas.

Despite the shift in philosophy about urban problems represented by specialists such as Moynihan and Banfield, the suburban-oriented programs of the 1970s kept federal aid to metropolitan areas high. Federal aid comprised 15 percent of state and local spending in 1960, 19 percent in 1970, and 25 percent by 1975. Severe reductions did not come until after the election of Ronald Reagan in 1980. Cities and city residents absorbed approximately two-thirds of the federal budget cuts in the 1981–82 budget. The new administration's first National Urban Policy Report, issued in the summer of 1982, took direct slaps at older cities. Provisions for accelerated depreciation of factories and equipment in the 1981 tax act encouraged the abandonment of central-city plants in favor of new suburban facilities.

Federal-aid patterns favored both the economic independence and political power of America's suburbs. By 1975, suburbanites occupied the largest block of seats in the House of Representatives—131 suburban districts, 130 rural, 102 central city, and 72 mixed. In 1982, reapportionment based on the 1980 census produced a House that was even more heavily suburban. For a seat in the U.S. Senate, politicians in earlier generations needed either rural roots or a big-city power base. By the late 1970s and early 1980s, however, the Senate included residents of such suburbs as Mill Valley, California, Aurora, Colorado, Island Park, New York, and Winter Park, Florida.

School integration controversies in the 1970s reconfirmed the suburban separatism of the 1950s and 1960s. In the case of *Swann* v. *Charlotte-Mecklenburg Board of Education* (1971), the U.S. Supreme Court held that crosstown busing was an acceptable solution to de facto segregation within a single school district. Integration through busing occurred peacefully in Charlotte, Detroit, Seattle, Los Angeles, Norfolk, and dozens of other cities. Nonetheless, it remained intensely unpopular among whites. For most Americans, the effect of busing to achieve racial integration was symbolized by the violent reaction in 1975 of the white South Boston community when black students were bused to the neighborhood high school.

Because the Supreme Court ruled in a separate decision that busing programs were to stop at the boundaries of individual school districts (unless one district was directly responsible for segregation in another), suburban residents remained relatively free from the pressures to integrate their schools. Busing during the 1970s thus accelerated the movement of whites from central cities to suburbs, accounting for an extra year's worth of outmigrants. It also caused suburbanites to fiercely defend their political independence. In Denver, for example, a bitter debate over busing lasted from 1969 until court-ordered enforcement in 1974. Byproducts of the court order included incorporation or expansion of several large suburbs and a state consti-tutional amendment that made further expansion of the city of Denver (and thus of the Denver school district) virtually impossible.

Upper-status suburbs resisted the "wrong" kind of neighbors as strongly as they resisted the "wrong" kind of schoolchildren. Short-story writer John Cheever described a white family that might have lived in one of the expensive suburbs outside New York.

> The Wrysons wanted things in the suburb of Shady Hill to remain ex-actly as they were. Their dread of change—of irregularity of any sort—was acute, and when the Larkin estate was sold for an old people's rest home, the Wrysons went to the Village Council meeting and demanded to know what sort of old people these old people were going to be. The Wrysons' civic activities were confined to upzoning, but they were very active in this field, and if you were invited to their house for cocktails, the chances were that you would be asked to sign an upzoning petition before you got away. . . . They seemed to sense that there was a stranger at the gates—unwashed, tirelessly scheming, foreign, the father of dis-orderly children who would ruin their rose garden and depreciate their real-estate investment.

As the Wrysons knew well, locally controlled land-use zoning was a powerful suburban self-defense tool. Restrictive building codes, requirements for large lots, and expensive subdivision and utility hookup fees could price all but the affluent out of the local housing market. Many suburbs refused to zone land for apartments. Others refused to cooperate with federal programs for subsidized moderate- and low-income housing. Petaluma, California, and Ramapo, New Jersey, experimented with severe controls on the rate of housing con-struction. Together, the various limitations added up to what critics called exclusionary zoning or "snob zoning." In the view of one Con-necticut suburbanite, for a moderate-income family to hope to move into a proper suburb was "like going into Tiffany and demanding a ring for $12.50. Tiffany doesn't have any rings for $12.50. Well, Green-wich is like Tiffany."

In a handful of states, exclusionary zoning was limited by legislation (as in California and Oregon) or state court action (as in New Jersey's 1975 *Mount Laurel* case). Greater change, however, has come from the slow lowering of barriers to African Americans in real estate rental and purchase. Federal civil rights legislation in the late 1960s ended the most blatant racial discrimination in housing, while the slowing of black migration to northern cities in the 1970s reduced pressures of neighborhood turnover. In addition, the number of blacks in suburban rings jumped by 43 percent in the 1970s—from 4.3 million to 6.2 million.

In a number of cities black suburbanization was little more than the spillover of ghettos beyond city limits. In other cities with large African American middle and professional classes, however, a move to the suburbs meant what it has to millions of whites—an escape from the problems of the inner city. In 1980, nearly half the metropolitan Washington blacks lived outside the District of Columbia; Prince Georges County, Maryland, for example, was 37 percent black. And in prosperous San Diego, thousands of middle-class African Americans lived in new neighborhoods on the rolling hills southeast of the city. The only difference from more prestigious white suburbs was the relative affordability of housing.

The Vitality of the Everyday City

In the middle and late 1970s, Americans rediscovered the value of the commonplace in their cities. With the growing independence of suburbs and the increasing failure of efforts to develop governmental institutions spanning entire metropolitan areas, it was clear that sweeping plans and grand programs were as likely to fail as to succeed. Making a virtue of necessity, urban planners and policymakers began to think small. They found the strength of American cities in the vitality and character of distinct areas within the metropolitan framework. The 1970s and early 1980s brought less concern with "the city" or "the public interest" and more attention to the improvement and promotion of neighborhoods, districts, and cityscapes.

In the 1970s, downtown planners faced a choice between ambitious pursuit of office construction and efforts to retain the historic

diversity of central business districts. Especially in the boom cities of
the West, proliferating downtown office buildings filled skylines with
the tracery of steel skeletons and with twenty-story cranes. The explosive growth often brought immediate prosperity at the expense of
many of the attractions of city living. Downtown Denver, Dallas,
Houston, and Tulsa were filled with office workers during the day,
but were empty shells at night. At their worst, as geographer Michael
Conzen has remarked, large-scale downtown office developments
"engross huge tracts of land, deprive the streetscape of its human scale
and pedestrian traffic (except during rush hours), and transfer increasing amounts of downtown to corporate control."

In some cases, the economic development impulse resulted in
what journalist Calvin Trillin astutely defines as municipal *dome-ism.*
Named for the Houston Astrodome and New Orleans Superdome, the
term described the tendency of cities to deal "in symbols of progress
so large that general-obligation bonds are required to meet the construction costs." These expensive stadiums, convention centers, and
downtown malls are intended to give a city a reputation as a fast-
moving glamour center and incidentally to boost local retail sales. "It
seemed for a while," Trillin has noted, "that boosters in expansion
cities in any part of the country were following a kind of checklist of
what was required for true major-league status—a big-league baseball franchise, of course, and a big-league stadium and a big-league
symphony and an airport so big-league that it could be called 'international.'"

The alternative was to build on the natural diversity of historic
business centers. The most common expedient was to recover waterfront areas that had frequently become seedy and run-down when
business centers moved inland and uphill. In Cincinnati, new riverfront
parks were created. Many other cities chose to designate historic districts that embraced the three-and four-story commercial buildings of
the nineteenth century. Still other cities tried to combine improved
waterfront access with adaptive reuse of old buildings and new tour-
ist-oriented facilities. These approaches often involved using the Urban Development Action Grant program (created in 1977) and taking
advantage of the favorable tax treatment for historic preservation em-
bodied in the 1976 and 1981 tax reform laws. By the early 1980s,

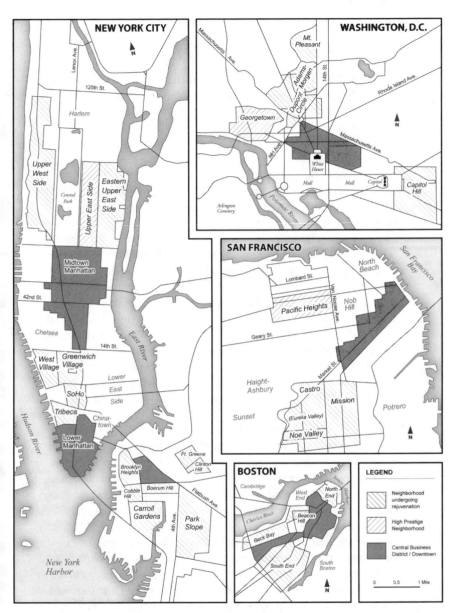

Revitalizing Neighborhoods in Major Cities in the 1970s. In most American cities, several neighborhoods close to the downtown core experienced significant housing rehabilitation and revitalization during the 1970s. From Christopher Winters, "The Social Identity of Evolving Neighborhoods," *Landscape*, 23, No. 1 (1979). Reprinted with the permission of *Landscape*.

revitalization efforts had reached even such unexpected places as Indianapolis and Cleveland.

One of the most complete examples of diversified downtown revitalization was Boston. From 1930 to 1960, Boston had attracted
virtually no private investment into its historic core. One banker stated
flatly in 1957 that "no one can buy land within the city of Boston, put
up an office building, and make money." In the 1960s, the city took
the first steps by using the urban renewal program to clear several
blocks in the tacky Scollay Square district for a new City Hall and
office buildings. In the 1970s, the redevelopment was extended to the
city's virtually abandoned waterfront, where nineteenth-century
wharves and huge granite warehouses still overlooked the harbor.
Redevelopment included a waterfront park, a new aquarium as a tourist attraction, and reuse of many of the historic structures for condominiums and restaurants. Between the City Hall and waterfront, the
historic Faneuil Hall market reopened in 1976 as an upscale "festival
market" for tourists and suburbanites. Renewed public attention helped
to trigger a private building boom that roughly doubled downtown
office space and supported the continued viability of the retail core.
Downtown Boston by 1980 was cramped, crowded, and somewhat
confusing; it was also a diverse and lively mixture of old and new
buildings, districts, and people.

In the 1970s, a number of cities decided to support their downtown districts with new public transit facilities. The creation of the
Urban Mass Transit Administration in 1968 within the new Department of Transportation (1966) provided funds with which public transit
agencies were able to acquire dozens of failing private bus companies
and save basic city transit systems. The late 1960s and early 1970s
brought a series of "freeway revolts," with citizens and neighborhood
groups blocking new construction or extensions of urban freeways
that would have devastated entire neighborhoods and commercial districts. Boston, New Orleans, and San Francisco took the lead in blocking downtown freeways. Cities from Baltimore to Portland followed,
successfully resisting proposed freeways that would have destroyed
viable neighborhoods.

Many replacements for expressways were new public transit facilities that radiated toward and away from central business districts.

Portland, Denver, and Minneapolis built bus malls through their downtowns to facilitate transfers and speed operations. New subway/rail systems opened in San Francisco in 1972, in Washington in 1976, and in Atlanta in 1979. The combined bill for forty-eight miles of the Washington Metro line, sixteen miles of the Metropolitan Atlanta Regional Transit Authority, and seventy-one miles of the Bay Area Rapid Transit system totaled roughly $10 billion by the beginning of the 1980s.

Even more important, the 1970s brought the transfer of a degree of power or influence from centralized municipal bureaucracies and politicians to neighborhoods and community-based organizations. One city after another went through some form of neighborhood revolution involving what were often uneasy coalitions among members of the white middle class, working-class communities, and minority populations. Although individual neighborhood agendas often varied, the unifying goal was to utilize residential concentration as a political resource to promote the interests and independence of individual city neighborhoods. Specifically, the new style of politics included the creation of city council districts, neighborhood associations, and a community.

In many white working-class neighborhoods, neighborhood politics was protective and parochial, a renewal of allegiance to the old ethnic community. Residents in Slavic neighborhoods in Baltimore, Italian neighborhoods in St. Louis, and Irish neighborhoods in Boston were essentially interested in protecting established communities against unwanted change. Depending on the problems of the moment, they might resist busing for school integration, redlining by local banks, freeway plans, or city proposals for land clearance and redevelopment on the fringe of a downtown.

With existing social networks as a starting place, the same neighborhoods also provided fertile ground for efforts at community economic development and self-help projects that bypass downtown bureaucracies. Residents organized the Southeast Baltimore Community Organization in 1971 to fight city policies that encouraged neighborhood decline. The organization was soon responsible for local health care services, housing rehabilitation, and economic development projects. The Neighborhood Housing Services program, which originated in Pittsburgh's North Central neighborhood, provided the model for scores of similar efforts nationwide. The NHS model requires participation of private lenders, local government agencies, and neighborhood groups in housing and community rehabilitation efforts that remain under neighborhood control. The National Commission on Neighborhoods in 1979 found that the most common examples of public services delivered and controlled at the neighborhood level included child care, services for the elderly, health care, crime prevention, job training, housing rehabilitation, and small business assistance.

Middle-class supporters of the new neighborhood politics tended to be participants in the "postindustrial" economy. Scientists, professors, government workers, and executives of national corporations are "cosmopolitan in outlook and pecuniary interest," as sociologist Harvey Molotch has pointed out. They depend on statewide or national markets for their talents rather than on local markets for their goods and services. They view the city more as a residential environment than as an economic machine. Salaried employees who were caught in the inflation of the 1970s, they were also intensely interested in the availability of affordable and convenient housing.

Between 1970 and 1980, members of this professional-managerial middle class made their mark on American cities by leading the revitalization of selected inner-city neighborhoods. Most "gentrifiers" were relatively young individuals and couples with downtown white-collar jobs. They were attracted by undervalued older neighborhoods that offered convenient locations along with interesting and affordable housing. Some of the most striking cases of gentrification date back to the 1960s, with Society Hill in Philadelphia and Capitol Hill in Washington as prime examples. By 1975, however, activity was apparent in at least half of the country's major cities. The wave of reinvestment in close-in neighborhoods paralleled the burgeoning national interest in historic preservation, and many gentrified neighborhoods were designated historic districts. The price of such middle-class reinvestment was sometimes the displacement of the poor or the elderly who could no longer afford to live in neighborhoods where well-paid executives and civil servants were bidding up the costs of housing.

Middle-class neighborhood activists made the substantive contribution of pushing city officials to incorporate neighborhood groups into the government decisionmaking process. Dayton, Des Moines, Portland, and Kansas City were among the cities that gave official recognition to neighborhood associations. Fort Worth's district planning organizations gave neighborhoods a regular role in land use and development decisions. New York City systematically decentralized authority through community school districts and neighborhood planning boards.

The growth of political power among African Americans and Hispanics during the 1970s complemented the impact of white neighborhood activists. In the wake of the racial violence of the 1960s, many urban blacks turned to local politics as a means of taking control of their own communities. African Americans constituted a majority of the population in only a handful of central cities in 1970, most notably Newark, Washington, and Atlanta. By 1980, they were also a majority within the city limits of Detroit, Baltimore, New Orleans, Birmingham, and Richmond. The first black mayor in a major American city was Carl Stokes in Cleveland in 1967, followed closely by Richard Hatcher, victor in a bitterly contested race in Gary, Indiana. Kenneth Gibson won the mayor's office in Newark three years later. The 1973 election brought victories for Tom Bradley in Los Angeles, Maynard Jackson in Atlanta, and Coleman Young in Detroit. By 1983, the nation's second, third, and fourth largest cities had African American mayors (Harold Washington in Chicago, Wilson Goode in Philadelphia, and Bradley in Los Angeles). In the same year, blacks served as police chief in eight of the country's fifty largest cities.

The fact of minority mayors in the 1970s was sometimes more important for its symbolic value than for the transfer of real power. Efforts to restructure city council elections, however, struck directly at the balance of power within cities. Although many of the nation's old industrial cities had retained the nineteenth-century custom of electing city councils by wards or districts, most middle-sized cities had abandoned ward systems for citywide council elections during the Progressive Era of the early 1900s, or in the era of growth politics of the 1940s and 1950s. At-large voting tended to shift power away from individual neighborhoods and geographically concentrated ethnic groups. It favored business interests that could claim to speak for the city as a whole but could assign most of the costs of economic growth to older and poorer neighborhoods.

In the 1970s, minority leaders and community activists realized that a return to ward voting could convert neighborhood concentration from a liability to a political resource. The federal Voting Rights Act of 1965, with its amendment and extension in 1975, allowed minorities to use the federal courts to require ward systems when at-large voting effectively eliminated the impact of their votes. African Americans in Richmond and Mexican Americans in San Antonio both used the Voting Rights Act to reestablish city council districts in the late 1970s and early 1980s. Fort Worth, Phoenix, Atlanta, Albuquerque, Grand Rapids, and San Francisco were among a score of other cities that made the same switch.

Atlanta showed the way in which the different forces coalesced to produce local politics oriented to neighborhood interest. The city entered the 1970s with the downtown growth coalition program intact. Although elected with the help of 92 percent of the black vote in 1969, Mayor Sam Massell pushed projects that served established business projects including the new subway and the construction of I-485, a freeway connector that promised to gut half a dozen east side neighborhoods. He lobbied for a substantial annexation that would have diluted African American voting power via the votes of white suburbanites. In response, younger black leaders advocated a charter change in which aldermen would be elected in and by districts. Resistance to I-485 created an anti-freeway alliance among a set of middle-class white neighborhoods that effectively killed the route in 1973.

Both the development of an independent political agenda for African American Atlanta and the rise of neighborhood militancy reflected the demography of the city in the 1970s. Grant Park, Inman Park, Morningside–Lenox Park, Virginia Highlands, and Ansley Park were parts of an entire tier of east side neighborhoods that experienced reinvestment by a new generation of urbanites who a decade or two earlier would have moved to the suburbs as they built careers and families. At the same time, the steady increase in the city's African American population (from 38 percent in 1960 to 66 percent in 1980) provided the political resource for transforming growing minority dissatisfaction into action.

The municipal election of 1973 brought the two trends together to produce a basic change in Atlanta politics. Maynard Jackson campaigned on the promise of increased citizen participation and consultation with neighborhoods, winning with 95 percent of the black vote and 18 percent of the white. Neighborhood activists also applied their organizing skills to several city council races. The new city charter created a city council of twelve districts with two council members elected from each, plus six more elected at large. It also mandated that neighborhoods play a role in city development plans. During the last quarter of the century, the challenge would be for a city with increasingly democratic governance but also a decreasing proportion of white residents to claim a fair share of the economic growth that was doubling the population of the metropolitan area.

City Leaders

Left: Mayor of New York from 1933 to 1945, Fiorello LaGuardia brought political savvy and flamboyant style to his reform administration. The LaGuardia and Wagner Archives, LaGuardia Community College / The City University of New York. Right: Richard J. Daley, Chicago's longest-serving mayor from 1955 to 1976, epitomized the pluses and minuses of the big city political machine, presiding over a period of prosperity but ignoring the needs of minority communities. Courtesy Wikipedia.

Left: Maynard Jackson was one of the nation's most influential African American leaders as mayor of Atlanta from 1974 to 1982. His career was an important part of the broadening of urban politics in the South with the civil rights movement. Courtesy Wikipedia. Right: Mayor of San Antonio from 1981 to 1989, Henry Cisneros was part of a new generation of Latino officials whose rise to political office reflected the nation's changing demographics. Used by permission of Henry Cisneros.

Iconic Structures

Along with the Empire State Building (1931) and the RCA Building (now GE Building) in the Rockefeller Center complex (1933), New York's Chrysler Building (1930),was one of several stunning skyscrapers that symbolized the emergence of Midtown Manhattan as a center of the national economy. Library of Congress, LC-D41-7 DLC

Built in 1962 for the Century 21 Exposition in Seattle, the Space Needle was intended to represent Seattle's commitment to a science-based economy. It gave that city an instantly recognizable monument to compete with the backdrop of Mount Rainier. Photo: Seattle's Convention and Visitors Bureau.

Opposite top: In 1970 business leaders formed the Detroit Renaissance to revitalize their city. Their immediate aim was to stimulate building activity. A result was one of the largest privately financed real-estate projects in history, the Detroit Renaissance Center, which contains multi-use spaces and has become a landmark for downtown Detroit. Photo courtesy Archives of Michigan.

Opposite bottom: The Golden Gate Bridge was completed in 1937. Soaring gracefully over the entrance to San Francisco Bay, it quickly became one of the best-known structures in the world. Library of Congress, Prints and Photographs Division, American Buildings Survey, HAER CAL, 38-SANFRA, 140-4.

Above: The Arlington Memorial Bridge, shown under construction in the 1930s, connected the Lincoln Memorial to Arlington National Cemetery and the home of Robert E. Lee. It represented the unity of the United States three generations after the end of the Civil War and added to Washington's status as an open air cathedral of American patriotism. National Archives, Still Photographs Division.

Landscapes of Commerce

Opposite top: The New York Garment District, shown here in 1943, was an intense concentration of clothing manufacturers and wholesalers that thrived on the synergy of urban life. Library of Congress, John Vachan, photographer, LC-USW3-020227-E DLC.

Opposite bottom:This General Motors factory building on Marcellus Street in Syracuse, New York, was one piece in a vast complex of automobile assembly plants and parts suppliers that made Michigan and Ohio the heart of the industrial economy in the middle decades of the twentieth century. Library of Congress, Gilbert Ask, photog-rapher. HABS NY, 34-SYRA, 33-1.

Above: Omaha in the early twentieth century was a railroad gateway between the agriculture of the Great Plains and the markets of the Northeast. As in Kansas City, Fort Worth, Minneapolis–St. Paul and similar cities, shippers and wholesalers controlled this trade from downtown office and warehouse buildings dating from the early decades of the twentieth century. From the collections of the Omaha Public Library.

Top: Billings, Montana, is a city made by the railroad. Tracks of the Northern Pacific Railroad (now the Burlington Northern–Santa Fe Railroad) draw a straight line east-west through the city, flanked by warehouses and then by downtown buildings to the left in this aerial view. Photograph by Roy Swann. Montana Historical Society, Helena.

Bottom: This crowd of shipyard workers in Portland, Oregon, with half a dozen ships under construction in the background, were part of the industrial labor force that transformed the economies of many southern and western cities during World War II. Courtesy Oregon Historical Society.

Top: The suburban shopping mall, pioneered in the 1950s and reaching full
development in the 1970s and 1980s, remade the metropolitan landscape by
providing an alternative to the traditional downtown. Image courtesy of the Mount
Prospect Historical Society, Mount Prospect, IL.

Bottom: Times Square in 1933 lay at the heart of New York's theater district. Following economic decline after 1950, new investment in the 1990s pushed out many of
the downscale uses. Library of Congress, Samuel Herman, photographer, LC-G612-
T01-19590 DLC.

Residential Neighborhoods

Top: Developed in the 1910s and 1920s, Laurelhurst in Portland, Oregon, was similar to upper-middle-class neighborhoods in growing cities across the country. This idealized view shows both automobiles and streetcars at a time when urban transportation was in the process of change. OrHi 63786, Oregon Historical Society.

Bottom: Rear view of houses in an African American district in Richmond, Virginia, in 1927. Although New York tenements attracted the greatest attention, much more sub-standard housing in American cities resembled this low-rise neighborhood. General Research & Reference Division, Schomburg Center for Research in Black Culture, The New York Public Library, Astor, Lenox, and Tilden Foundations,. No. 1169851.

Top: Middle-class bungalows in Denver were typical of many western cities. Their relatively open floor plans were designed for families without servants and anticipated the preferences of families after World War II. Photo courtesy of author.

Bottom: Larimer Street was Denver's skid road district that served the needs of transient laborers. This corner includes both a cheap restaurant and a loan company. Workers and the down-and-out could also find cheap hotels, bars, missions, stores selling work clothes, and employment offices for day laborers.

Urban renewal replaced run-down housing, often from the nineteenth century, with new high-rise housing, as in this view from the south side of Chicago in the 1950s. Photograph Mildred Mead. Courtesy Metropolitan Planning Council.

In the 1990s, many cities began to experience a boom in upscale downtown housing for both yuppies and empty-nesters. Shown are the Metropolis condominiums in Atlanta. Courtesy of Wood Partners.

Landscapes of Conflict

The Chicago Race Riot of July 1919 ravaged the city for five days. Here a photographer caught a mob chasing a black man through alleys and backyards a few moments before they stoned him to death. ICHi-31915, Jun Fujita, Chicago Historical Society.

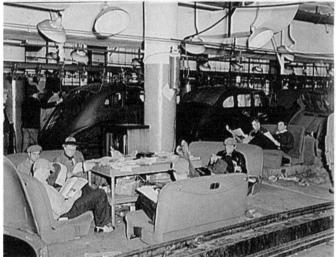

In 1937, members of the United Auto Workers staged sit-down strikes in General Motors plants in Flint, Michigan. Relying on food and supplies passed through the windows, they refused to leave the factories until GM negotiated a contract. Library of Congress, #LC-USZ62-131617 DLC.

Transportation

Opposite top: The Chicago Circle, shown here in 1961 near the beginning of the Interstate Highway era, brought together three major expressways just west of downtown and for a number of years gave its name to the new University of Illinois at Chicago, "Circle Campus." Courtesy Portland Cement Association.

Opposite bottom: Cities in the 1920s and 1930s began the long process of making room for automobiles by constructing high-volume parkways and expressways and setting aside large tracts of land for parking. Here workers in Portland, Oregon, widen West Burnside Street through downtown by slicing off the sides of existing buildings. OrHi 46673, Oregon Historical Society.

Above: BART, the subway-rail service operated by the San Francisco Bay Area Rapid Transit began operating in 1972 as one of several new rail transit systems built for large, fast-growing cities. In 2006 it operated on 104 miles of tracks linking downtown San Francisco and Oakland to outlying communities on both sides of the bay. Courtesy of Andrew Rolle.

People

The northward migration of hundreds of thousands of southern African Americans in the 1910s and 1920s remade the social landscape of northern cities. Library of Congress.

The Chicago area counted more than 600,000 residents without jobs at the depths of the Great Depression. CD372 2, DN-0085377, Chicago Historical Society.

Top: *The explosive growth of suburban communities of single family houses after World War II increasingly separated places of residence from places of work and led to new social patterns and rituals. These women are participating in an early Tupperware party in 1954. Brownie Wise Papers, Archives Center, National Museum of American History, Smithsonian Institution.*

Bottom: *The Immigration Reform Act of 1965 opened the United States to large-scale immigration from Asia. One result was the growth of Asian American communities not only in coastal states but all across the nation, as indicated by this Japanese mall in suburban Arlington Heights west of Chicago, sponsored by a store owned by Japan's largest supermarket chain. Courtesy Lucy Herz.*

CHAPTER FOUR

Prosperity and Poverty

The movie version of *West Side Story*, which hit the screen in 1962, opened with a stylized skyline of New York, cut to a fast sequence of aerial shots of the thriving city—bridges, highways, skyscrapers, Yankee Stadium—and then zoomed suddenly down to a single asphalted playground where the teenage toughs of the Jets are hanging out, snapping their fingers, and waiting for trouble. Originally a Broadway show with lyrics by Stephen Sondheim and music by Leonard Bernstein, *West Side Story* reenacts *Romeo and Juliet* on the streets of the city. As the European American Jets confront the Puerto Rican Sharks, the musical explores racial and ethnic conflict but celebrates immigration as the central story of urban America.

Thirty-six years later, novelist and social critic Tom Wolfe's novel, *A Man in Full* (1998), used a flyover of booming Atlanta to present his own version of the urban story that highlights the power of economic change and the depth of racial difference. The modern city—New York and Atlanta—is so big that it has to be viewed from above. In one of the early scenes, real estate magnate Charlie Croker takes off from Atlanta in his private Gulfstream aircraft:

In the distance the sun was exploding off the towers of Downtown and Midtown Atlanta and the commercial swath on the eastern side of Buckhead. Charlie knew them all by sight. He know them not by the names of their architects–what were architects but neurotic and 'artistic' hired help?–but by the names of the developers. . . . There was Mack Taylor and Harvey Mathis's Buckhead Plaza. There was Charlie Ackerman's Tower Place. . . . Many was the time that the view from up here in the G-5 . . . had filled him with inexpressible joy. *I did that! That's my handiwork! I'm one of the giants who built this city!*

Charlie's Atlanta is a city divided by money and race. It is erupting northward, with real estate development flowing like a sea of lava. Development has spread from downtown to Midtown, then to Buckhead, then to Perimeter Center and Cumberland Mall. Further north still, Forsyth County is changing from a "Redman Chewing Tobacco rural outback into Subdivision Heaven." But left behind in the outward surge of real estate and jobs are many of Atlanta's African Americans, who have power in city government but not in the economy. Like Wolfe's earlier novel, *Bonfire of the Vanities*, set in New York, the plot of *A Man in Full* revolves around the gaps of understanding between whites and blacks. It is also a telling comment on the changing character of urban development that *West Side Story* swoops from its helicopter shots to the streets, gyms, and tenements of working-class New York, while Wolfe sets his scenes in board rooms, city offices, law chambers, and private clubs.

The Age of Real Estate

Charlie Croker was a fictional participant in a real estate boom that remade American cityscapes in the 1980s. The boom would pause briefly in the early 1990s, when Croker was struggling to work his promotional magic once again, and then take off into the new century. The median sales price of a new, single family house doubled in the course of the 1980s (from $65,000 to $123,000). The jump paced the consumer price index and reflected surging suburbanization that supported buildings like Atlanta's Southern Bell Center, Promenade Two, and Charlie Croker's own "Phoenix Center." It also fed on growing

expectations for bigger and bigger houses with more and more amenities—this was the decade, after all in which "Lifestyles of the Rich
and Famous" became a television staple, and even public television's
"This Old House" began to take on fancier and fancier remodeling
projects.

Commercial real estate investing took a temporary hit at the end
of the decade with the savings-and-loan scandal. Savings and Loans
(S&Ls) had traditionally been conservative financial institutions that
funneled individual savings into safe home mortgages. The years of
the Reagan Administration, however, were a time of deregulation when
Congress and the executive departments removed constraints on the
private market. Under new rules in the early 1980s, S&Ls began to
compete for deposits by offering high interest rates and reinvested the
money in much riskier commercial real estate. Risky behavior triggered a financial crisis in 1990. Bad loans destroyed hundreds of S&Ls,
especially in the Southwest. American taxpayers were left to bail out
depositors to the tune of hundreds of billions of dollars to prevent a
cascading collapse of the nation's financial and credit system. Novelist Jonathan Franzen caught the spirit of the times in *The Twenty-
Seventh City* (1988), in which a St. Louis building contractor muses
about risky ventures: "The North Side boom was built on paper, on
being in the middle, on buying low and hoping, later, to sell high. The
spirit of the renaissance was the spirit of the eighties: office *space*,
luxury *space*, parking *space*, planned not by master builders but by
financial analysts."

The real estate market did come back strong in the mid-1990s as
the nation enjoyed eight years of continuous economic growth from
1992 to 2000. Both Democrat Bill Clinton and then Republican George
W. Bush made increasing homeownership rates a major goal of their
presidential administrations. The data showed success. After holding
steady in the 1980s, the share of Americans who own or are buying
their own homes rose steadily to a record level of 69.2 percent by
2004, even as housing prices on the east and west coasts spiraled upward in what looked by 2004–05 like a speculative bubble.

The vast majority of new development took place in the outer
districts of metropolitan areas, filling in established suburbs and push-

TABLE 4.1 Greatest Population Gains & Losses, 1990–2000: Metropolitan Statistical Areas

GAINS

New York-Northern New Jersey-Long Island	1,477,000
Atlanta	1,179,000
Dallas-Fort Worth	1,172,000
Los Angeles-Long Beach-Santa Ana	1,092,000
Phoenix	1,013,000
Houston	998,000
Miami-Fort Lauderdale	951,000
Chicago	916,000
Washington	673,000
Riverside-San Bernardino	666,000
Las Vegas	634,000
Denver	512,000
Seattle-Tacoma	484,000
San Francisco-Oakland	437,000
Minneapolis-St. Paul	430,000
Orlando	420,000
Portland-Vancouver	404,000
Austin	404,000

LOSSES

Pittsburgh	-37,000
Buffalo	-19,000
Utica-Rome	-17,000
Scranton	-15,000
Binghamton	-12,000
Weirton-Steubenville	-11,000
Youngstown	-11,000
Johnstown	-10,000
Syracuse	-10,000

ing the subdivision frontier even farther into farms, forests, and deserts. Growth continued to be most rapid in the South and West, with pockets of decline remaining in the Northeast (see Table 4.1). In aggregate, 28.5 percent of the nation (80.3 million people) lived in central cities in 2000. Suburban cities and counties housed 145.9 million people. That total accounted for 51.8 percent of all Americans—a symbolic milestone as important as the census finding in 1920 that the nation had shifted from majority rural to majority urban. The pattern was essentially the same under a new definition of metropolitan areas that the Census Bureau implemented in 2003. Under the new categories, 92.6 million people in 2000 lived in "principal cities" (32.9 percent) and 140 million lived in suburbs (49.8 percent).

As Tom Wolfe's novel reminds us, much of the real estate action came in very large metropolitan counties that continued the long-standing trend toward suburban self-sufficiency. They have a full range of land uses and economic functions, but remain low-slung and far-flung landscapes. Many of these counties doubled in population from 1980 to 2000 and some grew even faster. Six of them counted more than 1 million people by the end of the century despite lacking a traditional large central city—Orange, San Bernardino, and Riverside counties in California, Broward and Palm Beach counties in Florida, and Tarrant County in Texas. Gwinnett County north of Atlanta went from 167,000 people in 1980 to 588,000 in 2000. Denton County north of Dallas went from 143,000 to 433,000.

Beyond these well-established regions, the wave of urbanization continued to wash into areas thirty and forty miles from historic metropolitan centers as builders looked for vacant land and families hoped for affordable housing. Growth in Loudoun County, Virginia, far beyond Dulles Airport, brought the exurbs of Washington, D.C. within sight of historic Harpers Ferry at the mouth of the Shenandoah Valley. Denverites spilled south into the hills of Douglas County halfway to Colorado Springs. Columbus, Ohio, sprawled north into Delaware County. The booming San Francisco Bay area reached eastward over the Diablo Range to the farmlands of California's central valley. The town of Tracy is closer to Stockton and Modesto than to Silicon Valley jobs, but it boomed in the 1990s with new houses for long-distance commuters. There, work days start at 5 or 6 A.M. and end after 7 P.M. as cars stream back and forth over Altamont Pass on I-80. Tracy grew from 18,500 to 53,000 in the 1980s and 1990s as Woodfield Estates, Quail Meadow, Hidden Lakes, and dozens of other subdivisions sprouted on the dusty valley floor.

Many of the new suburban developments were privatized. City dwellers had long been accustomed to apartment and condominium buildings where access is controlled by locks, buzzers, or doormen, but limited-access housing now boomed in suburbia in the form of "gated communities." From 1980 to 1998, the number of condominium units nationwide grew from 2,541,000 to 5,079,000, but units in planned communities exploded from 3,838,000 to 10,563,000. These planned communities had varying degrees of private governance in which property-owner associations collect fees, regulate common areas, and enforce voluminous deed restrictions ("covenants, conditions, and restrictions" or CCRs in real estate jargon) that can run to such extremes a prohibiting outside clotheslines or colored Christmas lights. Perhaps 20–25 percent of the planned communities—and much larger proportions around Washington, Miami, Houston, Dallas, Phoenix, and Los Angeles—are also access-controlled with walls, gates, guardhouses, or internal security patrols that limit use of normally public spaces such as streets and sidewalks to residents only.

"Gated community" calls up the image of high-income residents circling the wagons against contact with the poor, a picture evoked by science fiction writers such as Neal Stephenson in *Snow Crash* (1992), who anticipates a city of *burbclaves*, each of which claims national sovereignty, enters into security treaties with neighboring burbs, and hires mercenaries from Metacops Unlimited and WorldBeat Security to keep out the skateboarders and pizza vans. However, surveys show that simple prestige is an equally important motivation for upper-income families. In addition, many public housing projects and manufactured housing parks also have their entry controlled by key cards or coded gates. According to census data first gathered in 2000, Hispanic householders are more likely to live in controlled entry communities than are white householders, a reminder that these communities were becoming popular across social and economic divides and that gates and walls may help working-class families avoid the social chaos of high-poverty neighborhoods. This is the spin in science fiction writer Octavia Butler's *Parable of the Sower* (1993), set in a future Los Angeles where middle-class families live in constant fear inside walled suburban cul-de-sacs. Adults venture outside on jobs or errands, but only in daylight and always on watch: "That's the rule. Go out in a bunch, and always go armed."

One thing that is clear is that "suburbia" in the 1980s and 1990s was increasingly differentiated by lifestyle choices as well as income. Geographer Larry Ford in *Metropolitan San Diego* (2004) described the way that family status and social values have as much influence as economic class on the social landscape of San Diego. Journalist David Brooks commented in *On Paradise Drive* (2004) that the typical American metropolis is parceled out among cool bike messenger neighborhoods for recent college graduates, politically liberal granola suburbs, older upscale suburbs full of sophisticated consumers ("Bistroland"), and newer suburban cul-de-sac developments for people who worry about raising a stable family:

> So let's get in the minivan. We will start downtown in an urban hipster zone; then we'll cross the city boundary and find ourselves in a progressive suburb dominated by urban exiles who consider themselves city folks at heart but moved out to suburbia because they needed more space. Then, cruising along tree-lined avenues, we'll head into the affluent inner-ring suburbs, those established old-line communities with doctors, lawyers, executives, and Brooks Brothers outlets. Then we'll stumble farther out into the semi-residential, semi-industrial zones, home of the immigrants who service all those upper-middle-class doctors, lawyers, and other professionals. Then we'll go into the heart of suburbia, the mid-ring, middle-class split-level and ranch-home suburbs, with their carports, driveway basketball hoops, and seasonal banners over the front doors. Finally, we'll venture out into the new exurbs, with their big-box malls, their herds of SUVs, and their exit-ramp office parks.

Someone like Brooks sees a residential landscape in which Americans live in self-selected communities, but generally at the same low density. In contrast, journalist Joel Garreau's take was quite different. In the highly influential *Edge City* (1991) Garreau argued that suburban areas had developed full alternatives to the old downtown. These new "edge cities" are destinations in their own right, developing around super regional shopping malls, beltways, and airports and including 5 million square feet of office space (more than downtown Fort Wayne or Topeka). In effect, Garreau argued, the suburbs in the 1970s and 1980s had been reurbanizing and creating alternate centers whose twenty-story glass towers rise over suburbia like clusters of acacia trees punctuate the African veldt. Garreau's prime examples were places such as Tyson's Corner and Bethesda outside Washington, King of Prussia outside Philadelphia, Galleria–Post Oak in Houston, Buckhead north of Atlanta, the North Central Expressway corridor of Dallas, and Walnut Creek northeast of Oakland.

The shift from trains to planes for business travel accentuated the trend. By the 1980s, salespeople, consultants, and executives arrived in airports located at the edge of town rather than at railroad stations in the city's center, and they wanted to do business with a minimum of extra travel. This pattern was first evidenced by Chicago's O'Hare International airport in the 1960s, but by the 1970s every major airport was growing a fringe of hotels, office parks, and corporate offices. The Los Angeles airport replaced downtown L.A. as a center for western Los Angeles. The Dallas–Fort Worth airport, which opened in 1974, brought flush times to the supersuburbs of Arlington, Irving, and Grand Prairie. In Orange County, California, the John Wayne Airport area that straddles Costa Mesa, Newport Beach, and Irvine includes the South Coast Plaza with over 2 million square feet of retail space and office space of 25 million square feet. The Denver International Airport is intended to have the same impact on the plains northeast of the Mile High City.

Garreau's book was in part a hymn to the energy and imagination of large-scale real estate developers, and Tom Wolfe has his character Charlie Croker muse on the way that Garreau's book put a name on his own business: "He had experienced the *Aha!* phenomenon. The book put into words something that he and other developers had felt, instinctively." However, Garreau was also trying to discern emerging patterns in the seeming chaos of suburban sprawl. His insights resonated with the desire of urban planners and public officials to bring order out of the randomness of the market. A number of cities in the later 1980s or 1990s adopted plans that promoted the development of outlying centers or nodes. Phoenix talked about promoting "urban villages." In Oregon, Portland's regional plan designated a hierarchy of "regional centers" and "town centers." The Puget Sound Regional Council in 1996 defined nine established downtowns in the Seattle-

Tacoma area and twelve suburban locations as "urban centers" that are to absorb most new employment and receive most transportation improvements.

There *are* Edge Cities in many of the places that Garreau identified, but such high-rise islands and oases account for only a fraction of metro-area employment and retailing. Instead, other experts depict a fractal landscape organized at a much finer grain. Robert Lang has described the evolution of "edgeless cities" in the form of office space sprawling along suburban highways and arterial streets such as central New Jersey's low-density employment landscape around routes 1, 27, and 206. The edgeless city is the ordinary landscape that we don't really notice—small office parks, scattered factories and warehouses, and highway-side strips where insurance agents, CPAs, and yoga studios sit next to take-and-bake pizza places and car stereo stores. It is the place where "office park dads" (a term coined by political consultants in 2002) are busy at work while their spouses are juggling the duties of "soccer moms."

These findings support Anne Vernez Moudon's argument that most clustering of activity in suburban zones is at a much smaller scale than Edge Cities. Instead, her research finds what are, in effect, suburban neighborhoods of 3,000–4,000 residents in which a commercial strip or small shopping center (perhaps with multiplex cinema) forms a core. Surrounding it are inward-turned sets of low-rise apartments that have urban densities but nothing of urban appearance and single family houses. The Seattle region, for example, has two or three Edge Cities such as Bellevue and the Kent Valley but roughly 100 suburban clusters.

This is the sort of landscape that fills the background of contemporary fiction. It would be familiar to the twentyish slackers of Douglas Coupland's novel *Generation X* (1991), college graduates who work dead-end service jobs in upscale Palm Springs, California while living in cheap two-story apartments that horseshoe around a swimming pool. It is the environment that Richard Ford captured in *Independence Day* (2001) a novel about a real estate salesman during the Reagan years whose territory includes a chunk of suburban New Jersey, somewhere between Princeton and New Brunswick. Here are subdivisions backed up to a minimum-security prison for white-col-

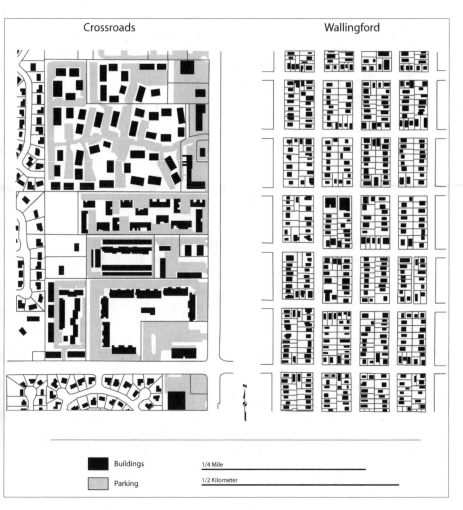

Crossroads   Wallingford

Buildings

Parking

1/4 Mile

1/2 Kilometer

Old and New Neighborhood Patterns. This diagram contrasts the fine-grain and inter-connected street pattern of early twentieth century neighborhoods with the superblocks typical at the end of the century. The examples here are the Wallingford neighborhood in Seattle and the Crossroads district in suburban King County. From Anne Vernez Moudon and Paul Hess, "Suburban Clusters," *Journal of the American Planning Association,* 66 (2000): 261. Reprinted by permission.

lar criminals; a declining mall with a Sears and a Cinema XII; a small town engulfed by suburbia where the town offices have been moved into a mini-mall along Route 1; a condo development that never quite caught on, with "low, boxy, brown-shake buildings set in what was once a farmer's field, now abutting a strip of pastel medical arts plaza and a half-built Chi-Chi's."

The suburban components may be similar, but the actual cityscapes of New Jersey and California actually followed very different paths of development. In the eastern two-thirds of the United States, there are few environmental restraints to prevent low-density development that leapfrogs over remnants of farm and forest in search of cheap land and spreads urban activities deep into the countryside. One indicator for "sprawl" is when a metropolitan area urbanizes rural land at a rate greater than its growth of population, meaning that the overall density of the metropolis drops. For example, the population of metropolitan Chicago grew by 1 percent from 1970 to 1990 while its total of urbanized land grew by 24 percent. The figures for Philadelphia were 5 percent population growth and 55 percent growth in its urbanized area. Dayton actually lost 10 percent of its metropolitan population over the two decades but its urbanized land still rose by 22 percent. The typical eastern or southeastern city intertwines into the surrounding region. As Charlie Croker noticed during his plane trip, "the trees stretched in every direction. They were Atlanta's greatest natural resource, those trees were. People loved to live beneath them. . . . for the past thirty years all sorts of people . . . had been moving beneath those trees, into all those delightful, leafy, rolling rural communities that surrounded the city proper."

The situation was different in the western third of the country, where rugged landscapes limit easy sprawl and arid climate encourages compact development around artificial water supplies. Look down on Phoenix from South Mountain or from an airplane circling to land at Sky Harbor Airport, residential subdivisions cluster tightly next to each other and the only vacant spaces are high, steep ridges. Phoenix is a typical southwest/far west metro area that has been holding its density while gaining population. Indeed, the entire "dry Sunbelt" of California, Arizona, Nevada, Colorado, Utah, and New Mexico added new developed land and population in roughly equal rates from 1982 to 1997, according to the National Resource Inventory. In the 1990s,

Charlotte converted forty-nine acres of rural land to housing for every 100 new residents and Nashville converted forty-two acres. In contrast, Las Vegas converted fifteen, Phoenix converted sixteen, and Salt Lake City converted nine acres.

Whereas eastern cities spread in all directions like ink droplets in water, many western cities have grown within tightly bounded corridors. Puget Sound and the Cascade mountains squeeze the Seattle-Tacoma-Olympia metropolis into a corridor eighty miles north-south but only twenty miles east-west. Greater Denver extends for a hundred miles along the base of the Front Range of the Rockies. In Utah, the Ogden–Salt Lake City–Provo metropolis runs ninety miles between the Wasatch Front on the east and Utah and Great Salt lakes on the west.

Beyond even these corridors and commuting zones were metropolitan spheres of influence that tied many superficially isolated small towns into urban economies. The half century after World War II was marked by the ubiquity of automobiles and levels of prosperity that allowed many middle-class families to acquire vacation properties and second homes in areas with scenic and recreational resources. Every large city staked out a "recreation shed" or "weekendland"— the Pocono Mountains and Jersey shore for Philadelphia, the Eastern Shore of Maryland for Baltimore and Washington, the Front Range of the Rocky Mountains for Denver. This mountain and coastal development has meant that few rural communities are isolated from the social and cultural forces of city people and their frequent desire to protect natural amenities from the continuation of the traditional resource economy. It also means that small towns in states like Vermont or Wisconsin that have enjoyed a "rural renaissance" are inextricably tied to economic systems and communication networks that continue to focus on urban centers. They benefit markedly from that contact compared to the cultural and physical isolation of small towns in previous generations.

Entrepreneurial Cities

American cities entered the 1980s with a political system that can best be described as metropolitan pluralism. The late 1960s and 1970s had been an era of frequently confrontational politics, with issues defined as absolute choices between downtown development or neighborhood revitalization, growth or livability, white or black mayor. By the mid-1980s, the increasing conservatism of national politics was reflected in a renewed interest in businesslike, growth-oriented city government. Quality-of-life liberals aged and became quality-of-life consumers, and "yuppies" replaced granola eaters. More important, newly empowered minorities began to press for a fair share of an expanding pie. Mayors all over the country proclaimed that their town was open for business.

At first glance, this newest generation of urban leaders sounded remarkably like the "new breed" of neoprogressive mayors that *Fortune* had described in the 1950s. However, there was an essential difference. The political rebalancing of the 1970s meant that politicians in the early 1980s faced strong pressures to assure equitable distribution of the benefits and burdens of growth. Denver and San Antonio offer good examples. In each case, a young Hispanic politician brought new ideas into city government. Henry Cisneros of San Antonio defeated a representative of the downtown establishment in 1981; Denverite Federico Peña ousted crusty, sixteen-year incumbent Bill McNichols with the help of armies of volunteers. If the campaigns had come in 1976 or 1978, they would probably have resulted in deep community division. In the 1980s, however, Peña and Cisneros were able to run on positive platforms as advocates of planned growth.

Other cities followed the same middle-of-the-road path. In 1983, Bostonians chose between white and African American candidates for mayor without making race a major issue. Mayor Andrew Young of Atlanta, elected in 1981, benefitted from the same black support that had previously elected Maynard Jackson, but he moved quickly to mend fences with the Atlanta establishment and helped the city out of the economic doldrums of the late 1970s. Albuquerque, New Orleans, Houston, and San Francisco made similar choices, looking for leaders interested in conserving the strengths of their cities while promoting diversified economic expansion.

The prominence of get-it-done mayors continued in the 1990s. City leaders accepted the painful fact that most cities lacked the resources to provide social services, rebuild infrastructure, and generate jobs on their own. With declining federal contributions, the realistic options were to cut budgets and court the suburbs—an agenda that was shared by leaders across all ethnic backgrounds.

In Detroit, for example, Dennis Archer had been a respected state supreme court justice before jumping into city politics. The heart of his agenda as mayor (1994–2001) was to rebuild cooperation between Detroit and its suburbs and to attract reinvestment into the city—as represented by new baseball and football stadiums. However, he was more popular among white and Hispanic voters than among fellow African Americans, who remembered the patronage-rich administration of Coleman Young,

In Philadelphia, Ed Rendell (1992–2000) was a gregarious politician with a mixed record of success and failure when he won the first of two terms as mayor in 1992–2000. He was a flamboyant but realistic leader who took charge of a city that ran a budget deficit of $250 million and was unable to sell bonds or maintain its pension fund. He pushed for efficiencies in city services by cutting jobs and contracting out, and then was able to offer tax cuts. His efforts slowed but did not stop job flight. In recognition of his efforts to pull the city up by its own bootstraps, *Time* magazine called him "the Rocky Balboa of American mayors."

While central cities such as Detroit and Philadelphia scrapped and scraped for financial survival, cities with stronger economies competed for growing high-tech industries. Having seen what the computer industry did for Boston and San Jose, every place wanted to be the next Silicon Valley. While Seattle spawned hundreds of "Microsoft millionaires" who benefitted from generous stock options, other cities and states competed for branch plants of Californian and Asian electronics companies. Portland talked about its Silicon Forest, Phoenix about its Silicon Desert, and Dallas about its Silicon Prairie. In the mid-1980s, Austin won a fierce competition for Sematech, a federally sponsored consortium of high-tech corporations that aimed to develop commercial applications for technical innovations.

High-tech futures, including the multimedia industries that sprang up to utilize computing capacity for entertainment and advertising, depended on highly educated workers. A major research university was a plus for attracting and holding these workers. So was a city with the amenities to appeal to what Richard Florida called the "creative class." These are the artists, scientists, academics, architects, entertainers and other "idea workers" who are thought to be young, highly educated, and geographically mobile. They seem to gravitate to cities that are both prosperous and cool—"diverse, tolerant, and open to new ideas" in Florida's words.

Austin is one of the cities with what it takes to attract the creative class. It has a topnotch university, a pleasant setting, a great music scene, and a critical mass of high-tech companies and research labs, all of which put it in the top tier of new economy cities as defined by the Progressive Policy Institute in 2001. San Francisco, San Diego, and Boston were also high on the list, as were smaller metropolitan areas such as Madison, Albany, and Albuquerque.

Only some cities could market themselves to young creative types, but everyone could compete for tourism and convention business. Tourism was one of the fastest-growing segments of the national economy in the 1980s and 1990s, reflecting high levels of disposable income and the democratization of air travel. Travelers brought in their dollars from outside, spent money in hotels, restaurants, theaters, and shops, and demanded few city services in return. Every mayor wanted bigger and better convention facilities. Smaller cities tried to cut into New York's convention business. Chicago, New Orleans, Washington, Las Vegas, and San Francisco remained top draws. But Columbus and Charlotte added new convention-center space in an exhibit hall arms race, as did Kansas City and Memphis, St. Louis, Seattle, and Salt Lake City.

The creative class, conventioneers, and business travelers are most likely to pay attention to a city's downtown. Picture a business traveler landing on a transcontinental flight to Seattle-Tacoma International Airport. She grabs a taxi outside the Sea-Tac terminal and heads north into the city. Traffic builds as she covers the twenty miles into town and the towers of downtown Seattle begin to pierce the horizon. There's the Space Needle from the 1962 world's fair, but it is dwarfed by newer hotel and bank towers. Topping a rise, she spots the Qwest Stadium for the Seattle Seahawks of the National Football League and Safeco Field for the Seattle Mariners. Her downtown exit takes her past the Washington State Convention and Trade Center before the cab swings into the courtyard of the tastefully modernized Olympic Hotel.

Our traveler has arrived in the heart of another real estate success story. Downtown Seattle, like city centers across the country, attracted a wave of public and private investment in the 1980s and especially after 1990. Some of the investment was in new office towers as the financial industry continues to value downtown locations, but much of it went to new facilities to enhance the downtown as a recreation and meeting zone for both locals and visitors. In Seattle's case, not only were a new convention center and professional sports facilities built but also a new art museum, library, symphony hall, and cruise-ship pier, with remodeled and upscale hotels as accompaniments.

It was not just Seattle where one of the symbols of the "hot" downtown was a new baseball stadium dropped into an old ware-house or light manufacturing district on the edge of downtown. When they were built, the Ballpark at Camden Yards in Baltimore (1992), Jacobs Field in Cleveland (1994), and Coors Field in Denver (1995) were immediate hits that attracted restaurants, bars, and trendy hous-ing to areas long overlooked. New downtown ball parks came to Phoe-nix in 1998, to Seattle in 1999, to Detroit and San Francisco in 2000, and to San Diego and Cincinnati in 2004. Minor league cities such as Dayton and Memphis jumped on the downtown baseball boom with new stadiums in 2000. The Dayton Dragons drew 590,000 fans in 2003 to a ballpark built on the site of an abandoned Sears store and parking lot. The Memphis Redbirds drew 749,000 fans to a stadium only blocks from the jazz clubs of Beale Street.

Some of the ball parks lived up to their billing as economic revi-talization tools and some did not, but they were all part of a concerted effort to bring "fun" and "action" back downtown. Investment in new cultural facilities such as museums and concert halls were built to attract the same market, aiming at suburbanites with disposable in-come. The same was true for new or refurbished parks and plazas with the food retailers and music festivals that filled them. Conven-tion centers and hotels chased a finite pool of national business, pro-fessional, and fraternal organization meetings. New York City offi-cials, scarcely in need of starting from zero, worked to transform Times Square from a natural attraction in a very sleazy part of town, into one much more carefully managed and well scrubbed. Commentators talked about the creation of "tourist bubbles" where visitors could have fun without rubbing elbows with the real city.

Some cities decided to create new downtowns from the ground up. Led by Mayor Tom McEnery, San Jose in the mid-1980s began to build a new downtown from scratch, including a convention center, a science museum, a performing arts center, new hotels, and a light rail line—at a total cost of more than $1 billion. The results were impressive, although perhaps not putting San Jose in the league of cities such as Zurich and Paris as some politicians enthused. Purely suburban communities from Schaumburg, Illinois, to Mountain View, California, got into the act with their own efforts to create urban centers where none previously existed. "People here want a downtown," said an official from Federal Way, Washington, a low-density suburb in the shadow of SeaTac Airport. "They want a city center."

Surrounding the office and entertainment core was new housing for young professionals who worked in downtown offices or empty nesters who wanted easy access to downtown activities. After decades of a declining core-area population (the result of urban residential renewal and the loss of low-cost housing), the 1990s brought downtown residential growth. In Seattle, for example, the Belltown district north of downtown was a neglected skid row in 1980 but a condoland by 2000, where trendy households were pushing out the last elderly poor and homeless shelters. Downtown Seattle grew from 0.4 to 0.7 percent in metropolitan area population in the 1990s, Chicago from 0.3 to 0.5, and Memphis from 0.7 to 0.8. Many of the new apartments and condominium units were in adapted office buildings, factories, and stores in which developers tried to recreate the style of New York "loft living." Where the market was strong, developers followed with new buildings in the loft style and with modern high-rise apartments. Hip, young workers in San Francisco's dot.com boom of the later 1990s priced auto repair shops and cheap single-room-occupancy hotels out of the SOMA district (*So*uth of *Ma*rket) and pushed into the historically Hispanic Mission District. New apartment and condominium buildings rose by the dozens on the edges of Chicago's North Loop and South Loop.

Despite the privileging of the private market, it is also interesting that the expanding core often benefitted from federal legislation in the form of requirements to clean up contaminated industrial sites ("brownfields" in real-estate lingo). The nastiest sites came under the

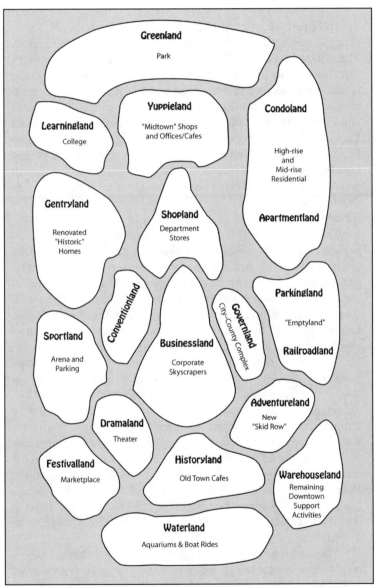

The Central City as Disneyland. This diagram illustrates and satirizes the way in which many American downtowns have developed into specialized zones for tourism, entertainment, and consumption. From Larry Ford, *Cities and Buildings*. Reprinted by permission of the author and the Johns Hopkins University Press.

federal Superfund program established by the Comprehensive Emergency Response, Compensation, and Liability Act (CERCLA) in 1980.
Much of the impetus for CERCLA, came from the political discovery
that minority and low-income Americans were most likely to live in
or near toxic and health-threatening waste dumps and polluters. In
the Louisiana petrochemical belt along the Mississippi River, African
Americans often lived downstream and downwind of noxious plant
fumes. In Buffalo, white working-class residents near the Love Canal
industrial site discovered in 1978 that an entire neighborhood had
been built on land contaminated by decades of chemical dumping. In
practice, however, cleanup of brownfields has often helped core-area
development reclaim old factories, industrial waterfronts, and rail yards
for upscale uses.

One result of this real-estate boom was to break traditional con-
ception of a boundary between the historic Central Business District
and its surroundings. In the classic model of urban form developed by
sociologists at the University of Chicago in the early twentieth century, the CBD was surrounded by a "zone in transition" filled with
cheap workers' housing, warehousing, transportation terminals, and
industry. By 2000, many of these zones had transitioned. Large cities
now have central districts that encompass the old CBD, recycled warehouse and waterfront areas, sports and convention venues with large
parking fields, close-in university campuses, uptown office clusters
two or three miles from the old financial district, and historic residential neighborhoods thriving as islands in the midst of development. In
this new model, for example, Milwaukee's core runs three miles from
Lake Michigan to Marquette University. Philadelphia's core includes
its long-established "Center City" (the local term for downtown) but
effectively extends two miles north-south and four miles from the
Delaware River westward through the University of Pennsylvania
campus. Denver's somewhat newer core reachers six miles from the
north side of the South Platte River to the Cherry Creek commercial
district.

These expansive downtowns pushed up against older neighborhoods where another selective entrepreneurial revival was in progress
with a selective push from the federal government. Enterprise Zones

and Empowerment Zones, which were efforts to attract private investment into poor neighborhoods, had only modest success. In contrast, locally based community development corporations leveraged neighborhood energy with small infusions of federal funds.

Enterprise Zones were the Reagan administration's effort to entice private businesses in to inner city neighborhoods. Copied from Great Britain, the program offered a variety of tax breaks and exemptions from regulations for companies that chose to locate in designated areas. Several states created their own versions to copy or supplement the federal initiative, although the results were less than hoped. The same was true of Empowerment Zones, an updated variation created in 1994.

Community development corporations (CDCs), in contrast, were nonprofit organizations that gave direct voice to neighborhood residents and tried to respond directly to local needs. The earliest CDCs, such as the Bedford-Stuyvesant Redevelopment Corporation in Brooklyn, organized in the late 1960s under the Economic Opportunity Act. They spread rapidly in the later 1970s and 1980s, tapping federal Community Development Block Grant funds that funneled through city governments. By the early 1990s, there were at least 2,000 CDCs in operation around the country. Like the earlier Model Cities program, their grassroots character made them important training grounds for low-income and minority women as well as men.

The typical Community Development Corporation was a small organization that focused its work on building or rehabilitating low-income housing within a single neighborhood or district. They have used federal tax credit programs to attract private investment to their projects and also have drawn funding and technical assistance from national foundations such as the Local Initiatives Support Corporation, set up under the umbrella of the Ford Foundation. Some of the larger CDCs have taken on additional programs such as small business assistance, the creation of housing for people with special needs, and commercial real-estate development. In Boston, the Dudley Street Neighborhood Initiative empowered the residents of one of the city's poorest neighborhoods, helping them to improve their surroundings. In Newark, the New Community Corporation had by the mid-1990s produced several hundred houses and apartments, owned a shopping center and supermarket building, and operated a day-care facility for children and a nursing home for elders.

The nationwide nonprofit organization Habitat for Humanity epitomized both the grassroots and entrepreneurial models. Founded in 1976, Habitat helps families earn home ownership by participating in the construction of own their houses, adding sweat equity to Habitat's expertise, funds, and volunteers. The organization began to grow rapidly in the 1980s after former president Jimmy Carter and Rosalyn Carter signed on as volunteers, finishing its 200,000th house in 2005. It operates in rural areas as well as cities, and overseas as well as in the United States, but its most visible impact has been on America's urban neighborhoods.

International Cities

Sixty years ago, sociologist Roderick McKenzie described the concentration of the economy's "center.work" and commented that "once a city becomes established as a regional distributing center its banking, transportation, and other facilities compel new concerns to select it for their point of operation."Although the Sunbelt boom augmented a regional system that had previously favored the Northeast, New York remained the national metropolis. In the 1980s, the New York region accounted for roughly a quarter of all major corporate headquarters. Indeed, New York's recovery from the verge of financial collapse in the 1970s and its economic vitality in the 1980s and 1990s has been one of the chief exhibits in the emergence of economic supercities. Variously called a "global city" or a "world city," New York remained a place where decisions are made about world investment and trade. Its interrelated complex of banks, stock-and-bond exchanges, corporate headquarters, advertising and public relations firms, management consultants, international attorneys, and national media receive, create, and direct huge flows of financial and economic information. It also has attracted a disproportionate number of trade associations, think tanks, and nonprofit organizations that work on a global scale.

Every description of the world urban system in the last twenty years has identified New York, London, and Tokyo as the three dominant cities. Saskia Sassen's *Global Cities* (1991) described them as a sort of three-headed capital of the world economy, "centers of finance . . . [and] for global servicing and management." To simplify their roles in the 1980s, Tokyo exported capital, London processed it, and New York made investment decisions. Visitors to all three come away with similar impressions of the intensity of city life. Workers and tourists crowd into their central districts by subways and surface streets. High-rise office towers, apartments, and hotels hover over the landscape. The bright lights of New York's Times Square, the neon glitter of Tokyo's Ginza, and the buzz of Piccadilly Circus entice twenty-four hour consumption. The message of each city is that economic change happens fast, and that instant information is the key to success.

At the heart of global cities are bifurcated economies. The economic decisionmakers and their technical support staff draw high incomes, live in expensive apartments, and spend their money in high-end stores and restaurants. A cosmopolitan business elite that moves easily through international business networks desires common amenities and cultural services, and the international district in Brussels is not vastly different from the higher-priced suburbs of Washington. Cleaning the apartments, washing the dishes, restocking the shelves, and looking after the kids are underpaid service workers, many of them recent immigrants. There is an international market for cultural leaders such as symphony orchestra conductors, but there is also an international market for Filipino nannies and kitchen help from Thailand.

In the 1980s and 1990s, it was not only New York that went global. Ambitious urban leaders around the country increasingly measured their cities against the ill-defined but even broader standard of the "world-class" city. City after city advertised itself as a new international leader. Mayors joined the jet set in search of special access to overseas markets and board rooms. Cartographic boosters revived "metro-centric" map projections that place *their* city at the center of the world. Ports have become "Worldports" while development officials have battled for direct air service to Seoul or Paris. *American City and County*, the trade magazine for city managers and public works directors, proclaimed a new era of international competition and cosmopolitan cities in 1992.

The new rhetoric reflected some very real changes from the parochial nation of the 1950s, when a foreign tourist or business traveler was a rare sight in the majority of American cities. The sources of change have been both institutional and technological, ranging from trade policy to a generation of American imperialism to the democratization of air travel. During the first year of the Eisenhower administration, there was one foreign tourist each year for every 654 Americans. By the end of the Reagan years, there was one foreign tourist for every twenty Americans. The relative value of imports and exports climbed steadily upward from 7 percent of the gross domestic product in 1965. By 2000, the value of exports was 14 percent of the gross domestic product and imports were 17 percent. Direct foreign investment as a proportion of the value of fixed capital shot upward after the oil crisis of the mid-1970s, and foreign bond buyers financed the huge federal government deficits in the early twenty-first century.

There are many ways to rank the importance of cities in the world economy. We might compare their number of foreign bank offices, value of exports, international conventions and events, immigrants, foreign tourists, or even direct flights overseas. Geographer P. J. Taylor and colleagues examined the offices of the world's 100 largest firms in accounting, advertising, banking, insurance, law, and management consulting. They placed New York second in the world in the density of its global network connections, Chicago seventh, and Los Angeles ninth (London, Tokyo, Paris, Milan, Toronto, Hong Kong, and Singapore were the other top scorers). Also in the top forty were San Francisco, Miami, Atlanta, and Washington.

Many cities that lack the comprehensive global reach of New York or Los Angeles have still developed specialized international roles. Business consultant Rosebeth Moss Kanter in *World Class: Thriving Locally in the Global Economy* differentiated *Thinkers, Makers,* and *Traders* (we could also term them *information cities, production cities,* and *gateway cities*). Houston and Detroit not only export petroleum products and automobiles but also sell relevant production expertise—oil field equipment and drilling supplies in the one case, software and robotics for manufacturing processes in the other. Houston's numerous foreign banks directly serve its international petrochemical business. Dallas and Atlanta have capitalized on

TABLE 4.2   Global Network Connectedness of U.S. Cities

	U.S. Rank	World Rank
New York	1	2
Chicago	2	7
Los Angeles	3	9
San Francisco	4	17
Miami	5	25
Atlanta	6	33
Washington	7	37
Boston	8	60
Dallas	9	61
Houston	10	62
Seattle	11	68
Denver	12	73
Philadelphia	13	76
Minneapolis	14	77
St. Louis	15	81
Detroit	16	85
San Diego	17	98
Portland	18	105
Charlotte	19	108
Cleveland	20	112

P. J. Taylor, G. Catalano, and D. R. F Walker, "Exploratory Analysis of the World City Network," *Research Bulletin* 50, Globalization and World Cities Study Group and Network.

their roles as gateways to large segments of the American domestic market. Foreign businesses have found it convenient to utilize their hub airports, railroads, interstate highways, wholesaling systems, regional banks, and business services.

Miami is another "trader" or "gateway city" that built on its location and ethnic mix to emerge as an economic center for the Caribbean. By the late 1970s, Cuban immigrants owned about one-third of the Miami area's retail stores and many of its other businesses. Their success in business made Miami a major Hispanic market and helped to attract 2 million Latin American tourists and shoppers to its stores and hotels during the 1980s. Access to the Caribbean and South America also made Miami an international banking and commercial center with hundreds of offices for corporations engaged in U.S.– Latin American trade. In the 1970s it began to attract "Edge Act" banks (subsidiaries of U.S. banks authorized to engage in international lending and financing of foreign trade). After changes in state and federal banking laws in the late 1970s, the city also added numerous agencies of Latin American banks. The same factors of location and local culture that have attracted bankers also make the city a good location for Latin American offices of U.S. businesses and for initial U.S. offices of Latin American companies. In effect, as journalist Joel Garreau has pointed out, Miami by the 1980s was less a part of the American South than the economic capital of the Caribbean.

The Southwest has developed a different sort of cross-border metropolis around manufacturing production. The Mexican government in the mid-1960s began to encourage a "platform economy" by allowing companies on the Mexican side of the border to import components and inputs duty-free as long as 80 percent of the items were re-exported and 90 percent of the workers were Mexicans. The intent is to encourage American corporations to locate assembly plants south of the U.S. border. Such *maquila* industries can employ lower-wage workers than in the U.S. and avoid strict antipollution laws (leading to serious threats to public health on both sides of the border). *Maquiladora* plants proliferated, especially after devaluation of the peso in 1982 and the adoption of the North American Free Trade Agreement (NAFTA) in 1993. In 2005, roughly 3,000 maquiladora plants employed 1.2 million workers, mostly in border communities. Sets of cities such as Brownsville, Texas, and Matamoros, Mexico, El Paso, Texas, and Juarez, Mexico, or San Diego, California, and Tijuana, Mexico, are "Siamese twins joined at the cash register." Employees with work permits commute from Mexico to the United States. American popular culture flows southward. Bargain hunters and tourists pass in both directions.

Greenville-Spartanburg, South Carolina developed as yet another type of international manufacturing center. German, Swiss, and Aus-

trian textile manufacturers wanting a toehold in the United States began to locate their sales, distribution, and service offices in the
Greenville region, attracted by presence of similar industry in the Carolinas. They expanded by opening factories to make textiles and textile
machinery and were soon followed by unrelated manufacturing companies from the same nations. More than 40,000 residents of
Greenville-Spartanburg worked for European corporations at the end
of the century, and the metropolitan area was increasingly bilingual
in English and German.

Tourism is a different approach to international specialization.
Honolulu and Las Vegas are major destinations for international tourists as well as for Americans. Las Vegas in 2000 received 2,260,000
foreign visitors for a metropolitan area of 1,376,000 inhabitants and
Honolulu 2,234,000 for a population of 876,000. Honolulu has been
especially attractive to East Asian visitors and investors because of its
proximity to Asia and ethnic mix. Indeed, Hawaiian statehood in the
1950s was promoted as creating a "bridge to Asia" for Cold War
America.

Washington, D.C., provides a final example of an international-
ized city as the control center for the coordination of economic policy,
diplomatic initiatives, and a vast system of military bases and alliances. If the hundreds of U.S. embassies, consulates, and military
bases can be viewed as the dispersed production sites for global influence, the Pentagon and State Department buildings were the federal
equivalent of Wall Street office towers. By the 1980s, Washington
area employment in international agencies ranged from hundreds of
workers with the Arms Control and Disarmament Agency or the Council for International Economic Policy to thousands with the United
States Information Agency and tens of thousands with the Department of Defense.

A vast private and semipublic information industry grew up around
this set of governmental agencies. Since World War II, international
governmental and nongovernmental organizations have spread widely
from their European homeland where the rules and forms of diplomacy were created. Their worldwide numbers are now so great that
the *Yearbook of International Organizations* divides them among eight
different categories. As late as 1962, Washington housed the head-

quarters or regional office of only forty-seven international organizations compared with 164 for New York. By 1985, in contrast, Washington had the principle secretariat of 462 such organizations and a secondary or regional secretariat of forty-five more, largely closing the gap on New York's 701. In total numbers, Washington passed such historic centers as Zurich and Geneva to rank sixth among world cities.

In the 1980s, international corporations and foreign lobbyists followed governmental and nonprofit organizations, sharing K Street office buildings with domestic lobbyists. For U.S. firms with international interests, argued the Greater Washington Board of Trade in 1987, "greater Washington offers a community of worldwide investment and trade organizations that create an entree to the far corners of the earth. For international firms, Washington offers the U.S. base of operations close to the government regulatory agencies which oversee import/export trade." A prominent business consulting firm ranked Washington fourth among sixty world cities as a desirable location for international headquarters, following Singapore, London, and New York. Washington's attraction, of course, is the ease of monitoring the changing U.S. policy environment, lobbying for access to domestic markets, and maintaining contact with state governments, national business and trade associations, and international organizations.

Back in the 'Hood: Poverty and Place

It took two full decades for the rising tide of the entrepreneurial city to begin reaching some of the poorest inner-city neighborhoods. Despite the enthusiasm of enterprising mayors and the growing community development movement, concentrated poverty and the accompanying social ills continued to get worse through the 1980s before showing improvement toward the end of the 1990s. At the same time, the nation's growing international connections were adding new ethnic groups and communities to the urban scene, creating new tensions and opportunities within increasingly diversified cities.

Most obvious to anyone visiting American cities in the 1980s was the abandonment of entire inner-city neighborhoods. Corporations walked away from outmoded factory buildings, retailers closed their doors, and landlords let apartments deteriorate until tearing them down was the only option. Sections of North Philadelphia and the South Bronx, of Camden, New Jersey, and St. Louis, Missouri, looked as if they had been bombed out. Some experts talked about urban triage—writing off entire districts and shrinking the coverage of public services. Jonathan Franzen's description of St. Louis in the mid-1980s in *The Twenty-Seventh City* caught the sense of devastation as one of his characters drives out of downtown:

> Spaces open up on either side of him where houses have been punched out of rows. . . . In half a mile Clarence has passed three squad cars. They're guarding nothing. No pedestrians, no businesses, just dogs and stripped vehicles. And property. High fences run along the street guarding bulldozed tracts and plywood windows. . . . square *miles* fenced and boarded, not *one* man visible, not *one* family left.

Abandoned neighborhoods were easy to see, but poor people were often less visible. The proportion of Americans living in poverty had declined steadily from the early 1960s to a low of 11 percent in 1978. It moved back to 15 percent during a severe recession in 1982–83, dropped to 13 percent and again reached 15 percent in 1993 before falling with the prosperity of the Clinton years. Most of the poor lived in households where adults held jobs. In the early 1990s, nearly one-fifth of all full-time jobs did not pay enough to lift a family of four out of poverty.

The national statistics found especially troubling expression in abjectly poor neighborhoods. The standard definition for a neighborhood of concentrated poverty is a census tract (a subdivision of metropolitan areas containing approximately 3,000–4,000 residents) in which more than 40 percent of the residents fall below the federal government's poverty level. In 1970 there had been roughly 1,000 such tracts. The number climbed to 2,800 by 1990 before falling to 2,510 in 2000. Even with this improvement, 7.9 million Americans still lived among concentrated poverty. Half were African Americans, a quarter were Hispanic, and a quarter were non-Hispanic whites. Most of the reduction of poverty-level tracts came in the Middle West and South. Some central cities showed improvement, but some older suburbs gained pockets of intense poverty. The poverty rate in both 1990 and 2000 was 9 percent in suburbs and 18 percent in central cities.

Concentrated poverty not only meant individual hardship and families struggling to get by on inadequate funds. It also fueled a pernicious slum culture. Sociologist William Julius Wilson pointed out in *The Truly Disadvantaged* (1987) that children growing up in high-poverty neighborhoods have few positive role models. Instead, they are left to observe and learn from models of dysfunctional be- haviors—or behaviors that are functional only in poor neighborhoods but not in the larger society. They have to cope with high crime levels and police stereotyping of neighborhood residents as inherent crimi- nals. Their parents are also physically separated from job opportuni- ties in growing and prosperous parts of their metropolitan area and thus isolated from the informal networks through which most work- ers find their employment—a problem confirmed in detailed studies of Atlanta and other cities.

At worst, the results were neighborhoods dominated by gangster culture. Crack cocaine spread rapidly as a new drug in the mid-1980s, offering a quick high and gaining dozens of street names. New gangs of young toughs and criminals took over crack sales and distribution. Violence escalated in inner-city neighborhoods as groups battled for business with drive-by shootings. Bloods and Crips, rival Los Ange- les gangs, colonized other cities or spawned imitators. By the 1990s, African American, Latino, and Asian gangs were far more threaten- ing that the Jets and Sharks of *West Side Story. Boyz in the Hood* (1991) was the best of many films that commented on the new inner- city dangers, while ride-along cop shows introduced television view- ers to one "felony flats" neighborhood after another. At the same time, some of the most troubled neighborhoods and housing projects were the creative centers for African American music. The same sorts of neighborhoods that produced doo wop and soul music in the 1950s and 1960s brought together the African Americans and Caribbean im- migrants who created rap and hip hop styles in the 1980s and 1990s as a way to comment on the social evils of their own world.

In the 1980s, commentators experimented with the term *under- class* to describe people mired in persistent poverty. Journalist Ken

Auletta, for example, used it in writing about welfare families. Members of the underclass were supposedly people who were disconnected from mainstream society—permanently unemployed and unemployable, undereducated, criminal or simply dysfunctional. In effect, the underclass was a restatement of Edward Banfield's fears about the unassimilable poor. The more scholars probed the concept, however, the more the idea of a monolithic underclass seemed unhelpfully to lump together people with too many different problems and needs.

Despite its analytical weakness, the term underclass did seem particularly apt for the growing numbers of homeless Americans. Large cities have always had a population of derelict alcoholics, transient laborers, and voluntarily homeless hobos. In the 1980s, several factors made homelessness more visible and pressing. A new approach to the treatment of the mentally ill reduced the population of mental hospitals from 540,000 in 1960 to only 140,000 in 1980. Deinstitutionalized patients were supposed to have community-based support, but many ended up in overnight shelters and on the streets. New forms of self-destructive drug abuse, such as crack and meth addiction, joined alcoholism. The boom in downtown real estate destroyed old skid-row districts with their bars, missions, and dollar-a-night hotels.

These factors tripled the number of permanently homeless people during the early and middle 1980s. There have always been individuals who prefer to live on their own without permanent shelter, but an increase in the number of homeless, from 200,000 to somewhere between 500,000 and 700,000, was the result of structural changes in the economy. Twice or three times that many may have been homeless for part of a given year. For every person in a shelter on a given night, two people were sleeping on sidewalks, in parks, in cars, and in abandoned buildings. Because homeless people made middle-class Americans uncomfortable, it was reassuring to them to assume the homeless were outsiders attracted by local conditions, such as tolerant attitudes (as some claimed in Seattle) or mild a climate (as some claimed in Phoenix). In fact, few among the down-and-out have the resources to move from town to town. Bag ladies, panhandlers, working people, and yuppies were all parts of the same communities, neighbors in the broadest sense.

One of the consequences of chronic poverty and separation from mainstream society was the renewed outbreaks of urban riots. After a relatively quiet time during the 1970s, Miami opened the new decade with a three-day disturbance over May 17–19, 1980. The trigger was the acquittal of four police officers changed with beating black motorist Arthur McDuffie to death. Coming at a time when many of Miami's African Americans saw themselves being pushed aside by economically and politically successful Cubans, the disturbance mirrored the riots of the mid-1960s, with looting, arson, and violence against whites until the National Guard ringed the neighborhoods on the third day of unrest. Eighteen people died in the course of the riot. A year-and-a-half later, the Overtown ghetto, located just west of downtown Miami, against exploded during Orange Bowl week.

The MOVE disaster in Philadelphia soon followed. MOVE was a small group of African American militants with a back-to-nature philosophy. They were bad neighbors and belligerent citizens with a longstanding feud with city authorities. On May 13, 1985, Philadelphia police tried to serve arrest warrants at the MOVE house, whose residents responded with gunfire. After hours of a pitched battle, the police decided to drop an incendiary bomb on the house. Their justification was an attempt to destroy a turret on the roof, but the result was a fire that engulfed the entire block, killing six adults and five children from the MOVE group.

The "Rodney King riot" of April 1992 in Los Angeles was another reminder of the nation's inattention to the problems of race and poverty and of the continued antagonism between police and minorities. Rodney King was an African American motorist who had been savagely clubbed and kicked by police officers while being arrested after a car chase on March 3, 1991. A nearby resident had captured the beating on videotape from his apartment. Within two days, the tape was played and replayed on national television. The grainy pictures shocked the nation and confirmed African Americans' worst fears about the biased L.A. police. Early the next year, the four officers stood trial before a suburban jury for unjustified use of force. The televised trial and the unexpected verdict of not guilty on April 29 stirred deep anger that escalated into four days of rioting.

The disorder revealed multiple tensions among ethnic groups and was far more complex than the Watts outbreak of 1965. African Americans from south central Los Angeles participated, but so did Central American and Mexican immigrants in adjacent districts, who accounted for about one-third of the 12,000 arrests. The rioting spread south to Long Beach and north to the edge of upscale neighborhoods in Westwood and Beverly Hills. Rioters assaulted the downtown police headquarters, city hall, and the *Los Angeles Times* building. As in 1965, some targets were white passers-by and symbols of white authority. But members of competing minority groups were also victims as angry African Americans targeted hundreds of Korean and Vietnamese merchants as symbols of economic discrimination. Four days of disorder left fifty-eight people dead, mostly African Americans and Latinos.

One reaction to the L.A. riots was to construct what critic Mike Davis called "the carceral city," meaning a city of imprisonment. Writing about Los Angeles in *City of Quartz* (1990), Davis described the threatening result of continuous police surveillance of minority neighborhoods, closed-circuit television monitoring, expanded prisons, Immigration and Naturalization Service detention centers, and armored buildings as elements of an increasingly fortified landscape. The image of Los Angeles as an urban jungle was portrayed in movies like *Falling Down* and *Pulp Fiction*. The dangers of Miami were played up in television crime shows such as "Miami Vice" and "CSI-Miami".

Nationwide, states diverted funds from education and health to create the carceral society by building and staffing more prisons. The number of people serving sentences of a year or longer in state and federal prisons grew from 316,000 in 1980 to 740,000 in 1990 and 1,368,000 in 2002, with another 658,000 being held for shorter periods in local jails. The federal government's concerted "war on drugs," begun in the 1980s, was the biggest contributor to the prison boom. As the drug war dragged on through the 1990s, the federal government poured billions of dollars into efforts to stop illegal drugs from being carried across the Mexican border or brought by boat or airplane to the Southeast. Aggressive enforcement of domestic laws against drug possession or sales supplied convicts to fill American prison cells. The antidrug campaign hit minorities hardest. Connecticut, for example, required mandatory jail sentences for selling or possessing drugs within two-thirds of a mile of a school, day-care center, or public-housing project. Because these criteria encompassed nearly all the neighborhoods in Hartford and New Haven with large minority populations, minority offenders arrested on drug charges were nine times more likely than white offenders to end up serving time in jail.

In fact, crime began to fall steadily for a decade after reaching a peak in 1991. The rate of violent crime (murder, rape, robbery, aggravated assault) fell by 33 percent from 1991 to 2000. The rate of major property crimes (burglary, larceny-theft, and motor vehicle theft) fell by 30 percent. Easing fears and escalating costs combined to cause some states to rethink the reliance on prison terms. California voters adopted a measure that provides for drug treatment rather than prison terms for many drug offenders. A handful of states adopted measures legalizing marijuana for medical use.

Rudolph Giuliani, mayor of New York from 1993 to 2001, took a different tack. He built his administration around the "broken windows" theory of law enforcement, which argued that permitting small signs of disorder and petty crimes sends the message that nobody is paying attention to public safety, and thereby promotes more serious crime. Giuliani cracked down on street peddlers, panhandlers, graffiti "artists," and subway stalkers. Crime in New York fell by 57 percent during his time in office, faster than the national decline.

Federal policy also emphasized "tough love" in the form of welfare reform. In 1996, President Bill Clinton signed bi-partisan legislation to "end welfare as we know it." The new program of Temporary Assistance to Needy Families (TANF) replaced Aid to Families with Dependent Children (AFDC). TANF had strict requirements that aid recipients seek work or enroll in schooling to obtain assistance, and it set a time limit on it. By 2001, the number of public-assistance recipients had declined 58 percent from its 1994 high, but there are doubts that many of the former recipients have found jobs adequate to support their families.

In fact, much of the reduction in concentrated poverty came not from federal policies but from the entrepreneurial energy of immigrants, who continued in the 1980s and 1990s to account for more than one-third of the national population growth. The total of legally recorded immigrants for 1981 through 1990 was 7,336,000. For 1991 through 2000 it was 9,095,000. For 2001 and 2002 the numbers were even higher, with 1,064,000 immigrants arriving each year. More than 12 percent of the U.S. population at the start of the twenty-first century were born in another country, the highest percentage since 1920. As in the 1970s, the largest immigration flows (35 percent of the total) were from Asia, Mexico, Central America, and the Caribbean (41 percent of the total), and South America and Eastern Europe. After recording decades of declining population and neighborhood abandonment, the 2000 census had the surprising news that many older core cities had grown in the 1990s—and immigration was the major reason. Denver reversed twenty years of decline in its population, jumping from 468,000 to 555,000, with many of the new residents Hispanics. New York City had lost 850,000 residents in the 1970s, but it began to turn around in the 1980s and added 700,000 people in the 1990s. By 2005, the 3.2 million immigrants (both legally documented and undocumented) within New York's city limits helped to push the city's population to a historic high.

Many of the new American families found their way to the suburbs as well as city neighborhoods. The minority share of suburban population in 2000 reached to 27 percent—12 percent Hispanic, 9 percent African American, and 5 percent Asian. Some of the numbers come from a further spillover of African American ghettos or Hispanic barrios across city limits, continuing the trend of the 1960s and 1970s but also include immigrant families deliberately opting for the suburbs. In the Washington area, the African American share of Prince Georges County, Maryland, continued to increase, but Arlington, Virginia grew increasingly multiracial—African American, Vietnamese, Cambodian, Honduran, and Mexican.

There were still "Ozzie-and-Harriet" families (two parents and children in the same household) in metropolitan areas, but they were most likely to be living in the suburbs and to be named Nunez or Nguyen rather than Nelson. They might have picked a new planned community in Chula Vista, outside of San Diego. The population of Eastlake Greens, for example, consisted of 3,822 whites, 2,380 Hispanics, 2,383 Asians, and 465 African Americans. The nearly identical new houses, the strict design controls, and the curving streets and cul-de-sac layouts offer the newly successful immigrant family economic security in a location without embedded ethnic tensions.

Suburbanization was one of the reasons for hope about racial desegregation. Racial segregation levels in 2000 were at the lowest level since 1920, continuing a trend first evident in the 1970s. Nationwide, the segregation rate (index of dissimilarity by census tracts) fell from 74 in 1980 to 69 in 1990 and 65 in 2000. The decline reflected an increasing racial variety in heavily white areas as middle-class African Americans and Latinos took advantage of less discriminatory housing markets. The segregation index by 2000 had dropped below 50 for Charleston, Norfolk, Raleigh-Durham, Greenville, and Riverside, although it was still much higher in old industrial cities.

Unfortunately, school segregation in the 1990s moved in the opposite direction, reversing the progress of the 1970s and 1980s. The U.S. Supreme Court in 1991 relaxed the standards for rescinding desegregation orders. In response, federal judges in many cities allowed magnet school and school-choice plans to replace busing programs, especially those that involved both city and suburban schools. Rollbacks in desegregation plans occurred in Seattle and Cleveland, Milwaukee and Columbus, Tampa and Charlotte. As a result, African American schoolchildren were increasingly likely to be in schools with few white or Asian children, raising the old challenge of whether separate education could be equal education.

Planning Compact Cities

Despite the continuing concern about social divisions and the isolation of poverty, most theorists and propagandists of urban planning in the last decades of the twentieth century centered their attention on the overall patterns of metropolitan growth. Proponents of regional growth management, advocates of metropolitan policies, and the practitioners of "new urbanism" all worked in the large-scale tradition of early twentieth-century Garden City advocates, so-called "City Beautiful" planners, and theorists of balanced regional development such as Lewis Mumford and Frank Lloyd Wright. Their analyses of the problem and resulting solutions, however, reversed previous concerns. From the mid-nineteenth century to the mid-twentieth century, planners and reformers viewed urban congestion and overcrowding as their central problem, arguing for decentralization and suburbanization as solutions. At the end of the twentieth century, the arguments reversed: sprawl and automobile dependence became the problem, and compact growth the solution.

The "compact city" ideal brought together architects, planners, policy analysts, and portions of the land development and real estate industry. It drew in environmentalists because compact growth reduces the demand for developable land and reduces the urban "footprint" on the landscape. It appealed to banks and other lenders, as well as to community activists, because focusing demand on developed areas helps to maintain the value of real estate on which loans have been made. It attracted local government officials because the costs of providing public services are less with compact growth than with sprawl, as has been repeatedly documented in reports beginning with *The Costs of Sprawl* (1974). And, finally, it struck a cord with people who found the modern metropolis ugly and alienating in daily life—the theme of James Howard Kunstler's passionate, acerbic, and widely read indictment *The Geography of Nowhere* (1993).

One of the most comprehensive summaries of the compact-city model came not from a planning theorist but from the California-based Bank of America, which published *Beyond Sprawl: New Patterns of Growth To Fit the New California* in 1995. The report inventoried the damage that sprawl does to public budgets, natural resources, and social cohesion, arguing that cost inefficiencies and irreplaceable resources required new approaches to managing land development. "We can no longer afford the luxury of sprawl," said the report. "This is not a call for *limiting* growth, but a call for California to be *smarter* about how it grows."

In practice, planning theory since the 1980s has involved three complementary approaches. The "New Urbanism" has tended to work from the bottom up, emphasizing improvements in neighborhood layout and design. In contrast, growth management and regional planning efforts have started with the shape of entire metropolitan regions and the distribution of growth within entire states. In effect, the goal of growth management is to provide the metropolitan framework, and that of New Urbanism is to color inside the lines. Overlapping with the interests of growth management, with its interest in the patterns of land development was a "new regionalism" that emphasized the economic and political connections among cities and their suburban rings.

The movement known as "New Urbanism" burst onto the planning scene at the end of the 1980s. The driving force was a group of architects who wanted to revive the art of urban design and envisioned ways to combine the positive lessons of neighborhood conservation with the lessons—both positive and negative—that could be learned from the New Town experience. They excoriated some of the absurdities of suburban design such as the unwalkability of suburban neighborhoods and the increasing distances between schools, shopping areas, and housing. In place of traditional suburban design, New Urbanists call for "neo-traditional" planning that tries to reintroduce some of the benefits of early twentieth-century neighborhoods. Practitioners of the growing movement came together in 1993 as the Congress for the New Urbanism and in 1996 issued a manifesto for their ideas titled "Charter of the New Urbanism." The CNU defines itself as "an urban design movement" that is involved "at all aspects of real-estate development." The Congress in 2004 had more than 2,000 members and identified several hundred new urbanism projects built or under construction. The Charter speaks to the three scales of region, neighborhood, and block. However, much of new urbanist practice has centered at the smaller scales, with efforts to design neighborhoods that encourage walking, focus on public spaces, and allow for a mixture of housing and other uses.

An example is Miami-based architect Andres Duany, one of the most articulate and energetic spokesmen for New Urbanism. In hundreds of speeches around the country and in *Suburban Nation: The Rise of Sprawl and the Decline of the American Dream*, a book he co-authored with Elizabeth Plater-Zyberk and Jeff Speck (2000), he called for changes to zoning and building codes to allow for narrower streets, smaller lots, a clustering of housing, and accessibility to stores and other services to promote walking. The book demonstrates the great differences between standard suburb-building and neo-traditional planning. The authors know what they dislike—streets are "traffic sewers," for example. They also know what needs to be done: reform the way that local governments regulate new construction and open the eyes of developers to unserved markets.

Peter Calthorpe is the other most prominent name in New Urbanism. Also an architect, he is very concerned with reforming neighborhood patterns and streetscapes. Calthorpe, however, also has a more comprehensive regional vision in which walkable neighborhoods are grouped together as the parts of a compact metropolis and ideally tied together by rail transit. In *The Regional City: Planning for the End of Sprawl* (2001) written with planning consultant William Fulton, Calthorpe envisions metropolitan regions as a hierarchy of centers, from neighborhood corners to vital suburban downtowns. Planning for all parts of the regional city should follow "a common design ethic: that communities at the regional or neighborhood scale should have active centers, should respect their history and ecology, and should husband diversity. The challenge is to clarify the connections and shape both neighborhood and region into healthy, sustainable forms."

Most new urbanist development in the 1990s and early twenty-first century consisted of freestanding residential communities, inciting the criticism that it is simply prettier sprawl and reminding critics of some of the less successful New Towns of the 1970s. The oldest and best known example is Seaside, Florida, a resort community on the Gulf Coast designed by Duany. Its inviting town center and closely packed houses were the setting for the movie, *The Truman Show*, raising the obvious criticism that New Urbanism produces stage sets rather than natural communities. Other early efforts on previously undeveloped "greenfield" sites include Kentlands in Maryland, with many similarities to Radburn, New Jersey, and Celebration, Florida, developed by the Walt Disney Company near Disney World. Houses in Celebration are limited to six styles chosen from a pattern book, and a ready-made downtown with a more-than-passing resemblance to Disneyland's Main Street, U.S.A. These sorts of projects have raised the criticism that the movement is really the "new suburbanism."

Advocates counter with an impressive roster of mixed-use projects on redeveloped urban sites, retooled shopping malls, and similar efforts to improve existing communities and better utilize surplus land close to city centers. One of the largest of such projects has been the reuse of Denver's Stapleton Airport site after the city opened a new airport and terminal twenty miles out of town in prairie-dog country. At full build-out, Stapleton projected 33,000 residents in 8,000 houses and 4,000 apartments, plus 3 million square feet of retail space and 10 million square feet of office space.

Most of the impetus for the compact city has come from the private sector, with some help from state and local government. One of the few relevant federal programs is the Hope VI program for the replacement of rundown public-housing projects. Congress responded to the recommendation of the National Commission on Severely Distressed Public Housing by allocating money for local housing authorities to demolish and replace their worst projects, including high-rise towers. In some cases the replacement projects evicted the very poor from increasingly valuable land which was reallocated for moderate-income households. In other cases, the redevelopment followed New Urbanist principles, as at New Columbia, an 850-unit Hope VI project in Portland, Oregon.

Whereas New Urbanist projects can be undertaken within the private market, regional growth management has required state legislation—the only way to overcome governmental fragmentation and rivalries among cities and counties within individual metropolitan areas. A glance at the record confirms the problem. In 1960s and 1970s, individual suburban communities that experimented with moratoriums on growth (such as Petaluma, California, and Ramapo, New Jersey) found that developers simply moved their construction to neighboring communities. Boulder, Colorado's greenbelt and open-space preservation program, begun in 1967, preserved environmental amenities and limited growth of Boulder itself, but demand for new construction spilled over into neighboring communities at the same time that Boulder housing prices zoomed.

The most effective growth management response has been Oregon's systematic requirement that cities and counties develop and enforce land-use plans that match statewide goals. The Oregon system represents a coalition that spans rural and urban economic interests in the Willamette Valley. The original goal of Oregon Trail emigrants, the valley contains the state's richest farmland, its three largest cities of Portland, Salem, and Eugene, and 70 percent of its population. The movement for state-mandated planning originated in efforts by Willamette Valley farmers to protect their livelihoods and communities from urban engulfment and scattershot subdivisions, with their disruptive effects on agricultural practices. One Republican legislator recalled that "at the time, I was a dairy farmer terribly concerned with what was happening around me, because of the houses moving in around me out there." As the effort moved through several legislative versions between 1970 and 1973, fear of California-style sprawl attracted Willamette Valley urbanites to the legislative coalition.

Governor Tom McCall energized the movement with a brilliant address to the legislature in January 1973. "There is a shameless threat to our environment and to the whole quality of life—the unfettered despoiling of the land," he thundered. "Sagebrush subdivisions, coastal condomania, and the ravenous rampage of suburbia in the Willamette Valley all threaten to mock Oregon's status as the environmental model for the nation. . . . The interests of Oregon for today and in the future must be protected from grasping wastrels of the land." The final land use measure that emerged from the back rooms drew overwhelming legislative support from all parts of the Valley—and very little initial support from rural eastern or coastal Oregon, whose residents worried about lack of development rather than an excess.

Formally adopted in 1974, the statewide goals linked urban-planning concerns to environmentalism and changed a purely reactive effort to fend off erosion of the state's farm economy to a positive attempt to shape compact cities and towns. Most important have been goals requiring the preservation of farmland and open space, access to affordable housing, orderly development of public facilities and services, energy-efficient land use, and clear separation of urbanizable from rural lands. For urban planning, the key is the requirement that every city or metropolitan region adopt an Urban Growth Boundary (UGB). The intent is to prevent sprawl by providing for "an orderly and efficient transition from rural to urban use." Within the UGB, the burden of proof rests on opponents of land development. Outside the boundary, the burden rests on developers to show that their land is easily supplied with necessary services, that it has little worth as resource land or farmland, and that it is the only practical location for needed development.

The Oregon system was a bridge between earlier initiatives and a new generation of state-planning programs in the 1980s and 1990s.

Its perceived success helped to convince Florida, Maine, Georgia, Washington, Maryland, Tennessee, New Jersey, and Rhode Island to adopt their own statewide planning programs or standards. So did threats to particularly valued natural resources such as the Everglades in Florida, Puget Sound in Washington, and Chesapeake Bay in Maryland. In some cases, such as Washington's, the specific approach mirrors that of Oregon. In other cases, such as Florida's and Maryland's, there is also an important emphasis on "concurrency," or the idea that development should be paced to meet the capacity of local infrastructure. Maryland's "Smart Growth" program, for example, is an incentive program that defines areas appropriate for urbanization or development and limits state aid for infrastructure to those areas. Unfortunately, it was closely identified with Governor Parris Glendenning (1995–2003) and largely ignored by his successor. Tennessee's Growth Policy Act (1998) matches many of the goals of the American Planning Association's "Growing Smart" program, utilizing both regulatory and incentive approaches.

A continuing boom in rail transit complemented growth management efforts—at least in theory. After San Francisco (1973), Washington (1976), and Atlanta (1979) pioneered a new generation of heavy rail/subway system, most cities turned to less expensive "light rail" systems running on surface streets or elevated tracks. Seven cities opened light rail lines in the 1980s (San Diego, Miami, Buffalo, Pittsburgh, Portland, Baltimore, and Sacramento). More opened from 1990 through 2005, including Los Angeles, San Jose, Minneapolis, Memphis, Houston, St. Louis, Denver, and Dallas, and voters continued to approve new systems or expansions. At their most successful, in cities such as San Diego and Portland, light rail provides an alternative to extra freeway lanes and catalyzes development around transit stations—thereby promoting compact growth. In cases such as Salt Lake City, however, the lines have gotten a handful of commuters out of cars and otherwise have been pleasant conveniences for getting students to university campuses or customers to sports venues, but they have not significantly changed development patterns.

Transportation has been one of the other areas of urban policy where the federal government was proactive in the 1980s and 1990s. Federal dollars were essential for many urban rail projects. The

Intermodal Surface Transportation Efficiency Act of 1991 (ISTEA for short) required unified metropolitan transportation planning as a prerequisite for federal funding and shifted a portion of that funding from highway projects to alternatives such as improving conditions for bicyclists and pedestrians. Its continuation in 1998 with the Transportation Equity Act for the 21st Century (TEA-21) requires regions to consider social, economic, energy, and environmental costs of transportation decisions, opening doors for advocacy groups.

Linking the specific arguments about growth management and New Urbanism have been a set of policy advocates who have tried to deal with the social and political impacts of a century of suburbanization. Beginning in the 1990s, these "New Regionalists" have revisited the mismatch between core-city problems and suburban resources that led to metropolitan consolidation efforts in the 1950s and 1960s. Their central argument is that "we're all in it together" and that wide disparities between older and new parts of the metropolis drag down the economic performance of the whole region. In *Cities without Suburbs* (1993), David Rusk drew on his experience as mayor of Albuquerque to argue that cities that can annex surrounding communities are more prosperous than those that cannot. Political scientist Alan Altshuler found that high levels of racial segregation result in a 3–6 percent reduction of metropolitan-area productivity, while also increasing public service and public safety costs. Journalist Neal Peirce argued that the most important unit in the global economy is the metropolitan "citistate" that functions as a single entity.

A comprehensive response to this situation has been to develop city-suburb political alliances. A number of experts argue that social activists and business interests therefore share a common agenda of promoting growth through equity. Analysts such as Myron Orfield, a former member of the Minnesota legislature, have further refined this point by showing that central cities and older suburbs often share common interests that can be served by regional approaches to housing and transportation. In the Twin Cities region, he found a receptive audience in Jesse Ventura, who served as mayor of an inner-ring suburb between his stints as a professional wrestler and governor of Minnesota.

Important innovations in regional governance were found in the Twin Cities, Portland, and Atlanta. The Metropolitan Council of Minnesota covers the seven-county region of Minneapolis–St. Paul. The Minnesota legislature created the Council in 1967 and strengthened its powers in subsequent laws. The Council has seventeen members, appointed by the governor to represent districts. It operates transit, wastewater, regional parks, and affordable housing programs, and coordinates transportation planning. Portland's Metro has the distinction of being the only elected regional government in the U.S., with a governing council elected by districts that overlap municipal and county boundaries. Voters of the three core metropolitan counties created Metro in 1978 and strengthened its powers in 1992. Metro acquires and operates regional parks and recreation facilities, manages solid-waste disposal, controls the urban-growth boundary, has certain abilities to levy taxes, and develops regional land-use and transportation plans that set basic requirements for local plans. Another important regional agency is the Georgia Regional Transportation Authority. After high air-pollution levels triggered the loss of federal highway funds in 1994, the state created a new superagency to manage transportation planning for thirteen counties.

Finally, a major accomplishment of the New Regionalism has been a new generation of metropolitan plans that range from statewide work by the State of New Jersey to scenario building for the Salt Lake City area by Peter Calthorpe. Commonalities include an emphasis on concentrating development in a hierarchy of centers, prevention of sprawl, concern with effective public transportation, and the desire to protect open space and environmentally sensitive land. The San Francisco Bay area pursued a comprehensive effort to acquire new parkland and open space before it was built over. The *Third Regional Plan for the New York–New Jersey–Connecticut Metropolitan Area*, published by the Regional Plan Association in 1996, defined strategies for environment, land use, equity, and governance. The Chicago Commercial Club, which sponsored Daniel Burnham's famous plan for Chicago in 1908, helped to issue *The Metropolis Plan: Choices for the Chicago Region* early in the new century. The plan considered scenarios for fitting 1.6 million more people into the region by 2030, and called for investing in strong "regional cities" and rail transit, helping communities build more walkable neighborhoods and business districts, and restoring and protecting prairie reserves, woodlands, and wetlands.

Ambitious regional plans and architects' drawings of bustling new neighborhoods were balanced by important challenges of political implementation. Advocacy of compact cities came from specific interests such as environmentalists, large developers, and local officials, rather than from the general public. Demand for traditional suburbs remained strong, fueled in part by economically successful immigrant families. The U.S. Supreme Court in *Dolan* v. *City of Tigard* (1994) limited the sorts of tradeoffs a community can require in return for allowing property owners to develop their land. At the same time, defenders of private property rights chipped away at planning initiatives with state legislation requiring compensation for regulations that reduce potential property values by limiting development options.

Overlaid on property rights and regional plans, finally, the federal Endangered Species Act brought additional and unanticipated limitations on land development. When Congress passed the measure in 1973, senators and representatives were surely thinking of grand species in the distant wilderness—golden eagles, grizzly bears, whales, and the like. In fact, the ESA became an important constraint on urban regions as they have grown into surrounding mountains and wetlands. The need to protect songbirds has limited development in the Hill Country around Austin. Protected prairie dog habitat may be a check on Denver's eastward sprawl onto the High Plains. Cities around Puget Sound have to preserve free-flowing streams for migratory salmon.

The ESA reminds us of the long reach of American cities. In 2005, the researcher Robert Lang and the Lincoln Institute of Land Policy revisited Jean Gottmann's idea of the megalopolis as reshaped by a half century of Interstate Highways. They defined ten Megalopolitan Areas, each of which has a distinct historical and regional identity, is organized around high-volume transportation corridors, and is projected to have at least 10 million people by 2040. They include the Boston-to-Washington and Chicago-to-Pittsburgh clusters that observers identified as early as the 1960s, with 50 million and 40 million residents respectively. They also include the 7.5 mil-

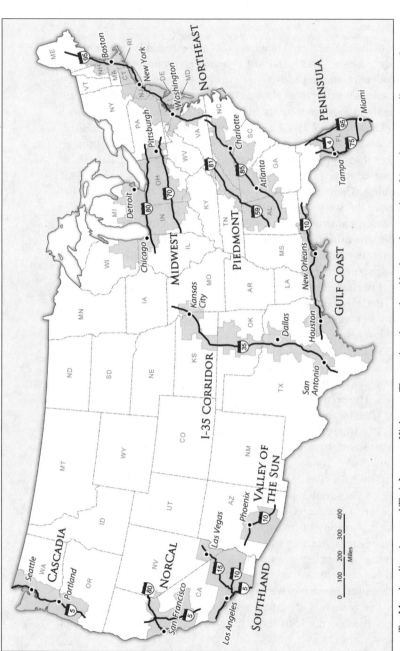

Ten Megalopolitan Areas and Their Interstate Highways. The continued growth and horizontal expansion of American metropolitan areas has created constellations of urbanized areas connected along major transportation corridors. Map by Robert Lang from *Land Lines* (July 2005). Reprinted by permission of Lincoln Institute of Land Policy.

lion people currently in Cascadia (Seattle-Portland) and 4.5 million in the Valley of the Sun (Phoenix-Tucson). Other relatively compact clusters are the Florida Peninsula, the Gulf Coast along I-10, the Los Angeles–San Diego "Southland," and North Central California from San Jose to Sacramento. Far more sprawling are the Piedmont Megalopolis and the I-35 Megalopolis from San Antonio to Kansas City.

Megalopolitan growth shapes the value of city real estate and the future of neighborhoods. It creates opportunities for immigrants and continually redistributes the population of the fifty states among economically troubled and booming cities. Cities reach far into the countryside for food, clean water, energy, and building materials. They restructure the lives of rural residents in weekendlands. For better or worse, they reshape valleys and hillsides and impinge on the lives of deer and condors, mountain lions and sea lions. They are the inescapable fact of twenty-first century America.

The Promise of Urban Life

> I am an American, Chicago born—Chicago, that somber city—and go as I have taught myself, free-style, and will make the record in my own way: first to knock, first admitted; sometimes an innocent knock, sometimes a not so innocent.
>
> —Saul Bellow, *The Adventures of Augie March*

The opening lines from *The Adventures of Augie March* capture one of the essential elements of the twentieth-century city. The hero of Saul Bellow's novel about growing up during the 1920s and 1930s knew that cities are places where things happen. They are indispensable centers of opportunity that bring people together to exchange goods, services, ideas, and human company. Even when Americans think that they prefer small towns, it turns out that most really want to maintain access to all the advantages of urban living—a fact that is confirmed by the continued growth of metropolitan regions since the early decades of the last century.

At their best, American cities are now among the most livable environments in the world. We have solved or know how to solve

Table P.1   Populations of Twelve Largest Metropolitan Areas, 1920 and 2000

1920: Metropolitan Districts

New York	7,910,000
Chicago	3,179,000
Philadelphia	2,407,000
Boston	1,772,000
Pittsburgh	1,208,000
Detroit	1,165,000
St. Louis	952,000
Cleveland	926,000
San Francisco–Oakland	891,000
Los Angeles	879,000
Baltimore	787,000
Minneapolis–St. Paul	629,000

2000: Combined Statistical Areas

New York-Newark-Bridgeport	21,362,000
Los Angeles-Long Beach-Riverside	16,374,000
Chicago-Naperville-Michigan City	9,312,000
Washington-Baltimore-Northern Virginia	7,538,000
San Jose-San Francisco-Oakland	7,092,000
Philadelphia-Camden-Vineland	5,834,000
Boston-Worcester-Manchester	5,716,000
Detroit-Warren-Flint	5,358,000
Dallas-Fort Worth (metropolitan statistical area)	5,346,000
Miami-Fort Lauderdale-Miami Beach	5,008,000
Houston-Baytown-Huntsville	4,815,000
Atlanta-Sandy Springs-Gainesville	4,548,000

many of their physical problems of traffic, pollution, and deteriorated housing. Failures come from lack of commitment and political will, not from problems inherent in our great cities. The real dilemma in urban areas, of course, is our willingness to use parts of metropolitan areas as dumping grounds for social problems. People with limited abilities to help themselves are shunted into cities and then blamed for their own ills. The poor are expected to tax themselves to pay for public services that they cannot afford as private citizens. Alcoholics, the mentally ill, voluntary dropouts, and other social discards end up on each city's skid row—a visible area with a homeless population that amounts to about one in four hundred residents of every city. When affluent households flock to revitalized downtowns and inner neighborhoods, they casually shove poorer families outward into old and cheaper suburbs. None of these situations in acceptable. In any realistic assessment, society itself is damaged and limited when we allow the well-being of individuals to be jeopardized by poverty, crime, and ignorance.

The solution is not to abandon public concern, but rather to develop cities as centers of opportunity. Augie March saw his city as a set of possibilities that could "make a nobility of us all." At the start of the last century, political reformer Frederic Howe proclaimed that the city was the "hope of democracy" because it had the ability to assure a fair start to everyone through public education, public health, and social services. To fulfill this promise, all of us need to share responsibility as individuals and as a nation for the special problems that our society has concentrated in cities.

What cities do best is to protect diversity. The key to urban vitality is variety in economic activities, in people, and in neighborhoods. Geographer Brian Berry has argued persuasively that American cities are "mosaics." They are not so much centrally structured units as they are sets of neighborhoods and districts arranged in complex patterns. Residents can choose among communities that vary "in their racial, ethnic, and socio-economic composition and thus in their available life styles; in their physical features, which can be used to create images and boundaries; and in their historic claims to a distinct reputation or identity." Residential neighborhoods range across working-class communities, ghettos, ethnic centers, affluent apartment complexes, family-oriented suburbs, and centers for artists and intellectuals.

Such an analysis implies that the several parts of the city are roughly equivalent in inherent worth, as long as each meets particular economic and social needs. Residential hotels for pensioners on the fringe of downtown, an upgrading neighborhood of Victorian row houses, and family-oriented suburbs filled with 1960s split levels all offer necessary residential choices. A district of low-rent warehouses and affordable storefronts for start-up businesses can be just as valuable to a vital city as a gleaming high-rise office cluster. Some of us, including this writer, make strong arguments for the social and environmental benefits of compact growth, but we also understand that the multicentered metropolis built around automobiles and freeways has been a logical expression of American city building. In the words of historian Sam B. Warner, Jr., it offers "the potential of a range of personal choices and social freedoms for city dwellers if we would only extend the paths of freedom that our urban system has been creating."

Livable cities are those that have accepted the imperatives of variety and learned to deal with their character as mosaics. They preserve multifunctional downtown districts that serve as everyone's neighborhood. They retain and value ethnic variety, and they conserve their everyday neighborhoods. Central to this approach is a concern with the smaller social and physical units through which individuals relate to the larger metropolitan area. Neighborhood communities, independent suburbs, and architecturally distinct districts each provide a sense of belonging and a source of cultural identity. They also provide the avenues for direct citizen participation in local decisions.

We can talk about the urban mosaic in terms of political pluralism or as an expression of multiculturalism. Diverse groups, defined variously by ethnicity, social class, or residential location, have developed the political capacity to pursue their goals through neighborhoods, suburbs, and interest areas. Pluralistic politics has allowed the recognition of groups and communities that were previously ignored in public and private decisions about metropolitan growth and services. However, cities still need strong areawide institutions that can facilitate the equitable sharing of problems as well as opportunities. Neighborhood politics and suburban self-sufficiency both require the balance of a metropolitan vision that recognizes the value of distinctive communities within a metropolitan framework.

The language of multiculturalism highlights the cultural dynamism of cities. New ideas emerge most easily when people of different backgrounds rub up against each other. Urban sociologists long ago understood that urban variety undermines unthinking allegiance to old values and requires conscious choices. Some may choose to reaffirm old ways, others to embrace new ideas and ways of life. Cities remain the focal points of American culture, creativity, economic change, and innovation—whether the Harlem Renaissance or hip hop music, medical advances or experiments with multimedia communication.

In the first years of the twenty-first century, U.S. cities experienced two disasters that challenged the social fabric. One of them exposed the persisting fault lines of urban society, while the other reaffirmed its strength.

At the end of August 2005, the backwash of Hurricane Katrina devastated New Orleans. It first it looked as if the huge storm had spared the city, driving head-on at the coast of Mississippi, but the rain and storm surge unexpectedly overtopped and undermined the levees protecting much of New Orleans. A city precariously located below sea level in many areas, New Orleans had long feared such a disaster. As flood waters inundated low-income neighborhoods, the city proved ill-prepared. Wealthier residents had evacuated, but many of the city's poor had not. Federal, state, and local officials all fumbled rescue and relief efforts while hundreds of people died and refugees huddled on rooftops and crammed into the Superdome and the Convention Center. The city's social fabric had long been frayed and tattered, with deep gaps between the tourist bubble of the French Quarter and the realities of housing projects, and the Katrina disaster highlighted the mutual distrust.

The story was different in New York on September 11, 2001, when Al Qaeda terrorists crashed a jetliner into each of the twin towers of the World Trade Center, 110-story buildings that housed 50,000 workers at the peak of the workday. Tens of millions of Americans were jolted out of morning routines by riveting television coverage and watched in horror as first one tower and then the other disintegrated into itself. The death toll from the tragedy as of November 2003 was at 2,752, including 479 police officers, firefighters, and other emergency workers. The buildings may have imploded but the city proved immensely resilient. Thousands of volunteers rushed to assist the rescue or contribute to relief efforts. A few commentators muttered that the era of the big-city downtown was over, but most Americans were impressed by the courage and unity of the great city in the face of crisis.

We are left with a narrative of urban development that has plenty of drama but no clear outcome. Is New Orleans the future? We hope not. Can we take heart from New York? Let us hope so. The implicit choice that Jane Jacobs suggested more than four decades ago remains just as meaningful today:

> Dull, inert cities . . . contain the seeds of their own destruction and little else. But lively, diverse, intense cities contain the seeds of their own regeneration, with energy enough to carry over for problems and needs outside themselves.

BIBLIOGRAPHICAL ESSAY

Previous books on the historical development of the modern American city are Blake McKelvey, *The Emergence of Metropolitan America: 1915–1966* (New Brunswick, NJ, 1968); William Wilson, *Coming of Age: Urban America, 1915–1945* (New York, 1974); Jon C. Teaford, *The Twentieth-Century American City: Problem, Promise, and Reality* (Baltimore, 1986); and Kenneth Fox, *Metropolitan America: Urban Life and Urban Policy in the United States, 1940–1980* (Jackson, MS, 1986). Henry Bedford, *Trouble Downtown: The Local Context of Twentieth Century America* (New York, 1978) traces broad themes through case studies of individual cities in periods of crisis and change from Detroit in the 1930s to Montgomery, Alabama, in 1955.

The era of the modern city is defined and discussed in a number of comprehensive historical analyses including Blaine Brownell and David Goldfield, *Urban America: From Downtown to No Town* (Boston, 1979); Sam B. Warner, Jr., *The Urban Wilderness* (New York, 1972); Bayrd Still, *Urban America: A History with Documents* (Boston, 1974); Peter Gluck and Richard Meister, *Cities in Transition:*

Social Changes and Institutional Responses in Urban Development (New York, 1979); and Eric Monkkonen, *America Becomes Urban: The Development of U.S. Cities and Towns, 1780–1980* (Berkeley, CA, 1988). The transition to the modern era is also the subject of Richard Wade, "America's Cities Are (Mostly) Better than Ever," *American Heritage* (Feb./Mar. 1979): 6–13, while Michael Conzen points toward the end of that era in "American Cities in Profound Transition: The New City Geography of the 1980s," *Journal of Geography* (May–June 1983): 94–101.

A highly influential geographical perspective on the emergence of the modern city is provided by John Borchert, "American Metropolitan Evolution," *Geographical Review* 57 (1967): 301–32. James Lemon, *Liberal Dreams and Nature's Limits: Great Cities of North America since 1600* (New York, 1996) is another wide-ranging interpretation by a historical geographer.

The genre of "urban biography" experienced a revival in the 1980s with a number of studies of cities that achieved much of their growth in the twentieth century. For southern and western cities, see Michael J. McDonald and William Bruce Wheeler, *Knoxville, Tennessee: Continuity and Change in an Appalachian City* (Knoxville, 1983); Don Doyle, *Nashville in the New South, 1880–1930* and *Nashville since the 1920s* (Knoxville, 1985); Bradford Luckingham, *The Urban Southwest: A Profile History of Albuquerque, El Paso, Phoenix, Tucson* (El Paso, 1982); David McComb, *Houston: A History* (rev. ed., Austin, TX, 1981); E. Kimbark MacColl, *The Growth of a City: Power and Politics in Portland, Oregon, 1915 to 1950* (Portland, 1979); Thomas G. Alexander and James B. Allen, *Mormons and Gentiles: A History of Salt Lake City* (Boulder, CO, 1984); Eugene Moehring, *Resort City in the Sunbelt: Las Vegas, 1930–2000* (Reno, 2000); Hal Rothman, *Neon Metropolis: How Las Vegas Started the Twenty-First Century* (New York, 2002); Patricia Hill, *Dallas: The Making of a Modern City* (Austin, TX, 1996); and Stephen Leonard and Thomas Noel, *Denver: Mining Camp to Metropolis* (Boulder, CO, 1990).

For recent biographies of industrial cities, see Carol Hoffecker, *Corporate Capital: Wilmington in the Twentieth Century* (Philadelphia, 1983); James B. Lane, *City of the Century: A History of Gary,*

Indiana (Bloomington, IN, 1978); Mark Goldman, *High Hopes: The Rise and Decline of Buffalo, New York* (Albany, 1983) and Russell Weigley, ed., *Philadelphia: A 300-Year History* (New York, 1982).

A valuable source for comparative analysis of urban growth and structure after midcentury is a set of twenty metropolitan profiles from the Comparative Metropolitan Analysis Project of the Association of American Geographers. Published under the comprehensive title of *Contemporary Metropolitan America* (Cambridge, MA, 1976), the four volumes carry the titles *Cities of the Nation's Historic Metropolitan Core, Nineteenth Century Ports, Nineteenth Century Inland Centers and Ports,* and *Twentieth Century Cities.* Among the outstanding sketches are those by Pierce Lewis on "New Orleans," by David Meyer on "From Farm to Factory to Urban Pastoralism: Urban Change in Central Connecticut," and by Howard Nelson and William Clark on "The Los Angeles Metropolitan Experience."

A new series of "Metropolitan Portraits" offers new reflections on the growth and character of important cities. Published through 2005 are Larry Ford, *Metropolitan San Diego: How Geography and Lifestyle Shape a new Urban Environment* (Philadelphia, 2005); Sam Bass Warner, Jr., *Greater Boston: Adapting Regional Traditions to the Present* (Philadelphia, 2001); and Carl Abbott, *Greater Portland: Urban Life and Landscape in the Pacific Northwest* (Philadelphia, 2001).

Several cities are also the subjects of detailed and scholarly city encyclopedias: Cleveland, Indianapolis, New York, Chicago. See David D. Van Tassel and John J. Grabowski, eds., *The Encyclopedia of Cleveland History* (Bloomington, IN, 1987); David J. Bodenhamer and Robert G. Barrows, eds., *The Encyclopedia of Indianapolis* (Bloomington, IN, 1994); Kenneth T. Jackson, ed., *The Encyclopedia of New York City* (New Haven, 1995); James Grossman, Ann Keating, and Janice Reiff, eds., *The Encyclopedia of Chicago* (Chicago, 2004).

The American Urban System

Classic descriptions of the national system of cities in the twentieth century United States are Roderick McKenzie, *The Metropolitan Community* (New York, 1933); Otis Duncan et al., *Metropolis and Region*

(Baltimore, 1960); Edward Ullman, "Regional Development and the Geography of Concentration," *Papers and Proceedings of the Regional Science Association* 4 (1958): 179–98. The descriptions were updated for the 1970s in John Borchert, "The Changing Metropolitan Regions," *Annals of the AAG* 62 (June 1972): 352–73; Brian Berry, *Growth Centers in the American Urban System* (Cambridge, MA, 1973); and Thomas Stanback and Thierry Noyelle, *The Economic Transformation of American Cities* (Totowa, NJ, 1984).

The urban pattern in the twentieth-century South is discussed in Rupert B. Vance and Nicholas Demerath, eds., *The Urban South* (Chapel Hill, NC, 1954); Blaine Brownell, "The Urban South Comes of Age, 1900–1940," and Edward Haas, "The Southern Metropolis, 1940–76," both in Blaine Brownell and David Goldfield, eds., *The City in Southern History* (Port Washington, NY, 1977); and David Goldfield, *Cottonfields and Skyscrapers: Southern City and Region, 1607–1980* (Baton Rouge, LA, 1982).

The characteristics of western cities are discussed in Ray B. West, ed., *Rocky Mountain Cities* (New York, 1949); Neil Morgan, *Westward Tilt: The American West Today* (New York, 1963); Gerald Nash, *The American West in the Twentieth Century: A Short History of an Urban Oasis* (Englewood Cliffs, NJ., 1973); and Carl Abbott, *The Metropolitan Frontier: Cities in the Modern American West* (Tucson, 1993).

The Middle West is treated in Daniel Elazer, *Cities of the Prairie: The Metropolitan Frontier and American Politics* (New York, 1970), a unique book that compares patterns of growth and politics in a set of smaller cities located between the Appalachians and the Rockies. Also see Jon Teaford, *Cities of the Heartland: The Rise and Fall of the Industrial Midwest* (Bloomington, IN, 1993).

The rise and character of the American Sunbelt as a distinct region is the subject of Carl Abbott, *The New Urban America: Growth and Politics in Sunbelt Cities* (Chapel Hill, NC, 1981); Kirkpatrick Sale, *Power Shift: The Rise of the Southern Rim and Its Challenge to the Eastern Establishment* (New York, 1975); Kevin Phillips, *The Emerging Republican Majority* (New Rochelle, NY, 1969); and Alfred J. Watkins and David C. Perry, eds., *The Rise of the Sunbelt Cities* (Beverly Hills, CA, 1977).

Shaping the Metropolis

For the pattern of land uses before 1940, see Robert W. Park, Ernest W. Burgess, and Roderick D. McKenzie, *The City* (Chicago, 1925) and Homer Hoyt, *The Structure and Growth of Residential Neighborhoods in American Cities* (Washington, 1939).

The evolving patterns of residence and economic activity in metropolitan New York can be traced in Edgar Hoover and Raymond Vernon, *Anatomy of a Metropolis* (Cambridge, MA, 1959); Jean Gottmann, *Megalopolis: The Urbanized Northeastern Seaboard of the United States* (New York, 1961); and John Mollenkopf, *New York City in the 1980s: A Social, Economic, and Political Atlas* (New York, 1993). The physical development of Chicago is treated in Harold Mayer and Richard Wade, *Chicago: The Growth of a Metropolis* (Chicago, 1969) and two volumes by Carl Condit: *Chicago, 1910–29: Building, Planning, and Urban Technology* (Chicago, 1973) and *Chicago, 1930–70: Building, Planning, and Urban Technology* (Chicago, 1974).

The physical form of the newer, more dispersed metropolis of southern California is the subject of Rayner Banham, *Los Angeles: The Architecture of the Four Ecologies* (New York, 1971); Mel Scott, *Metropolitan Los Angeles* (Los Angeles, 1949); Michael J. Dear, E. Eric Schockman, and Greg Hise, eds., *Rethinking Los Angeles* (Thousand Oaks, CA, 1996); Allen J. Scott and Edward Soja, eds., *The City: Los Angeles and Urban Theory at the End of the Twentieth Century* (Berkeley, CA, 1996); and Michael J. Dear, ed., *From Chicago to L.A.: Making Sense of Urban Theory* (Thousand Oaks, CA, 2002).

For the impact of the automobile on American cities, see John B. Rae, *The Road and Car in American Life* (Cambridge, MA, 1971); Mark Foster, *From Streetcar to Superhighway: American City Planners and Urban Transportation, 1900–1940* (Philadelphia, 1981); Howard Preston, *Automobile Age Atlanta: The Making of a Southern Metropolis, 1900–1935* (Athens, GA, 1979); Paul Barrett, *The Automobile and Urban Transit: The Formation of Public Policy in Chicago, 1900–1930* (Philadelphia, 1980); Joel Tarr, *Transportation Innovation and Changing Spatial Patterns in Pittsburgh, 1850–1934* (Chicago, 1978); and Scott Bottles, *Los Angeles and the Automobile*

(Berkeley, CA, 1987); Richard Longstreth, *City Center to Regional Mall: Architecture, the Automobile, and Retailing in Los Angeles, 1920–1950* (Cambridge, MA, 1997) and *The Drive-in, the Supermarket, and the Transformation of Commercial Space in Los Angeles, 1914–1941* (Cambridge, MA, 1999). For contrast, the persisting effect of railroad systems on urban form is the subject of John Stilgoe, *Metropolitan Corridor* (New Haven, 1983), and the expansion of mass transit is described in Zachery Schrag, *The Great Society Subway: A History of the Washington Metro* (Baltimore, 2006).

The shaping of townscapes and cityscapes is the topic of Carole Rifkind, *Main Street: The Face of Urban America* (New York, 1977) and Mary Proctor and Bill Matuszeski, *Gritty Cities: A Second Look at Allentown, Bethlehem, Bridgeport, Hoboken, Lancaster, Norwich, Paterson, Reading, Trenton, Troy, Waterbury, and Wilmington* (Philadelphia, 1978). Larry Ford, *Cities and Buildings: Skyscrapers, Skid Rows, and Suburbs* (Baltimore, 1994) is an insightful description of the continuing evolution of distinct districts within cities. John Findlay, *Magic Lands: Western Cityscapes and American Culture after 1940* (Berkeley, CA, 1992) examines the development of new forms for the postwar city.

The evolution of central business districts is detailed in Robert Fogelson, *Downtown: Its Rise and Fall, 1880–1950* (New Haven, 2001) and Alison Isenberg, *Downtown America: A History of the Place and the People Who Made It* (Chicago, 2004). Downtowns as targets of real estate development are discussed in Bernard Frieden and Lynn Sagalyn, *Downtown, Inc.: How America Rebuilds Its Cities* (Cambridge, MA, 1989); Lynn Sagalyn, *Times Square Roulette: Remaking the City Icon* (Cambridge, MA, 2001); Alexander Garvin, *The American City: What Works, What Doesn't* (New York, 1996); Carol Willis, *Form Follows Finance: Skyscrapers and Skylines in New York and Chicago* (New York, 1995); and Janet Daly Bednarek, *The Changing Image of the City: Planning for Downtown Omaha, 1945–73* (Lincoln, NE, 1992).

The development of urban housing is treated in Glendolyn Wright, *Building the Dream: A Social History of Housing in America* (New York, 1981); Anthony Jackson, *A Place Called Home: A History of Low-Cost Housing in Manhattan* (Cambridge, MA, 1976); Dolores

Hayden, *Redesigning the American Dream: The Future of Housing, Work, and Family Life* (New York, 1984); and Charles Abrams, *The City Is the Frontier* (New York, 1965). Gail Radford, *Modern Housing for America: Policy Struggles in the New Deal Era* (Chicago, 1996) examines the origins of public housing policy and Robert Fairbanks, *Making Better Citizens: Housing Reform and the Community Development Strategy in Cincinnati, 1890–1960* (Urbana, IL, 1988) analyzes its applications.

For general historical views of the development of city planning, see Mel Scott, *American City Planning since 1890* (Berkeley, CA, 1969); John Hancock, "Planners in the Changing American City, 1900–1940," *Journal of the American Institute of Planners* 33 (Sept. 1967): 290–304; and Donald Krueckeberg, ed., *Introduction to Planning History in the United States* (New Brunswick, NJ, 1983). Robert Walker, *The Planning Function in Urban Government* (Chicago, 1941) and National Resources Committee, *Urban Planning and Land Policies: Vol. II of Supplementary Report of the Urbanism Committee* (Washington, 1939) depict the status of planning at the start of World War II.

Case studies of planning and development in specific cities include Alan Altshuler, *The City Planning Process* (Ithaca, NY, 1965), on Minneapolis–St. Paul; Carl Abbott, *Portland: Planning, Politics and Growth in a Twentieth Century City* (Lincoln, NE, 1983); Christopher Silver, *Twentieth Century Richmond: Planning, Politics and Race* (Knoxville, TN, 1984); Patricia Burgess, *Planning for the Public Interest: Land Use Controls and Residential Patterns in Columbus, Ohio, 1800–1970* (Columbus, Ohio, 1994); Robert Fairbanks, *For the City as a Whole: Planning, Politics, and the Public Interest in Dallas, Texas, 1900–1965* (Columbus, OH, 1998); Howard Gillette, Jr., *Between Justice and Beauty: Race, Planning and the Failure of Urban Policy in Washington, D.C.* (Baltimore, 1995); and Thomas Hanchett, *Sorting Out the New South City: Race, Class, and Urban Development in Charlotte, 1875–1975* (Chapel Hill, NC, 1998).

The origins and functions of state land use planning systems are covered in Jerry Weitz, *Sprawlbusting: State Programs to Guide Growth* (Chicago, 1999). For specific states and communities see Carl Abbott, Deborah Howe, and Sy Adler, eds., *Planning the Oregon Way:*

A *Twenty Year Evaluation* (Corvallis, OR, 1994); Gerrit Knaap and Arthur C. Nelson, *The Regulated Landscape* (Cambridge, MA, 1992); Connie Ozawa, ed., *The Portland Edge: Challenges and Successes in Growing Communities* (Washington, 2004); and Gregory Squires, ed., *Urban Sprawl: Causes, Consequences, and Policy Responses* (Washington, 2002).

The neighborhood revitalization movement of the 1970s is analyzed in Phillip L. Clay, *Neighborhood Renewal* (Lexington, MA, 1979); Robert Cassidy, *Livable Cities* (New York, 1980); Richard Nathan and Michael Schill, *Revitalizing America's Cities* (Albany, 1983); Shirley Laska and Daphne Spain, *Back to the City: Issues in Neighborhood Renovation* (New York, 1980); Roger S. Ahlbrandt, Jr., and Paul C. Brophy, *Neighborhood Revitalization* (Lexington, MA, 1975); and Sharon Zukin, *Loft Living: Culture and Capital in Urban Change* (Baltimore, 1982). The role of neighborhoods in the social life of modern cities is the subject of Suzanne Keller, *The Urban Neighborhood: A Sociological Perspective* (New York, 1968); Albert Hunter, *Symbolic Communities: The Persistence and Change of Chicago's Local Communities* (Chicago, 1974); and Ida Susser, *Norman Street: Poverty and Politics in an Urban Neighborhood* (New York, 1982). For discussions of neighborhood roles in city politics and government, see Robert Fisher, *Let the People Decide: Neighborhood Organizing in America* (Boston, 1984) and George Frederickson, ed., *Neighborhood Control in the 1970s* (New York, 1973). The community development movement is evaluated in Peter Medoff, *Streets of Hope: The Fall and Rise of an Urban Neighborhood* (Boston, 1994) and Randy Stoecker, *Defending Community: The Struggle for Alternative Development in Cedar-Riverside* (Philadelphia, 1994).

Suburbs and Suburbanization

The baseline of information on suburban patterns at the start of the automobile era can be established from Harlan P. Douglass, *The Suburban Trend* (New York, 1925) and Chauncy Harris, "Suburbs," *American Journal of Sociology* 49 (July 1943): 1–13. Historical perspective on the evolution of twentieth-century suburbs can be found in Kenneth T. Jackson, *Crabgrass Frontier* (New York, 1985). Studies of individual suburbs include Carol O'Connor, *A Sort of Utopia: Scars-*

dale, 1891–1981 (Albany, NY, 1982) and Zane Miller, *Suburb: Neighborhood and Community in Forest Park, Ohio, 1935–76* (Knoxville, 1982). In contrast to the image of white middle class suburbia are the findings of Andrew Wiese, *Places of Their Own: African American Suburbanization in the Twentieth Century* (Chicago, 2004) and Becky Nicolaides, *My Blue Heaven: Life and Politics in the Working Class Suburbs of Los Angeles* (Chicago, 2002).

Experiments with planned suburbs in the 1920s and 1930s are the topic of Roy Lubove, *Community Planning in the 1920s: The Contribution of the Regional Planning Association of America* (Pittsburgh, 1963); Joseph Arnold, *The New Deal in the Suburbs: A History of the Greenbelt Town Program, 1935–54* (Columbus, OH, 1971); Daniel Schaffer, *Garden Cities for America: The Radburn Experience* (Philadelphia, 1980); and Cathy Knepper, *Greenbelt Maryland: A Living Legacy of the New Deal* (Baltimore, 2001).

Postwar suburban society was probed in William H. Whyte, *The Organization Man* (New York, 1954) and Maurice Stein, *The Eclipse of Community* (Princeton, NJ, 1960). Leo Schnore, *The Urban Scene: Human Ecology and Demography* (New York, 1965) analyzes the postwar shift of population from city to suburbs. Two of the most prominent of the new suburbs are the subject of Barbara Kelly, *Expanding the American Dream: Building and Rebuilding Levittown* (Albany, NY, 1993) and Gregory Randall, *America's Original G. I. Town: Park Forest, Illinois* (Baltimore, 2000). Greg Hise, *Magnetic Los Angeles: Planning the Twentieth Century Metropolis* (Baltimore, 1997) examines the building of Los Angeles suburbs such as Lakewood, which is also the subject of D. J. Waldie, *Holy Land: A Suburban Memoir* (New York, 1996). Lizabeth Cohen, *A Consumer's Republic: The Politics of Mass Consumption in Postwar America* (New York, 2003), places suburban development in the broad context of cultural change.

In the 1960s, negative evaluations of postwar suburbs gave way to a more balanced view represented in studies such as William Dobriner, *Class in Suburbia* (Englewood Cliffs, NJ, 1963); Herbert Gans, *The Levittowners: Ways of Life and Politics in a New Suburban Community* (New York, 1967); Bennett Berger, *Working Class Suburb* (Berkeley, CA, 1968); and Scott Donaldson, *The Suburban Myth* (New York, 1969).

By the 1970s, it was clear that many suburban areas were losing their dependence on central cities. See especially Louis Masotti and Jeffrey Hadden, eds., *The Urbanization of the Suburbs* (Beverly Hills, CA, 1973) and Peter Muller, *Contemporary Suburban America* (Englewood Cliffs, NJ, 1981). Joel Garreau extended and popularized these insights in *Edge City: Life on the New Frontier* (New York, 1991). Recent examinations of metropolitan settlement patterns are Anne Vernez Moudon and Paul Hess, "Suburban Clusters: The Nucleation of Multifamily Housing in Suburban Areas of the Central Puget Sound," *Journal of the American Planning Association* 66 (Summer 2000): 243–64; Peter Gordon and Harry Richardson, "Beyond Polycentricity: The Dispersed Metropolis," *Journal of the American Planning Association* 62 (1996): 289–95; Robert Lang, *Edgeless Cities: Exploring the Elusive Metropolis* (Washington, 2003); and Bruce Katz and Robert Lang, *Redefining Urban and Suburban America* (Washington, 2003).

Suburban politics are discussed in Robert Wood, *Suburbia: Its People and Their Politics* (Boston, 1958) and *1400 Governments: The Political Economy of the New York Metropolitan Region* (Cambridge, MA, 1961); Frederick Wirt et al., *On the City's Rim: Politics and Power in Suburbia* (Lexington, MA, 1972); and Charles Haar, ed., *Report of the President's Task Force on Suburban Problems* (Cambridge, MA, 1974).

Efforts to establish metropolitan government institutions in the 1950s and 1960s are discussed in Edward Sofen, *The Miami Metropolitan Experiment* (Bloomington, IN, 1963); Brett Hawkins, *Nashville Metro: The Politics of City-County Consolidation* (Nashville, 1966); David Temple, *Merger Politics: Local Government Consolidation in Tidewater Virginia* (Charlottesville, VA, 1972); Scott Greer, *Metropolitics: A Study of Political Culture* (New York, 1963); and Jon C. Teaford, *City and Suburb: The Political Fragmentation of Metropolitan America, 1850–1970* (Baltimore, 1979).

The planning and construction of "New Towns" in the 1960s and 1970s is discussed in Gurney Breckenfeld, *Columbia and the New Cities* (Washington, 1971); William H. Whyte, *The Last Landscape* (Garden City, NY, 1968); Frederick Steiner, *The Politics of New Town Planning: The Newfields, Ohio, Story* (Athens, OH, 1981); Martha

Derthick, *New Towns In-Town* (Washington, 1972); Judith Martin, *Recycling the Central City: The Development of a New Town-In Town* (Minneapolis, 1978); Joshua Olsen, *Better Places, Better Lives: A Biography of James Rouse* (Washington, 2003); Nicholas Dagen Bloom, *Suburban Alchemy: 1960s New Towns and the Transformation of the American Dream* (Columbus, OH, 2001); and Ann Forsyth, *Reforming Suburbia: The Planned Communities of Irvine, Columbia, and The Woodlands* (Berkeley, CA, 2005).

African Americans

For many Americans, Harlem symbolized the African American urban experience in the decades between the world wars. Its development can be traced in Gilbert Osofsky, *Harlem: The Making of a Ghetto (New York, 1966),* Nathan Huggins, *The Harlem Renaissance* (New York, 1971); David L. Lewis, *When Harlem Was in Vogue* (New York, 1981); and Jervis Anderson, *This Was Harlem: A Cultural Portrait, 1900–1950* (New York, 1981).

Leading works on ghetto formation and evolution in Middle Western cities include Kenneth Kusmar, *A Ghetto Takes Shape: Black Cleveland, 1870–1930* (Urbana, IL, 1976); St. Clair Drake and Horace Cayton, *Black Metropolis: A Study of Negro Life in a Northern City* (New York, 1945); Thomas Philpott, *The Slum and the Ghetto: Neighborhood Deterioration and Middle Class Reform, Chicago, 1880–1930* (New York, 1978); Chicago Commission on Race Relations, *The Negro in Chicago* (Chicago, 1922); and David Allan Levine, *Internal Combustion: The Races in Detroit, 1915–1926* (Westport, CT, 1976).

Violence during and after World War I is the subject of William Tuttle, *Race Riot: Chicago in the Red Summer of 1919* (New York, 1970); Elliott Rudwick, *Race Riot at East St. Louis, July 2, 1917* (Carbondale, IL, 1964); and Scott Ellsworth, *Death in the Promised Land: The Tulsa Race Riot of 1921* (Baton Rouge, LA, 1982). Rioting during World War II is treated in Dominic J. Capeci, Jr., *The Harlem Riot of 1943* (Philadelphia, 1977) and, on Detroit, Alfred Lee and Norman Hum-phrey, *Race Riot* (New York, 1943).

Robert Weaver, *The Negro Ghetto* (New York, 1948); Kenneth Clark, *Dark Ghetto: Dilemmas of Social Power* (New York, 1965) and Harold Rose, *The Black Ghetto* (New York, 1971) are valuable general treatments of the black community after World War II.

Electoral and interest-group politics are treated in Harold Gosnell, *Negro Politicians: The Rise of Negro Politics in Chicago* (Chicago, 1935); James Q. Wilson, *Negro Politics* (Glencoe, IL, 1960); Jewell Belush and Stephen David, *Race and Politics in New York City* (New York, 1971); Arvah Strickland, *History of the Chicago Urban League* (Urbana, IL, 1966); Paul Kleppner, *Chicago Divided: The Making of a Black Mayor* (DeKalb, IL, 1985); and Pierre Clavel and Wim Wievel, eds., *Harold Washington and the Neighborhoods* (New Brunswick, NJ, 1991).

Race and neighborhood are the central theme in C. S. Johnson, *Patterns of Negro Segregation* (New York, 1943); Arnold Hirsch, *Making the Second Ghetto: Race and Housing in Chicago, 1940–1960* (New York, 1983); Edward Banfield and Martin Meyerson, *Planning, Politics, and the Public Interest: The Case of Public Housing in Chicago* (Glencoe, IL, 1955); Harvey Molotch, *Managed Integration: The Dilemmas of Doing Good in the City* (Berkeley, CA, 1972); Richard Elman, *Ill-At-Ease in Compton* (New York, 1967); and Karl Taeuber and Alma Taeuber, *Negroes in American Cities: Residential Segregation and Neighborhood Change* (Chicago, 1965).

The racial violence of the 1960s is analyzed in Robert Fogelson, *Violence as Protest: A Study of Riots and Ghettos* (Garden City, NY, 1971); Joseph Boskin, "The Revolt of the Urban Ghettos, 1964–67," *Annals of the American Academy of Political and Social Science* 382 (March 1969): 1–14; Morris Janowitz, "Patterns of Collective Racial Violence," in Hugh Davis Graham and Ted Robert Gun, eds., *Violence in America* (Washington, 1969); National Advisory Commission on Civil Disorders (Kerner Commission), *Report* (New York, 1968).

The impact of the civil rights movement on southern cities can be followed in William Chafe, *Civilities and Civil Rights: Greensboro, North Carolina and the Black Struggle for Freedom* (New York, 1980); Elizabeth Jacoway and David Colburn, eds., *Southern Businessmen and Desegregation* (Baton Rouge, LA, 1982); and Robert A. Goldberg, "Racial Change in the Southern Periphery: The Case of San Antonio, Texas, 1960–65," *Journal of Southern History* 49 (August 1983): 349–74. David Colburn, *Racial Change and Community Crisis: St. Augus-*

tine, Florida, 1877–1980 (New York, 1985) also focuses on the civil rights campaign of the 1960s.

The texture and character of aspects of African American life in the postwar decades are described in both positive and negative terms in Carol Stack, *All Our Kin: Strategies for Survival in a Black Community* (New York, 1974); Elijah Anderson, *Streetwise: Race, Class and Change in an Urban Community* (Chicago, 1990); Nicholas Lemann, *Promised Land: The Great Black Migration and How It Changed America* (New York, 1991); J. S. Fuerst, *When Public Housing Was Paradise: Building Community in Chicago* (2005); and Sudhir Venkatesh, *American Project: The Rise and Fall of a Modern Ghetto* (Cambridge, MA, 2001).

Early trends toward greater housing integration are analyzed in Harold Rose, *Black Suburbanization* (Cambridge, MA, 1976); Robert Lake, *The New Suburbanites: Race and Housing* (New Brunswick, NJ, 1981); Thomas A. Clark, *Blacks in Suburbia: A National Perspective* (New Brunswick, NJ, 1979); and Larry Ford and Ernest Griffin, "The Ghettoization of Paradise," *Geographical Review* 69 (1979): 140–58. The countervailing problems of suburban housing discrimination are the subject of Anthony Downs, *Opening Up the Suburbs* (New Haven, CT, 1973) and Michael Danielson, *The Politics of Exclusion* (New York, 1976).

Earl Lewis, *In Their Own Interests: Race, Class and Power in Twentieth Century Norfolk, Virginia* (Berkeley, CA, 1991), Joe William Trotter, Jr., *Black Milwaukee: The Making of an Industrial Proletariat, 1915–45* (Urbana, IL, 1985), and Matthew Whitaker, *Race Work* (Lincoln, NE, 2005), emphasize self-determination and agency of black communities.

African American experiences in western cities are the subject of Shirley Ann Wilson Moore, *To Place Our Deeds: The African American Community in Richmond, California, 1910–1963* (Berkeley, CA, 2000); Josh Sides, *LA City Limits: African American Los Angeles from the Depression to the Present* (Berkeley, CA, 2003); Douglas Flamming, *Bound for Freedom: Black Los Angeles in Jim Crow America* (Berkeley, CA, 2005); Mark Wild, *Street Meeting: Multiethnic Neighborhoods in Early 20th Century Los Angeles* (Berkeley, CA, 2005); Gretchen Lemke-Santangelo, *Abiding Courage: African American*

Women and the East Bay Community (Chapel Hill, NC, 1996); and Quintard Taylor, *The Forging of a Black Community: Seattle's Central District from 1870 through the Civil Rights Era* (Seattle, 1999).

New Immigrants

General treatments of recent immigration include Alejandro Portes and Ruben G. Rumbaut, *Immigrant America* (Berkeley, CA, 1996); David Reimers, *Still the Golden Door: The Third World Comes to America* (New York, 1985); and Thomas Kessner and Betty Boyd Caroli, *Today's Immigrants* (New York, 1981).

Mexican Americans as an urban minority are discussed in Leo Grebler et al., *The Mexican-American People* (New York, 1970) and Franklin J. James, *Minorities in the Sunbelt* (New Brunswick, NJ, 1984). Ricardo Romo, *East Los Angeles: History of a Barrio* (Austin, TX, 1983); George Sanchez, *Becoming Mexican American: Ethnicity, Culture and Identity in Chicano Los Angeles, 1900–1945* (New York, 1993); and Douglas Monroy, *Rebirth: Mexican Los Angeles from the Great Migration to the Great Depression* (Berkeley, CA 1999) examines the evolution of the nation's largest Mexican American community. Edward Escobar, *Race, Police, and the Making of a Political Identity: Mexican Americans and the Los Angeles Police Department, 1900–1945* (Berkeley, CA, 1999) and Jose Obregon Pagan, *Murder at Sleepy Lagoon: Zoot Suits, Race, and Riot in Wartime Los Angeles* (Chapel Hill, NC, 2003) deal with the problems of discriminatory law enforcement.

Asian Americans are discussed in John Modell, *The Economics and Politics of Racial Accommodation: The Japanese of Los Angeles, 1900–1942* (Urbana, IL, 1977); Leland Saito, *Race and Politics: Asian Americans, Latinos, and Whites in a Los Angeles Suburb* (Urbana, IL, 1998); Hong Chen, *Chinese San Francisco: A Trans-Pacific Community, 1850–1943* (Stanford, 2000); Lon Kurashige, *Japanese American Celebration and Conflict: A History of Ethnic Identity and Festivals in Los Angeles* (Berkeley, CA, 2002); and Peter Kwong, *Chinatown: Labor and Politics, 1930–1950* (New York, 1979) and *The New Chinatown* (New York, 1987).

For immigrants from the Caribbean region, see Thomas D. Bosell and James R. Curtis, *The Cuban-American Experience: Culture, Im-*

ages and Perspectives (Totowa, NJ, 1984); Joseph Fitzpatrick, *Puerto Rican Americans* (Englewood Cliffs, NJ, 1971); Roy Bryce-Laporte and Delores Mortimer, eds., *Caribbean Immigration to the United States* (Washington, 1983); Glenn Hendricks, *The Dominican Diaspora* (New York, 1974); and Alejandro Portes and Alec Stepick, *City on the Edge: The Transformation of Miami* (Berkeley, CA, 1993).

Beyond the Melting Pot

European ethnic groups in the twentieth century city are the subject of Humbert Nelli, *Italians in Chicago, 1880–1930: A Study in Ethnic Mobility* (New York, 1970); Josef Barton, *Peasants and Strangers: Italians, Rumanians, and Slovaks in an American City, 1890–1950* (Cambridge, MA, 1975); John Bodnar, *Immigration and Industrialization: Ethnicity in an American Mill Town, 1870–1940* (Pittsburgh, 1977); and Edward R. Kantowicz, *Polish-American Politics in Chicago, 1888–1940* (Chicago, 1975). Stephen Thernstrom, *The Other Bostonians: Poverty and Progress in the American Metropolis, 1880–1970* (Cambridge, MA, 1973) and John Bodnar, Roger Simon, and Michael P. Weber, *Lives of Their Own: Blacks, Italians, and Poles in Pittsburgh, 1900–1960* (Urbana, IL, 1982) compare the experience of urban migrants and populations across racial categories. Gerald Suttles, *The Social Order of the Slum: Ethnicity and Territory in the Inner City* (Chicago, 1968), examines the internal dynamics of a multiracial community on the West Side of Chicago. Also see John T. McGreevy, *Parish Boundaries: The Catholic Encounter with Race in the Twentieth-Century Urban North* (Chicago, 1996) and Wendell Pritchett, *Brownsville, Brooklyn: Blacks, Jews, and the Changing Face of the Ghetto* (Chicago, 2003).

Daniel P. Moynihan and Nathan Glazer remind us of the survival of ethnic identities in *Beyond the Melting Pot: The Negroes, Puerto Ricans, Jews, Irish, and Italians of New York City* (Cambridge, MA, 1963). The ethnic city after 1950 is also the subject of Herbert Gans, *The Urban Villagers* (New York, 1962); it is treated in Richard Krickus, *Pursuing the American Dream: White Ethnics and the New Populism* (Garden City, NY, 1976) and Andrew Greeley, *Why Can't They Be Like Us? America's White Ethnic Groups* (New York, 1971). The crisis of school integration in Boston is examined in J. Anthony Lukas,

Common Ground: A Turbulent Decade in the Lives of Three American Families (New York, 1985) and Ronald Formisano, *Boston against Busing: Race, Class, and Ethnicity in the 1960s and 1970s* (Chapel Hill, NC, 1991).

Appalachian migrants to the Middle West are discussed in William Philliber and Clyde McCoy, eds., *The Invisible Minority: Urban Appalachians* (Lexington, KY, 1984); William Philliber, *Appalachian Migrants in Urban America: Cultural Conflict or Ethnic Group Formation* (New York, 1981); and Todd Gitlin and Nanci Hollander, *Uptown: Poor Whites in Chicago* (New York, 1970).

Lizabeth Cohen, *Making a New Deal: Industrial Workers in Chicago, 1919–39* (New York, 1990) offers an influential interpretation that links work life, community life, and ethnic politics. The texture of working class life is also the subject of Mary Murphy, *Mining Cultures: Men, Women and Leisure in Butte, 1914–41* (Urbana, IL, 1997); Laurie Mercier, *Anaconda: Labor, Community and Culture in Montana's Smelter City* (Urbana, IL, 2001); Julia Blackwelder, *Women of the Depression: Caste and Culture in San Antonio, 1929–39* (College Station, TX, 1984); and John Cumbler, *A Social History of Economic Decline: Business, Politics and Work in Trenton* (New Brunswick, NJ, 1989).

The Federal Government and Public Policy

The changing outlines of the federal role in urban policy are traced in Mark Gelfand, *A Nation of Cities: The Federal Government and Urban America, 1933–65* (New York, 1975) and Daniel Elazar, "Urban Problems and the Federal Government," *Political Science Quarterly* 82 (Dec. 1967): 505–25.

Urban affairs in the Great Depression are explored in Charles Trout, *Boston, the Great Depression, and the New Deal* (New York, 1977); August Meier and Elliott Rudwick, *Black Detroit and the Rise of the UAW* (New York, 1979); Sidney Fine, *Frank Murphy: The Detroit Years* (Ann Arbor, MI, 1975); William Mullins, *The Depression and the Urban West Coast* (Bloomington, IN, 1991); and Jo Ann Argersinger, *Toward a New Deal in Baltimore: People and Government in the Great Depression* (Chapel Hill, NC, 1988). The invaluable contemporary document is the National Resources Planning Committee, *Our Cities: Their Role in the National Economy* (Washington, 1977).

For the urban impact of World War II, see Phillip Funigello, *The Challenge to Urban Liberalism: Federal-City Relations during World War II* (Knoxville, TN, 1978); Charles W. Johnson and Charles O. Jackson, *City Behind a Fence: Oak Ridge, Tennessee, 1942–46* (Knoxville, TN, 1981); Gerald Nash, *The American West Transformed: The Impact of the Second World War* (Bloomington, IN, 1985); Roger Lotchin, ed., *The Martial Metropolis: American Cities in War and Peace* (New York, 1984); Roger Lotchin, *The Bad City in the Good War: San Francisco, Los Angeles, Oakland, and San Diego* (Bloomington, IN, 2003); Marilynn Johnson, *The Second Gold Rush: Oakland and the East Bay in World War II* (Berkeley, CA, 1993); Wesley Newton, *Montgomery in the Good War* (Tuscaloosa, AL, 2000); and Beth Bailey and David Farber, *The First Strange Place: The Alchemy of Race and Sex in World War II Hawaii* (Baltimore, 1994).

The policy and impacts of urban renewal are analyzed in Scott Greer, *Urban Renewal and American Cities* (Indianapolis, IN, 1965); Peter Rossi and Robert Dentler, *The Politics of Urban Renewal* (New York, 1961); Martin Anderson, *The Federal Bulldozer* (Cambridge, MA, 1964); James Q. Wilson, ed., *Urban Renewal: The Record and the Controversy* (Cambridge, MA, 1966); Leo Adde, *Nine Cities: The Anatomy of Urban Renewal* (Washington, 1969); Herbert Gans, "The Failure of Urban Renewal," *Commentary* (April 1965): 29–37; and Jon Teaford, *The Rough Road to Renaissance: Urban Revitalization in America, 1940–1985* (Baltimore, 1990).

The dimensions of the urban crisis of the 1960s are defined in Michael Harrington, *The Other America: Poverty in the United States* (New York, 1962); *The Editors of Fortune, The Exploding Metropolis* (Garden City, NY, 1958); James Q. Wilson, ed., *The Metropolitan Enigma* (Cambridge, MA, 1968); and Jeanne Lowe, *Cities in a Race with Time* (New York, 1967). Two very influential interpretations of the deep roots of urban inequality and political conflict are Thomas Sugrue, *The Origins of the Urban Crisis: Race and Inequality in Postwar Detroit* (Princeton, NJ, 1996) and Robert Self, *American Babylon: Race and the Struggle for Postwar Oakland* (Princeton, NJ, 2002).

Early efforts to provide social services are the subject of a collection of documents by David Rothman and Sheila Rothman, eds., *On Their Own: The Poor in Modern America* (Reading, MA, 1972) and of Clarke Chambers, *Seedtime of Reform: American Social Service and Social Action, 1918–33* (Minneapolis, 1963). Social service programs in the 1960s are discussed in Richard Coward and Francis Fox Given, *Regulating the Poor* (New York, 1971); Bernard Frieden and Marshall Kaplan, *The Politics of Neglect: Urban Aid from Model Cities to Revenue Sharing* (Cambridge, MA, 1975); and Daniel P. Moynihan, *Maximum Feasible Misunderstanding: Community Action in the War on Poverty* (New York, 1969). Inequities and inequalities in the allocation of public services within cities are analyzed in Frank S. Levy, Arnold J. Maltster, and Aaron Wildavsky, *Urban Outcomes: Schools, Streets, and Libraries* (Berkeley, CA, 1974) and Robert Lineberry, *Equality and Urban Policy: The Distribution of Municipal Services* (Beverly Hills, CA, 1977).

Galen Cranz, *The Politics of Park Design* (Cambridge, MA, 1982) and Martin Melosi, *Garbage in the Cities: Refuse, Reform and the Environment, 1880–1980* (College Station, TX, 1982) examine the provision of physical services to urban residents. For the federal role in transportation, see Mark Rose, *Interstate: Express Highway Politics, 1941–56* (Lawrence, KS, 1979). The popular revolt against urban freeway construction is described in Alan Lupo, Frank Colcord, and Edmund Fowler, *Rites of Way: The Politics of Transportation in Boston and the U.S. City* (Boston, 1971); Richard O. Baumbach, Jr., and William E. Borah, *The Second Battle of New Orleans: A History of the Vieux Carre Riverfront Expressway Controversy* (University, AL, 1981); Helen Leavitt, *Superhighway-Superhoax* (New York, 1971); and Richard Hebert, *Highways to Nowhere: The Politics of City Transportation* (New York, 1972). Jane Holtz Kay updates the indictment of the automobile in *Asphalt Nation* (New York, 1997).

Redefinitions of the urban crisis for the political climate of the 1970s and 1980s are found in Edward Banfield, *The Unheavenly City* (Boston, 1968) and William Julius Wilson, *The Truly Disadvantaged* (Chicago, 1987). Recent analyses of economic and demographic data from a progressive perspective are found in Douglas Massey and Nancy Denton, *American Apartheid: Segregation and the Making of the*

Underclass (Cambridge, MA, 1993); Paul Jargowsky, *Poverty and Place: Ghettos, Barrios, and the American City* (New York, 1997); John Yinger, *Closed Doors, Opportunities Lost: The Continuing Costs of Housing Discrimination* (New York, 1995); and Peter Dreier, Todd Swanstrom and John Mollenkopf, *Place Matters: Metropolitics for the Twenty-First Century* (Lawrence, KS, 2004).

Municipal Politics

General patterns in municipal politics are described for the 1920s and 1930s in Roger Lotchin, "Power and Policy: American City Politics between the Two World Wars," in Scott Greer, ed., *Ethnics, Machines and the American Urban Future* (Cambridge, MA, 1981) and for the 1950s in Edward Banfield and James Q. Wilson, *City Politics* (Cambridge, MA, 1963).

Politics in the multiethnic city between the world wars is the subject for Arthur Mann, *La Guardia: Fighter against His Times* (Philadelphia, 1959) and *La Guardia Comes to Power* (Philadelphia, 1965); Oscar Handlin, *Al Smith and His America* (Boston, 1958); J. Joseph Huthmacher, *Senator Robert Wagner and the Rise of Urban Liberalism* (New York, 1968), *Massachusetts People and Politics, 1919–1933* (Cambridge, MA, 1959); and "Urban Liberalism and the Age of Reform," *Journal of American History* 49 (Sept. 1962): 231–41; Ronald Bayor, *Neighbors in Conflict: The Irish, Germans, Jews, and Italians of New York City, 1929–41* (Baltimore, 1978); and Samuel Lubell, *The Future of American Politics* (New York, 1952).

Political bosses and the machine system in the twentieth century are analyzed in Harold Gosnell, *Machine Politics: Chicago Model* (Chicago, 1937); Alex Gottfried, *Boss Cermak of Chicago: A Study of Political Leadership* (Seattle, 1962); Roger Biles, *Big City Boss in Depression and War: Edward J. Kelly of Chicago* (DeKalb, IL, 1984); Lyle Dorsett, *The Pendergast Machine* (New York, 1968); Bruce Stave, *The New Deal and the Last Hurrah: Pittsburgh Machine Politics* (Pittsburgh, 1970); Mike Royko, *Boss: Richard J. Daley of Chicago* (New York, 1971); Roger Biles, *Richard J. Daley: Politics, Race, and the Governing of Chicago* (DeKalb, IL, 1995); and William Miller, *Mr. Crump of Memphis* (Baton Rouge, LA, 1964).

The growth-oriented politics of the 1950s and 1960s are theorized in Harvey Molotch and John Logan, *Urban Fortunes* (Berkeley, CA, 1987) and described in John Mollenkopf, *The Contested City* (Princeton, NJ, 1983); Frederick Wirt, *Power and the City* (Berkeley, CA, 1975); Robert Dahl, *Who Governs? Democracy and Power in an American City* (New Haven, 1961); Lorin Peterson, *The Day of the Mugwump* (New York, 1961); Edward Haas, *De Lesseps S. Morrison and the Image of Reform: New Orleans Politics, 1946–61* (Baton Rouge, LA, 1974); and Roy Lubove, *Twentieth Century Pittsburgh: Government, Business and Environmental Change* (New York, 1969). Robert Caro, *The Power Broker: Robert Moses and the Fall of New York* (New York, 1974) details the career of a bureaucratic entrepreneur who flourished in the political climate of the 1940s and 1950s; his interpretation is critiqued in Joel Schwartz, *The New York Approach: Robert Moses, Urban Liberals, and the Redevelopment of the Inner City* (Columbus, Ohio, 1993). For more recent New York politics, see John Mollelkopf, *A Phoenix in the Ashes: The Rise and Fall of the Koch Coalition in New York City Politics* (Princeton, NJ, 1992).

For the other side of the continent, Leonard Goodall, ed., *Urban Politics in the Southwest* (Tempe, AZ, 1967) and Richard Bernard and Bradley Rice, eds., *Sunbelt Cities: Politics and Growth since World War II* (Austin, TX, 1983) are collections of essays on the politics of various sunbelt cities. Amy Bridges, *Morning Glories: Municipal Reform in the Southwest* (Princeton, NJ, 1997) is comprehensive and insightful. Michael Logan, *Fighting Sprawl and City Hall* (Tucson, 1995); Stephen McGovern, *The Politics of Downtown Development* (Lexington, KY, 1998); and Richard DeLeon, *Left Coast City: Progressive Politics in San Francisco, 1975–91* (Lawrence, KS, 1992) explore political resistance to downtown development coalitions.

Studies of politics in individual sunbelt cities include David R. Johnson et al., *The Politics of San Antonio* (Lincoln, NE, 1983); for Houston, Chandler Davidson, *Biracial Politics: Conflict and Coalition in the Metropolitan South* (Baton Rouge, LA, 1973); David Tucker, *Memphis since Crump: Bossism, Blacks, and Civic Reform, 1948–68* (Knoxville, TN, 1980); Anthony Orum, *Power, Money, and the People: The Making of Modern Austin* (Austin, TX, 1987); Raphael Sonenshein, *Politics in Black and White: Race and Power in Los Angeles* (Princeton, NJ, 1993); and, for San Jose, Philip J. Trounstine and Terry

Christensen, *Movers and Shakers: The Study of Community Power* (New York, 1982). Atlanta politics and decision making have received special attention from Floyd Hunter, *Community Power Structure* (Chapel Hill, NC, 1953) and *Community Power Succession: Atlanta's Policy Makers* (Chapel Hill, NC, 1980); M. Kent Jennings, *Community Influentials: The Elites of Atlanta* (New York, 1964); Clarence Stone, *Economic Growth and Neighborhood Discontent: System Bias in the Urban Renewal Program of Atlanta* (Chapel Hill, NC, 1976); and Ronald Bayor, *Race and the Shaping of Twentieth Century Atlanta* (Chapel Hill, NC, 1996).

Lisa McGirr, *Suburban Warriors: The Origins of the New American Right* (Princeton, NJ, 2001) examines the development of Orange County, California, as a stronghold of conservative politics.

New Economies

Roger Lotchin, *Fortress California: From Warfare to Welfare, 1910–1962* (New York, 1992) is a richly detailed study of the role of the military budget in urban development. Ann Markusen, Peter Hall, Scott Campbell, and Sabina Deitrick, *The Rise of the Gunbelt* (New York, 1991) carries the story forward.

Margaret O'Mara, *Cities of Knowledge: Cold War Science and the Search for the Next Silicon Valley* (Princeton, NJ, 2005) and Annalee Saxenian, *Regional Advantage: Culture and Competition in Silicon Valley and Route 128* (Cambridge, MA, 1994) examine the origins and growth of Silicon Valley and competing efforts to build a high-tech economy. Glenna Matthews, *Silicon Valley, Women, and the California Dream* (Stanford, 2003) uncovers the social dimension of Silicon Valley's evolution.

The role of amenities and recreation on economic development is discussed in Harvey Newman, *Southern Hospitality: Tourism is the Growth of Atlanta* (Tuscaloosa, AL, 1999); Matthew J. Burbank, Gregory D. Andranovitch, and Charles Heying, *Olympic Dreams: The Impact of Mega-Events on Local Politics* (Boulder, 2001); and Richard Florida, *The Rise of the Creative Class* (New York, 2002).

Saskia Sassen, *The Global City: New York, London, Tokyo* (New York, 1991) is a key statement on the nature and implications of world cities. Comparative studies and planning and policy in world cities include Robert Beauregard, *Atop the Urban Hierarchy* (Totowa, NJ, 1989); Susan Fainstein, *The City Builders: Property Development in New York and London, 1980–2000* (Cambridge, MA, 1994); H. V. Savitch, *Post-Industrial Cities: Politics and Planning in New York, Paris, and London* (Princeton, NJ, 1988); Rosebeth Moss Kanter, *World Class: Thriving Locally in the Global Economy* (New York, 1995); and Carl Abbott, *Political Terrain: Washington, D.C., from Tidewater Town to Global Metropolis* (Chapel Hill, NC, 1999).

The Urban Physical Environment

The impact of urban growth on the natural environment is an increasingly popular historical topic. Key analyses include Adam Rome, *The Bulldozer in the Countryside: Suburban Sprawl and the Rise of American Environmentalism* (New York, 2001); Martin Melosi, *The Sanitary City* (Baltimore, 2000); and Robert Bullard, *Dumping in Dixie: Class, Race, and Environmental Quality* (Boulder, 1990).

Books dealing with individual cities include Joel Tarr, ed., *Devastation and Renewal: An Environmental History of Pittsburgh and Its Region* (Pittsburgh, 2003); Matthew Gandy, *Concrete and Clay: Reworking Nature in New York City* (Cambridge, MA, 2002); Sarah Elkind, *Bay Cities and Water Politics: The Battle for Resources in Boston and Oakland* (Lawrence, KS, 1998); Char Miller, *On the Border: An Environmental History of San Antonio* (Pittsburgh, 2001); Michael Logan, *The Lessening Stream: An Environmental History of the Santa Cruz River* (Tucson, 2002); Jared Orsi, *Hazardous Metropolis: Flooding and Urban Ecology in Los Angeles* (Berkeley, CA, 2004); Blake Gumprecht, *The Los Angeles River: Its Life, Death, and Possible Rebirth* (Baltimore, 2001); Mike Davis, *The Ecology of Fear: Los Angeles and the Imagination of Disaster* (New York, 1998); William Deverell and Greg Hise, eds., *Land of Sunshine: An Environmental History of Metropolitan Los Angeles* (Pittsburgh, 2005).

Thinking About Cities

For contrasting attitudes toward the new urban world of the 1920s, see Blaine Brownell, *The Urban Ethos in the New South, 1920–1930*

(Baton Rouge, LA, 1975) and Kenneth T. Jackson, *The Ku Klux Klan in the City: 1915–1930* (New York, 1967).

The construction of the Los Angeles image is a sprawling topic in itself. See William Deverell, *Whitewashed Adobe: The Rise of Los Angeles and the Remaking of Its Mexican Past* (Berkeley, CA, 2004); Mike Davis, *City of Quartz: Excavating the Future in Los Angeles* (New York, 1990); and Eric Avila, *Popular Culture in the Age of White Flight: Fear and Fantasy in Suburban Los Angeles* (Berkeley, CA, 2004).

Morton White and Lucia White, *The Intellectuals versus the City* (Cambridge, MA, 1962) and Park Dixon Goist, *From Main Street to State Street: Town, City, and Community in America* (Port Washington, NY, 1977) describe evolving attitudes toward urbanization among intellectuals and social scientists.

The twentieth-century United States has also produced a number of visionary statements about the future of American cities. For the ideas of Frank Lloyd Wright, see Wright, *The Living City* (New York, 1958) and Robert Fishman, *Urban Utopias in the Twentieth Century* (New York, 1978). Representative works of Lewis Mumford are *The Culture of Cities* (New York, 1938), *The Highway and the City* (New York, 1963), and *The Urban Prospect* (New York, 1968). Other key works of urban theory are Paul Goodman and Percival Goodman, *Communitas: Means of Livelihood and Ways of Life* (New York, 1947); and Jane Jacobs, *The Death and Life of Great American Cities* (New York, 1961) and *Cities and the Wealth of Nations* (New York, 1984).

Key discussions of the New Urbanism include Peter Calthorpe and William Fulton, *The Regional City* (Washington, 2001); Andres Duany, Elizabeth Plater-Zyberk, and Jeff Speck, *Suburban Nation: The Rise of Sprawl and the Decline of the American Dream* (New York, 2001); Peter Katz, *The New Urbanism: Toward an Architecture of Community* (New York, 1994); and Philip Langdon, *A Better Place to Live: Reshaping the American Suburbs* (Amherst, MA, 1994). James Howard Kunstler, *The Geography of Nowhere* (New York, 1993) is a scathing critique of late twentieth-century development patterns while F. Kaid Benfield et al., *Once There Were Greenfields: How Urban Sprawl is Undermining America's Environment, Economy, and Social Fabric* (Washington, 1999), is a more balanced, data-based discussion despite its title.

Aspects of political and economic regionalism are advocated and evaluated in Myron Orfield, *Metropolitics: A Regional Agenda for Community and Stability* (Washington, 1997); David Rusk, *Cities without Suburbs* (Washington, 1993) and *Inside Game/Outside Game: Winning Strategies for Saving Urban America* (Washington, 1999); Anthony Downs, *New Futures for Metropolitan America* (Washington, 1994); and Neal Peirce, *CitiStates: How Urban America Can Prosper in a Competitive World* (Washington, 1993).

INDEX

Note: Italicized page numbers indicate figures and tables.

African Americans: cultural life of, 35, 162; desegregation rollbacks and, 168; disenfranchisement of, 73–74; ghettoes and, 27, 30–35; housing issues and, 38, 41, 70–73, 125; job opportunities for, 70; migration of, 7, 27–30, 58, 68, 125; neighborhoods of, 86; police abuse of, 164–65; political power of, 131–33; 1970s immigrants and, 104; whites' exclusion of, 29–35. *See also* racial violence

agriculture, 27

AIP (American Institute of Planners), 51, 52

airplanes and aviation industry, 55–58, 141, 148

Akron: tire industry in, 11

Alabama Dry Dock Company, 59

Albany: attractions of, 148

Albuquerque: attractions of, 148; city council district in, 132; political pluralism in, 146; postwar political and civic reform in, 78

Allegheny Conference on Community Development, 75–76

Altshuler, Alan, 175

Amalgamated Clothing Workers, 35

American City and County (magazine), 155

American Institute of Planners (AIP), 51, 52

American Planning Association, 174

Anderson, Martin, 112

annexations, 87–88, 175

Appalachia: outmigration from, 68–69

Archer, Dennis, 147

Arlington: multiracial character of, 167

Arnow, Harriet, 69

Asheville: retirees' move to, 99

Asian immigrants, 103, 104–5

Atlanta: African American culture in, 35; African American majority in, 131, 132–33; annexations of, 88; business control of civic affairs in, 79; city council district in, 132–33; edge cities of, 141; freeway locations in, 86; global role of, 156–57; images of, 134–35; job locations in, 107–8; land boom in, 45; neighborhood militancy in, 132–33; political pluralism in, 146;

Urban America in the Modern Age:
From 1920 to the Present, Second Edition
Developmental editor: Andrew J. Davidson
Copy editor and Production editor: Lucy Herz
Proofreader: Claudia Siler
Cartographer: Jason Casanova, Pegleg Graphics
Indexer: Margie Towery
Printer: Versa Press, Inc.